Jim Graham's
Farm Family Cookbook
—— ∞ ——
For City Folks

Office of College Advancement
College of Agriculture and Life Sciences
North Carolina State University
Raleigh, North Carolina

$19.95
ISBN 0-9719219-0-3
Printed in the United States of America

9/02—5M—JMG—Source 4
G02-40396

Dedication

Jim Graham is arguably North Carolina's most beloved public figure. He grew up in Rowan County where he developed an appetite for agriculture and farm family cooking. His mother and father, Laura and Jim, sent him off to State College where he earned a degree in agriculture in 1942. After teaching school and managing a test farm, he went on to manage the Dixie Classic Fair in Winston-Salem and the Farmers Market  in Raleigh. Jim Graham ran for and won the office of North Carolina Commissioner of Agriculture in the fall of '64 and the rest is history. After 36 years of service as the state's Commissioner of Agriculture, Jim Graham now volunteers as Executive in Residence in the College of Agriculture and Life Sciences at NC State University, and we are pleased to dedicate this book to him.

−James L. Oblinger
Dean, College of Agriculture and Life Sciences
NC State University

Contents

Preface

The recipes for this book were solicited by the North Carolina Extension and Community Association, the North Carolina Farm Bureau Foundations, and the Office of College Advancement for the College of Agriculture and Life Sciences at NC State University. Recipes were submitted by North Carolinians from across the state.

Profits from the sale of this book will go to the James A. Graham Scholars Endowment and the North Carolina Extension and Community Association in NC State's College of Agriculture and Life Sciences, and the Farm Bureau Foundations.

The use of brand and trade names in this publication does not imply endorsement of products mentioned or criticism of similar ones not mentioned. Brand names are used as submitted to describe products and are included for the convenience of the reader.

Introduction

One of the earliest memories from my childhood is of our 250-acre farm in Rowan County. My father had 48 head of milk cattle. We grew grain and hay for the cattle and hogs we raised to eat. My most lasting memories of that wonderful childhood are of hard work, a big appetite, and the Sunday dinners my mother prepared. There wasn't a farmwife in the county who could outcook my mom. Sunday fried chicken with gravy, sweet potatoes, and black-eyed peas. Her pound cake with strawberries and whipped cream would melt in your mouth. And it wasn't just Sundays. We had a great meal to look forward to three times a day—breakfast, lunch, and dinner.

Did we work hard and work up big appetites? You bet, up at the crack of dawn and usually not in from the fields until dusk. My favorite breakfast was Mom's country ham, biscuits, red-eye gravy, and grits. At lunch we needed more than a sandwich to keep us going, and Mom would put on quite a spread. Most often it was two meats, potatoes, and gravy, all washed down with a big frosted glass of iced tea. At dinner when we'd come in from working that noon meal off we'd sit down to a table that looked like a Norman Rockwell painting...fried chicken, pork chops, fresh corn, and sliced tomatoes.

If you know me, you know that one of my favorite eating places is a country-cooking restaurant. The reason is simple. I love good farm food and home cooking.

Seeing farmers bring their fresh produce to the market and then sitting down to a lunch or dinner there takes me back to my childhood and those wonderful meals my mother prepared on our farm in Rowan County.

Can the people in these restaurants cook like my mother? Of course not; no one can. But I was sitting in a country restaurant one day eating a country-style steak. Across the room at another table were a man and his wife. You could just tell they were city folk. I watched them nodding as they enjoyed their meal, and it occurred to me that a whole heck of a lot of people haven't had the pleasures that I have—growing up on a farm and experiencing some of the best meals in the world three times a day. My next thought was this: wouldn't it be great if we could share recipes like the ones that my momma used to prepare.

The results of those thoughts are on the pages that follow—**Jim Graham's Farm Family Cookbook For City Folks**—more than 500 recipes fresh from North Carolina farms, most handed down generation to generation from one great cook to another. A few of these are so old timey—a pinch of this and a little of that—they aren't as precise as we'd like. But they looked so tasty that—for old time's sake—we went ahead and included them anyway.

And here's something else that makes them special. Agriculture and agribusiness are the state's No. 1 industry. The commodities grown right here on North Carolina's farms make us the third most diverse agricultural state in the nation, and these commodities make up the ingredients of the delicious recipes in this book—like my momma's Brunswick Stew and Corn Pudding.

Before you get into your apron and turn on the oven, you should know that these recipes were gathered and selected by two very special groups of North Carolina women from Farm Bureau and North Carolina's Cooperative Extension Service. And while I'm expressing my appreciation, I'd like to thank Ellen Miller and Carolyn Lackey, food and nutrition experts with the College's North Carolina Cooperative Extension Service. They made sure that our farm family recipes were accurate.

Now, put on your apron, and turn on the oven. You're about to experience a bit of North Carolina's heritage—homegrown, down-on-the-farm recipes just like my mother used to make.

—Jim Graham
Executive in Residence
College of Agriculture and Life Sciences
NC State University

Beverages
&
Appetizers

Beverages   Cheese Balls   Dips

Appetizers   Spreads

A Taste of North Carolina's Heritage

Food... For Thought!

**Food doesn't just come from a grocery store ...
it comes from farms!**

- Here in the United States, we spend less than 11 percent of our
  expendable income on food, making U.S. food the most
  affordable in the world.

- By February 9 of each year, the average American citizen has
  earned enough to buy food for the entire year. It takes the
  same citizen until May 9 to earn enough to pay annual taxes.

- The United States has less than 7 percent of the world's land
  but produces 13 percent of the world's farm commodities.

- Thanks to U.S. agriculture and agribusiness, those who eat
  U.S.-produced food enjoy the safest and most plentiful food
  supply in the world.

- A family of four eats about 5,000 pounds of food each year.

- In North Carolina, agriculture and agribusiness—food, fiber,
  and forestry—make up the state's No. 1 industry. Agriculture
  accounts for 22 percent of the $217 billion gross state product
  and for more than 750,000 jobs.

COMPANY ICED TEA

6 tea bags 1 1/2 cups sugar
2 quarts water 2 lemons

Steep tea bags in 1 quart of boiling water. Remove tea bags and add sugar to tea, stirring to dissolve. Add remaining water to make 1/2 gallon. After tea has cooled, squeeze the 2 lemons and mix juice with tea. Refrigerate before serving. Tea is best if served over crushed ice. Makes 1/2 gallon of tea. Serves 8.

Jane Stuart, Wake County

This tea was used in our family whenever company came for a meal. Mom always called it her "Company Tea."

EASY PUNCH

24 ounces white grape juice 12 ounces frozen lemonade
64 ounces pineapple juice   concentrate
32 ounces ginger ale

Chill all ingredients. Mix and serve.

Laura B. Wooten, Wake County

OLD-TIMEY BOILED GREEN PEANUTS

Wash in-the-shell peanuts thoroughly in cool water. Place the peanuts in a suitable saucepan and cover with medium brine (10 ounces salt to one gallon of water). Boil covered for 45 minutes or until the kernels are tender. Taste-test for preferred saltiness. (Allow peanuts to sit in brine to increase saltiness; drain as soon as desired degree of saltiness is achieved.) The peanuts are ready for shelling and eating immediately, or they may be held in the refrigerator for as long as 5 days.

Babs Wilkinson, Wake County

My father loves peanuts, and one of the ways our family enjoyed them was to "boil them in the shell" for a salty snack. It is one of my Dad's favorite ways to enjoy fresh green peanuts. We still go to the farmer's market every fall to find fresh peanuts in the shell so we can boil them. It's been a family tradition for several generations.

BOILED PEANUTS
(modified for Crock-Pot)

1 pound raw, shelled peanuts	4 to 5 tablespoons salt Water

Put peanuts in a 3-quart Crock-Pot. Fill with water. Allow peanuts to soak 8 hours or overnight. Peanuts will absorb a lot of the water, making it necessary to add water until the pot is filled. Add salt. Cook peanuts on low for 8 hours and then on high for 1 1/2 hours or medium for 4 1/2 hours. Drain. About 1 hour toward end of cooking time, taste peanuts. If not salty enough, add more salt and continue to cook. Yield: 1 pound of cooked, boiled peanuts.

Babs Wilkinson, Wake County

BOILED PEANUTS
(stove top version)

2 cups peanuts, raw and in the shell	4 cups water 1 1/2 teaspoons salt

Put in-the-shell peanuts into a saucepan; add water and salt. Bring to a boil. Reduce the heat to a good simmer and cook approximately 25 minutes. Time will vary, depending on the size and the freshness of the peanuts. When done, the kernel should have swollen to fill the pod well, and the taste of raw starch will have dissipated. The peanut will remain slightly chewy. Serve hot, still in the shell, or cold after draining. Yield: 2 cups of boiled peanuts.

Babs Wilkinson, Wake County

CHEESE STRAWS

1/2 teaspoon baking powder	1 cup sharp cheddar cheese, grated
1 cup flour	
1/2 cup butter	3 tablespoons cold water

Sift powder and flour in bowl. Cut in butter and cheese. Add water, and mix. Use cookie press to form cheese straws. Bake at 375° F. for 8 to 10 minutes. Cut into desired lengths after baking. Makes 3 dozen Cheese Straws.

Vicki Walton, Wake County

My mother used this recipe when she was in 4-H.

CHEESE STRAWS

1/2 cup margarine, softened
1 cup all-purpose flour
Pinch of salt
1 cup crispy rice cereal

1 8-ounce package grated
    sharp cheddar cheese
Cayenne, enough to taste

Cut softened margarine into flour until mixture has the appearance of coarse corn meal. Add remaining ingredients, and mix until thoroughly blended. Form into a ball. Roll dough out on floured board until about 1/4-inch thick. Cut into strips of desired width. Bake 15 minutes in a preheated 350° F. oven on a cookie sheet. Makes 3 dozen.

Lottie Lou Dickens, Nash County

Cheese Straws are very good for social events and snacks.

HOLIDAY MEATBALLS

1 1/2 pounds lean ground
    beef
1 cup corn flake crumbs
1 egg
1/4 cup parsley flakes
2 tablespoons
    Worcestershire sauce
1 medium onion, finely
    chopped
1/4 cup ketchup
1/2 teaspoon salt

1/2 teaspoon black pepper
1/2 teaspoon garlic salt
Sauce:
1 16-ounce can whole
    cranberry sauce
1 16-ounce bottle Hunt's
    Thick 'N' Chunky
    Barbeque Sauce (Original
    or Southern Flavor)
1/2 cup brown sugar

Mix all meatball ingredients thoroughly in large bowl. Pinch off bits and roll mixture into balls about 1 to 1 1/2 inches in diameter. Place meatballs on cookie sheet that has sides (to prevent grease from spilling into oven). Bake in preheated oven at 350° F. for 10 to 20 minutes until brown. Turn once while cooking. Meatballs may be made ahead, frozen, and used as needed. Mix sauce ingredients in a Crock-Pot, electric skillet, or heavy saucepan. Stir and let simmer until ingredients are blended. Add meatballs and heat for about 30 minutes in sauce before serving (until hot throughout). Do not overcook.

Susan Harper Britt, Nash County

Holiday Meatballs are delicious with this or other sauces. They are great for parties, since the meatballs can be prepared ahead and frozen until needed.

—

MISS EVELYN'S CRAB CAKES

3 slices of toast or stale
   bread
1/2 cup milk
1 egg, beaten
1 pound crab meat

1 teaspoon dry mustard
1/4 teaspoon Worcestershire
   sauce
1 tablespoon melted butter
Salt and pepper to taste

Soak bread in milk and egg mixture. Add remaining ingredients and mix well. Make into patties and fry in hot oil until brown on both sides. I use olive oil and my grandmother's cast iron skillet. Enjoy! Serves 8 to 10.

Rosie Patton, Dare County

My family loves seafood. The recipe that I'm sharing is one that was given to me by Mrs. Evelyn Styron of Hatteras Island. They're super crab cakes! You can add some Old Bay Seasoning or Texas Pete hot sauce if you want it spicy.

SHRIMP APPETIZER

1 8-ounce package light
   cream cheese
1/2 cup light sour cream
1/2 cup light mayonnaise
1 cup (8 ounces) seafood
   cocktail sauce
2 cups shredded light
   mozzarella cheese

2 4 1/2-ounce cans shrimp,
   rinsed and drained, or 1
   pound regular shrimp,
   cleaned and steamed
3 green onions, finely
   chopped
3/4 cup finely chopped
   tomato

Mix cream cheese, sour cream, and mayonnaise until smooth. Spread on 12-inch round serving platter. Cover with seafood sauce. Sprinkle with cheese, shrimp pieces, onions, and tomato. Cover and chill. Serve with reduced-fat crackers. Note: When arranged correctly, this looks like a pizza.

Georgine Armstrong, Pasquotank County

The president of the Pasquotank County Extension and Community Association serves these to her local club, Brite Meadows ECA.

SPINACH TARTS

1 medium onion, chopped
2 to 3 cloves garlic, chopped
1 cup fresh mushrooms, chopped
2 to 3 tablespoons oil
1 10-ounce package frozen chopped spinach, thawed and drained well
1/2 cup cheddar cheese
1/2 cup small-curd cottage cheese
1 egg slightly beaten
1/2 cup plain non-fat yogurt
1/2 teaspoon salt
1/2 teaspoon black pepper
1/4 teaspoon Cayenne pepper or crushed red pepper
3/4 cup Italian-style bread crumbs
1 can (10-count) flaky biscuits

In a large skillet, sauté onion, garlic, and mushrooms in oil until liquid cooks out. Add spinach and heat just through. Add cheddar and cottage cheeses and mix well. Beat egg lightly; add plain yogurt, salt, pepper, and cayenne. Mix into spinach mixture. Add bread crumbs. Separate each biscuit into two pieces. Push into miniature muffin pan to cover bottoms and sides. Add 1 tablespoon of spinach mixture to each cup of muffin tin. Bake at 350° F. for 18 to 20 minutes or until biscuits are brown and a knife inserted into the middle comes out clean. Serve warm. You can top with a dollop of sour cream if desired.

Ann Clarke, Lee County

STUFFED MUSHROOMS

1 pound hot bulk sausage
1/2 teaspoon hot sauce
8 ounces cream cheese
1 large package of large mushrooms

Brown and drain sausage. Mix hot sauce into sausage, and melt cream cheese together with sausage. Wash mushrooms, removing stems. Pat tops of mushrooms with a paper towel to dry. Fill mushrooms with mixture. Place mushrooms on a rack or cookie sheet. Place that rack or cookie sheet in a pan that contains a small amount of water. Cook in oven at 350° F. for 20 to 25 minutes. Serve hot. Makes 16 to 18 appetizers. Leftovers can be reheated in a microwave.

Kay Greene, Hertford County

WORLD'S BEST DEVILED EGGS

12 eggs	1 teaspoon dry mustard
1/2 cup mayonnaise	1/2 teaspoon paprika
2 tablespoons finely	1/2 teaspoon dillweed
chopped onion	1/4 teaspoon salt
1 teaspoon chives	1/4 teaspoon pepper
1 teaspoon parsley	1/4 teaspoon garlic powder

Place eggs in large saucepan, and cover with cold water. Bring to a boil. Reduce heat so water is just below simmering. Cover and cook 15 minutes. Drain, add cold water and ice. Let sit 10 minutes. Peel eggs. Split eggs in half. Remove yolks and mash with fork. Add all ingredients to yolks. Spoon mixture into egg whites. Cover and chill.

Nancy Johnston, Buncombe County

CHEESE BALL

2 8-ounce packages cream	1 teaspoon Worcestershire
cheese, softened	sauce
2 cups shredded sharp	1 teaspoon lemon juice
cheddar	Dash of cayenne pepper
1 tablespoon chopped	Dash of salt
pimiento (optional)	2 cups chopped pecans
1 tablespoon minced onion	

Combine softened cream cheese and cheddar, mixing until well blended. Add pimento, onion, Worcestershire sauce, lemon juice, pepper, and salt, and mix well. Shape into ball and chill for 30 minutes. Roll in chopped pecans.

Sue Arnette, Duplin County

DRIED BEEF BALL

3 8-ounce packages cream	2 2.25-ounce jars dried beef,
cheese, softened	chopped
8 ounces ranch dressing	Chopped pecans (optional)
1 small onion, grated	

Beat first three ingredients until blended. Stir in chipped beef. Form into ball and cover with chopped pecans, if desired. Serve with crackers.

Elizabeth Harper, Edgecombe County

HAM AND CHEESE BALL

3 packages of Carl Buddig
  ham
2 8-ounce packages cream
  cheese, softened

1 tablespoon Accent (MSG)
1 small grated onion
1 tablespoon
  Worcestershire sauce

Mix all ingredients except ham. Chop 2 packages ham. Add to
cheese mixture, and form into a ball. Chop remaining package of
ham. Roll ball in chopped ham. Chill and serve with crackers.

Ruth Morgan, Buncombe County

NUTTY CHEESE BALL

8 ounces sharp cheddar
  cheese, shredded
2 green onions, with onions
  chopped and tops in 1-
  inch pieces
1/4 green pepper, chopped
1 rib celery, chopped

16 ounces cream cheese at
  room temperature
Dash red pepper
2 teaspoons Worcestershire
  sauce
Dash salt
1/4 cup pecans, chopped
Shelled pecan halves

Mix all ingredients except pecans. Beat smooth and shape into ball.
Roll cheese ball in chopped pecans. Decorate with pecan halves.
Serve at room temperature. Store covered in refrigerator no longer
than 2 weeks. Serves 24.

Juanita T. Cannon, Gaston County

*I've made this cheese ball for many years, and all seem to enjoy it. I
make it year 'round.*

NUTTY FRUIT BALL

1 8-ounce Cracker Barrel
  sharp cheddar flavor cold
  pack cheese food
1 8-ounce package cream
  cheese, softened

2 tablespoons margarine at
  room temperature
1/2 cup chopped pecans
1 8-ounce can crushed
  pineapple, drained
3 tablespoons maraschino
  cherries, drained

Combine cheeses and margarine. Mix well. Stir in half of the pecans and all of the pineapple and cherries. Mix well. Shape into a ball. Roll in remaining pecans. Chill until firm.

Mary Alice Brooks, Union County

OLIVE CHEESE BALL

16 ounces cream cheese,
  softened
1 tablespoon of
  Worcestershire sauce

1 10-ounce jar of salad
  olives, drained and
  chopped
1 bunch green onions,
  chopped

Mix softened cream cheese with Worcestershire sauce. Add olives and onions. Mix well. Form into a ball or a log. Refrigerate 2 hours before serving.

Hannah Cox, Craven County

OLIVE-STUFFED CHEESE BALLS

1/2 cup sifted flour
1 cup grated sharp cheddar
  cheese
1/4 teaspoon paprika

2 tablespoons margarine,
  softened
1 teaspoon water
24 green olives

Mix flour, cheese, paprika, margarine, and water to make slightly stiff dough. Make small balls and then flatten in your hand. Place olive in center, and pinch dough around olive. Make sure you cover the entire olive. Bake on a cookie sheet for 15 minutes at 400° F. Serves 24.

Patricia Herring, Wayne County

ORANGE-DATE CHEESE BALL

4 8-ounce packages of
  cream cheese, softened
4 tablespoons Tang

8 ounces chopped dates
1/2 cup pecans, chopped

Mix all ingredients but pecans thoroughly, and roll into a ball. Roll ball in chopped pecans. Serve with windmill cookies or ginger snaps. Makes one large or two smaller cheese balls.

Hilda Ray, Columbus County

Perfect for that special occasion, wedding reception, or any other social function.

—

PARTY CHEESE BALL

8 ounces shredded New
  York cheddar cheese at
  room temperature
1 pound cream cheese
4 ounces blue cheese

1/2 teaspoon onion powder
1/2 teaspoon garlic powder
1/4 teaspoon cayenne
  pepper (optional)
3/4 cup chopped pecans

Allow all cheeses to reach room temperature. Mix all ingredients except pecans, and form into ball. Roll in chopped pecans. Serve with a variety of crackers.

Wilma B. McCollum, Union County

PEPPER JELLY CHEESE BALL

8 ounces cream cheese
1/2 cup mixed nuts

Heaping tablespoon pepper
  jelly

Combine cream cheese and jelly, and mix well. Roll into a ball. Roll in mixed nuts. Put in the icebox until firm.

Betty Wood, Craven County

CRAB SPREAD

1 pound crabmeat
2 tablespoons creamed
  horseradish
1 teaspoon lemon juice
Dash of Tabasco sauce
Dash Worcestershire sauce

1 cup mayonnaise
Salt to taste
Dash pepper
Dash of red pepper
1 cup grated cheddar cheese

Preheat oven to 350° F. Mix together all ingredients except cheese. Pour into 9-inch oven-proof pie plate. Spread cheese evenly over top. Cook 15 minutes or until bubbly. Serve on crackers.

Jennifer Britt Crumley, Nash County

Crab Spread is wonderful for a party or holiday dish, and it is simple to prepare.

PIMIENTO AND CHEESE

1 pound cheddar cheese, grated	6 tablespoons margarine
2 4-ounce jars pimiento, chopped	4 tablespoons sugar
	4 tablespoons vinegar
	1 teaspoon salt

Mix cheese and pimientos; set aside. Melt margarine. Add sugar, vinegar, and salt. Bring this mixture to a boil, and pour over cheese and pimiento. Mix well and store in refrigerator. Note: You will need to stir this before using because sometimes the mixture firms up. Or let mixture come to room temperature.

Juanita Fisher Lagg, Rowan County

My sister-in-law, who came from Winston-Salem, said her family had used this recipe for more than 50 years. It is of Moravian origin, has no mayonnaise, and is truly a Southern dish. It makes a great sandwich or stuffing for celery.

STRAWBERRY–BUTTER SPREAD

1 10-ounce carton frozen strawberries	1 cup unsalted butter, softened
	1/2 cup powdered sugar

Combine all ingredients in a bowl. Using either a blender or mixer, mix until well-blended and smooth. Store in refrigerator. Yields 1 3/4 cups.

Mrs. Doris B. Honeycutt, Columbus County

This spread is delicious on toast or hot biscuits.

VEGETABLE SANDWICH SPREAD

3/4 cup carrots	Salt and pepper to taste
1/4 cup celery	1/2 cup mayonnaise
1/4 cup green onions	1 8-ounce package cream cheese, softened
1/4 cup cucumber	
1 large tomato	

Grind vegetables, and add salt and pepper. In a separate bowl, blend mayonnaise and cream cheese. Add to vegetable mixture. Refrigerate 2 to 3 hours. Makes enough spread for 30 sandwiches.

Bee Simpson, Union County

ZESTY HOT CRAB SPREAD

1 8-ounce package cream
  cheese, softened
1 tablespoon milk
2 teaspoons Worcestershire
  sauce

1 7 1/2-ounce can or
  package of crabmeat,
  drained
2 tablespoons green onion,
  chopped
2 tablespoons toasted
  almonds, slivered

Thoroughly combine all ingredients except almonds. Turn into an 8-inch pie pan or small shallow baking dish sprayed with cooking spray. Top with toasted almonds. Place pie pan in a larger pan. Add boiling water to come halfway up the sides of the pie pan. Bake at 350° F. for 15 minutes or until heated through. Serve with assorted crackers.

Della Stephens, Forsyth County

CHEESE DIP

1 pound hamburger
1 pound sausage
1 large onion, chopped
2 pounds Velveeta cheese

1 can tomatoes and green
  chilies
1 can cream of mushroom
  soup

Brown hamburger and sausage in frying pan. After meat has browned, add onions and cook until tender. Drain and discard grease. Mix all ingredients together, and simmer on low heat for 30 minutes. Great over nacho chips.

Vickie Guin, Wake County

CHIP DIP

1 4-ounce jar Old English
  cheese spread, room
  temperature

1 8-ounce package cream
  cheese, room temperature
1 small onion, grated

Use a fork to blend Old English cheese and cream cheese together until very smooth with no lumps. Grate onion over dip to taste. Mix together. Refrigerate. Best if served with ruffled potato chips, as dip is very firm.

Wanda Simmons, Wake County

HOT ONION DIP

1 10-ounce package frozen
  chopped onions
1 8-ounce package shredded
  Parmesan cheese

1 cup mayonnaise
1 8-ounce carton sour
  cream

Mix all ingredients together, and pour into a baking dish. Bake at
350° F. for approximately 30 minutes, until golden brown and
bubbly. Serve with corn chips. Serves 10.

Tina Brown, Cabarrus County

*People ask me to bring my Hot Onion Dip to every gathering that I
attend.*

MEXICAN DIP

1 8-ounce package cream
  cheese, softened
1/4 cup sour cream
1 16-ounce jar of salsa,
  drained, leaving just a
  little juice

1 tomato, diced
1 green onion, stem and
  onion part chopped
1 16-ounce bag of shredded
  sharp cheddar cheese

Mix cream cheese, sour cream, and salsa. Spread in an ungreased
9 x 13-inch casserole dish. Top with diced tomato, chopped green
onion, and shredded cheese. Serve with tortilla chips. Keep in
refrigerator.

Kristy Easter, Surry County

SAUSAGE DIP

1 pound bulk sausage
2 8-ounce packages cream
  cheese

2 10-ounce cans Rotel
  chilies & tomatoes

Brown sausage and drain. Add cream cheese to sausage in hot
frying pan. Mix well, making sure there are no lumps of cream
cheese. Drain most of the juice off the can of chilies and tomatoes.
Add to sausage and cream cheese. Serve with tortilla chips or
French bread torn into bite-sized pieces.

Barbara Braswell, Union County

Soups, Salads, & Sauces

Soups   Congealed Salads   Sauces
Tossed Salads   Salad Dressings

A Taste of North Carolina's Heritage

Food ... For Thought!

Can you imagine wondering where your next meal might come from?

It could happen in the United States, the richest food society in the world, and it has! How about the last time a snow storm or a hurricane hit the world you live in? Do you recall banging grocery carts with your neighbors, elbowing your way down the aisle to capture the last loaf of bread, carton of milk, or dozen eggs? These are the times when we Americans appreciate the value of food.

Thanks to agricultural research, Americans enjoy an abundant, safe, and economical food supply. The more we understand what a good value our food is, the more we'll also appreciate the U.S. farmers who provide our food, as well as those who package, process, and deliver the products to market. And we'll see the ongoing value of institutions like North Carolina State University, where researchers and educators in the College of Agriculture and Life Sciences are using science and technology to ensure that food not only remains safe, economical, and plentiful, but also one of America's best buys.

BROCCOLI SOUP

1 can mushroom soup
1 can chicken soup
1 can cream of onion soup

1 10-ounce package frozen
broccoli, cooked
1 cup cheddar cheese,
shredded

Mix soups with three soup cans of water. Bring to boil, and add cooked broccoli. Add cheddar cheese, and heat until melted.

Mildred Moxley, Alleghany County

CABBAGE PATCH SOUP

1 1/2 pounds hamburger
3 medium onions, sliced
thin
2 medium stalks celery,
chopped
1 16-ounce can tomatoes
1 15-ounce can tomato
sauce

2 15-ounce cans pinto beans
1/2 to 1 cup bell pepper
1 1/2 quarts water
3 teaspoons chili powder
2 teaspoons salt
1/2 teaspoon pepper
2 cups coarsely chopped
cabbage

Brown hamburger. Pour off fat. Rinse to remove fat. Add onions, celery, tomatoes, tomato sauce, beans, bell pepper, and water. Add seasonings. Cook 15 minutes. Add cabbage last, and cook until cabbage is tender, about 10 to 15 minutes. More water may be added to make soup the desired thickness. Add more or less seasoning to suit your taste.

Pat James, Pitt County

This is one of my family's favorite soups. I sometimes add a package of frozen corn, which adds another flavor.

30-MINUTE CHICKEN AND RICE SOUP

6 cups water
2 10.75-ounce cans chicken
broth
1 1/2 teaspoons Italian herb
seasoning
1 teaspoon garlic powder
1 10-ounce package frozen
chopped spinach

15 ounces chopped carrots
1 14- or 15-ounce can sweet
peas
1 cup white rice, uncooked
3 chicken breasts, cooked
and cut into bite-sized
pieces

Mix water and broth in 5-quart pot. Bring to a boil. Add Italian seasoning and garlic. Reduce heat, cover, and simmer 5 minutes. Stir in spinach and carrots. Increase heat to medium and cook 5 minutes. Add peas and rice. Cook 20 minutes or until rice is tender. Add chicken to pot, and heat through. Serves 6.

Tara Crayton, Cabarrus County

This makes a wonderful dinner for a cold day. I serve it with corn bread and Parmesan cheese.

—

DOWN-HOME CHICKEN CHOWDER

4 slices cooked bacon,
  crumbled
1 small jar sliced
  mushrooms, drained
1/2 cup chopped onion
1/8 teaspoon crushed thyme
1 can chicken vegetable
  soup
1 soup can water

1 can cream of celery soup
1 1/2 cups chopped canned
  tomatoes
1 15-ounce can corn,
  drained
1/2 cup cooked diced
  chicken
1/8 teaspoon black pepper

In a large saucepan, cook bacon until crisp. Remove, blot with paper towel, then crumble. Pour off all but 2 tablespoons drippings. Brown mushrooms and onion with thyme in drippings until tender. Add bacon and remaining ingredients. Heat thoroughly.

Norma Chrisawn, Yancey County

This recipe came from my mother. She made it for Christmas Eve supper, and it has become a tradition for my family. It is served with assorted crackers and cheeses.

PENNSYLVANIA DUTCH CHICKEN CORN SOUP

1 chicken, cut up
1 onion
3 quarts water
1/2 teaspoon whole mixed
  pickling spice
2 teaspoons salt
2 stalks celery
2 cans corn, drained

2 hard-cooked eggs
Salt and pepper
Dough:
1 egg
1/4 cup milk
1 cup sifted flour
1/8 teaspoon salt

Put chicken in large kettle. Add onion, water, spice, and 2 teaspoons salt. Bring to boil, and simmer covered for 4 hours or until done. Remove chicken from broth and cool. Debone meat, and cut into small pieces. Strain broth. Add chicken, celery, and corn. Bring to boil and simmer 15 minutes. Add eggs, salt, and pepper to taste. Prepare dough: Beat egg and milk. Add to flour and salt. Mix well. Add small pieces of dough to soup, cover, and simmer 7 minutes.

Virginia Hodges, Ashe County

DOWN-EAST CLAM CHOWDER

2 to 4 slices bacon, chopped
2 large onions, chopped
2 32-ounce bags frozen
  Southern-style hash
  brown potatoes
8 6-ounce cans chopped
  clams in clam juice *or*
  1 large 51-ounce can

1 to 2 tablespoons chopped
  parsley, dried or fresh
1 tablespoon
  Worcestershire sauce
Salt and pepper to taste
Seasoned salt to taste (Joe's
  Mom's Seasoned Salt is
  good)
Tabasco sauce or Texas
  Pete hot sauce to taste

Cook bacon in large saucepan until lightly browned. Add onions. Cook until softened and lightly browned. Stir in potatoes, undrained clams, parsley, Worcestershire sauce, salt, seasoned salt, pepper, and Tabasco sauce. Add enough water to cover all the ingredients. Bring to a boil. Reduce the heat to low. Simmer, covered, for 45 minutes to 1 hour, or until desired consistency is reached.

Alice Graham Underhill, Craven County

MOM'S CORN CHOWDER

4 slices (about 2 ounces) salt
  pork, thinly sliced
1 tablespoon butter
  (optional)
3 large raw potatoes, diced
1 large onion, diced
1/2 cup uncooked macaroni

1 14.75-ounce can whole
  kernel corn
1 14.75-ounce can cream-
  style corn
1 can evaporated milk
1 can evaporated 2% milk
Salt and pepper to taste

Fry salt pork in skillet until browned. Deglaze pan with water. Add cooked salt pork and drippings. Add butter, potatoes, and onion, and cook for 10 minutes. Add macaroni, stirring once in a while so that macaroni doesn't stick. After macaroni is cooked, add corn. Cook through. Then add evaporated and 2% milk, and heat through. Season with salt and pepper. Serves 6 to 8.

Patricia L. Lique, Brunswick County

We were not well off, and Mom had to make healthy meals for us, a family of five. Macaroni was added so that we'd be full longer and not hungry an hour later. It is wonderful on a cold evening.

GAZPACHO

1 46-ounce can tomato juice
1/4 cup dry sherry
1/4 cup olive oil
1/4 cup wine vinegar
1 tablespoon Worcestershire
  sauce
Dash Tabasco hot sauce
1 teaspoon salt
1/4 teaspoon pepper
1 teaspoon MSG or Accent
  (optional)

1 teaspoon parsley flakes
1/2 teaspoon basil
1/2 teaspoon thyme
1/2 teaspoon celery salt
1/2 teaspoon garlic salt
1 mild onion, grated
3 cucumbers, peeled and
  diced
3 tomatoes, peeled and
  diced
2 green peppers, chopped

Combine liquid ingredients together in a large bowl. Add the spices, and stir until well blended. Add the fresh vegetables, and stir. Cover, and chill in the refrigerator until ready to serve, preferably 12 to 24 hours. The flavor improves the longer it sits. Garnish with crackers or croutons. Serves 8 to 10.

Alice Graham Underhill, Craven County

POTATO SOUP WITH CROUTONS

4 (green or spring) onions,
  or 1 small onion, chopped
1 stalk celery, finely
  chopped
4 tablespoons low-fat
  margarine

4 medium potatoes, diced
4 cups chicken broth
1 teaspoon salt, optional
1 teaspoon pepper, optional
1 cup skim evaporated milk
  or low-fat milk

Sauté (or microwave) the chopped onion and celery in margarine until translucent. Combine the potatoes, onions, chicken broth, salt, and pepper. Bring the mixture to a boil. Reduce heat and simmer for 40 minutes. Blend soup until smooth. Return soup to pot, and add milk. Serve either reheated or chilled, with Croutons (recipe below). Serves 6 to 8.

Melinda M. Houser, Lincoln County

CROUTONS

Use day-old French or Italian bread or a bread that is not soft, such as whole wheat. Cut into bite-sized pieces, and spread with melted low-fat margarine, or use one of the spray margarines. Place on baking sheet and sprinkle with some of your favorite herbs, such as garlic powder, parsley, oregano, basil, chili powder, sage, thyme, dill weed, or whatever herbs may be interesting and add flavor. Bake in a 250° F. oven until the bread is dry. Rotate the pan or stir the bread cubes around during the cooking time. Store croutons in a covered container in the refrigerator for up to a couple of weeks.

Melinda M. Houser, Lincoln County

SAUSAGE SOUP

1 pound Italian sausage	4 cups water
2 teaspoons vegetable oil	2 cups shell macaroni,
1 20-ounce can whole	uncooked
tomatoes	1 15- to 16-ounce can Great
2 chicken bouillon cubes	Northern white beans

Cook sausage in 2 teaspoons of oil. Add cut-up tomatoes with juice. Add bouillon cubes, water, and shell macaroni. Cook until macaroni is done. Add beans, and simmer covered for 5 minutes.

Tricie Brown, Cabarrus County

Sausage Soup is quick and easy. It is also inexpensive to make.

STUFFED GREEN PEPPER SOUP

1 pound ground beef or
  chuck, browned and
  drained
1/4 cup chopped onion
1/2 teaspoon garlic powder
1/2 teaspoon black pepper
2 14.5-ounce cans diced
  tomatoes (with green
  chilies, optional), not
  drained

2 beef bouillon cubes,
  dissolved in 1/2 cup hot
  water
1/2 green pepper, chopped
3 cups water, more if
  needed
1 tablespoon sugar
2 cups cooked rice, instant
  or long grain

Mix all ingredients in large skillet, cover and simmer for 15 minutes. If mixture is thick, add water. Serves 6.

Deane Avett, Cherokee County

A great soup for a cold winter night, and you have a full meal if you serve it with slaw or tossed salad and corn bread.

BLACKEYE PEA SALAD

1 15-ounce can blackeye
  peas, rinsed and drained
1 15-ounce can whole kernel
  corn, rinsed and drained
1/2 cup green pepper,
  chopped (optional)

1/2 to 1 cup onion, chopped
Marinade:
1/4 cup oil
2 tablespoons water
1/2 cup sugar
1/2 cup vinegar

Mix blackeye peas, corn, green pepper, and onion in a bowl. In a separate bowl, combine oil, water, sugar, and vinegar. Pour over vegetables and mix well. Chill in refrigerator 4 to 8 hours before serving. Serves 6 to 8.

Betty Weeks, Wake County
Pat Brafford, Wake County

Eat Your Vegetables

Increasing fruit and vegetable consumption is a central part of a healthier diet, and good overall nutrition lowers your risk for heart disease, stroke, cancer, and osteoporosis.

BETTY'S BROCCOLI SALAD

1 medium onion, chopped
fine
1 bunch broccoli, chopped
1 cup grated cheddar cheese

1/2 pound bacon, cooked
and crumbled
1/2 cup sugar
1 cup mayonnaise
1 tablespoon vinegar

Toss onion, broccoli, cheese, and bacon in a bowl. In a separate
bowl, combine sugar, mayonnaise, and vinegar. Pour over broccoli
mixture. Cover and refrigerate overnight.

Betty Evins, Granville County

BROCCOLI-APPLE SALAD

1 apple, diced
1 bunch broccoli, chopped
1 red onion, chopped
1/2 pound bacon, fried,
crumbled
1/2 cup pecans, chopped

Raisins to taste
Dressing:
3/4 cup mayonnaise
1/4 cup sugar
2 tablespoons vinegar

Toss apple, broccoli, onion, bacon, pecans, and raisins together. In a
small bowl, mix mayonnaise, sugar, and vinegar. Pour over salad,
and toss well.

Vickie Guin, Wake County

BROCCOLI-RAISIN SALAD

2 large stalks of broccoli,
florets only
1 red onion, sliced thin
12 slices bacon, cooked
crisp and crumbled
1 cup golden raisins

1 cup sunflower seeds
Dressing:
1 cup mayonnaise
1/2 cup sugar
2 tablespoons vinegar

In large bowl, toss broccoli, sliced onion, crumbled bacon, raisins,
and sunflower seeds. In a separate bowl, mix mayonnaise, vinegar,
and sugar. Pour dressing over broccoli mixture. Cover and
refrigerate for several hours or overnight. Serves 8 to 10.

Mildred Harper, Edgecombe County

This is a quick, easy, and delicious salad.

BROCCOLI-TOMATO SALAD

1 large bunch broccoli,
  separated into florets
2 large tomatoes, wedged
3/4 cup sliced fresh
  mushrooms
2 green onions, sliced, or 1/2
  Vidalia onion, sliced
Dressing:
1/2 cup olive oil
1/3 cup balsamic vinegar
2 tablespoons water

1 teaspoon lemon juice
1 teaspoon sugar
3/4 teaspoon dried thyme
1 garlic clove, minced
1/2 teaspoon celery salt
1/4 teaspoon Italian
  seasoning
1/4 teaspoon lemon pepper
1/4 teaspoon paprika
1/4 teaspoon dry mustard

Cook broccoli for 5 minutes; drain. Rinse with cold water; drain.
Place in large bowl. Add tomatoes, mushrooms, and onions.
Combine dressing ingredients in a jar, and shake well to mix. Pour
over vegetables and toss gently. Cover and chill 1 to 2 hours.

Jennifer W. Ballance, Wayne County

CALIFORNIA SALAD

1 head cauliflower, cut into
  pieces
1 bunch broccoli, cut into
  pieces
1 medium red onion, sliced
  into rings

1 bell pepper, cut into strips
1 jar pimiento, chopped
Salt to taste
Dressing:
1 cup mayonnaise
1/2 cup sugar

Mix first 6 ingredients in large bowl. *Prepare dressing:* Stir
mayonnaise and sugar until completely mixed. Pour over salad, and
toss to mix. Chill.

Dale Evans, Union County

Healthy Ingredients for Salads

*Vegetables like tomatoes, broccoli, peppers, and
cauliflower add flavor and nutritional value
without adding many calories.*

CORN BREAD SALAD

1 8-ounce box Jiffy corn
  bread mix, prepared and
  crumbled
1 medium bell pepper,
  chopped
1 medium onion, chopped

3 to 5 tomatoes, peeled and
  chopped
1 pound bacon, fried,
  drained, and crumbled
1 1/2 to 2 cups mayonnaise
1 tablespoon sugar
1/2 cup salad cube pickles

Make corn bread according to package directions. Crumble corn
bread to cover 1/2 inch in bottom of baking pan or dish, retaining
enough cornbread to sprinkle over top of casserole. Layer
vegetables and bacon in order given, retaining enough bacon to
sprinkle over top. Combine mayonnaise, sugar, and salad pickles.
Spread over vegetables and bacon. Sprinkle remaining cornbread
and bacon on top. Chill until served.

Jerrie Hasty, Union County

CUCUMBER SALAD

1/4 cup sugar
1/2 teaspoon salt
4 teaspoons vinegar
1/2 to 3/4 cup mayonnaise

Dill to taste
2 large cucumbers, peeled
and sliced

Mix sugar, salt, vinegar, mayonnaise, and dill. Pour over sliced
cucumbers. Refrigerate. Serves 4.

Brenda Hefner, Alexander County

This is great with any meal, or you can serve it as an appetizer.

DUTCH SLAW

1/4 cup water
4 tablespoons butter
1 1/4 pounds cabbage,
  coarsely grated or
  chopped

1/2 cup reduced-fat sour
  cream
1/4 teaspoon salt
Dash pepper
3 tablespoons vinegar
1 1/2 tablespoons sugar

Bring water and butter to a boil in a large skillet that has a tight-
fitting lid. Put cabbage in skillet. Cover and cook rapidly until
cabbage is just tender, about 5 minutes. Remove lid and cook

several more minutes, until skillet is just dry. Combine sour cream, salt, pepper, vinegar, and sugar. Pour over warm cabbage. Refrigerate for several hours. Slaw may be refrigerated for several days to a week.

Helen Kincaid Lackey, Cleveland County

This recipe has been passed down through the Kincaid family. We no longer know the significance of the name.

—

FARMER'S SALAD

1 pound bacon	*Dressing:*
1 head iceberg lettuce, torn	3/4 cup mayonnaise
into bite-sized pieces	3 tablespoons sugar
1 head fresh broccoli	1 tablespoon distilled white
florets, in bite-sized pieces	vinegar

Cook bacon in a large skillet over medium-high heat until evenly brown. Drain, crumble, and set aside. In a large bowl, combine lettuce and broccoli florets. *Prepare dressing:* Whisk together the mayonnaise, sugar, and vinegar. Pour dressing over lettuce mixture, and toss to coat evenly. Sprinkle with bacon, and refrigerate until chilled. Serves 8.

Tina Brown, Cabarrus County

This salad is really good on a hot summer day.

LAYERED CHEDDAR-FRUIT SALAD

1 1/2 cups shredded	3 cups seedless grapes,
cheddar cheese, divided	sliced
4 cups shredded lettuce	*Dressing:*
3 cups fresh peaches,	1/2 cup mayonnaise
peeled, pitted, and sliced	1/2 cup sour cream
3 cups fresh strawberries,	1 tablespoon honey
sliced	

In a large bowl, toss 1 cup of the cheese with the lettuce. In a 2 1/2-quart bowl, layer as follows: half of the lettuce mixture, peaches, remaining lettuce mixture, strawberries, grapes, remaining cheese. *Prepare dressing:* In a small bowl, whisk the mayonnaise, sour cream, and honey together. Spread dressing over the top of the salad or serve on the side. Chill salad and dressing well before serving. Makes 9 to 12 1-cup servings.

Tina Brown, Cabarrus County

This is a very light and refreshing salad on a hot North Carolina summer day.

—

MANDARIN ORANGE SALAD

1 large head lettuce, torn
4 small green onions,
** chopped**
1/4 cup celery, chopped
1 small can mandarin
** oranges, drained**

Dressing:
1/2 cup sugar
2/3 cup oil
1 to 2 tablespoons poppy
** seeds**
1/2 cup vinegar
1 teaspoon ground mustard
1 teaspoon salt

Prepare dressing first: Mix sugar, oil, poppy seeds, vinegar, mustard, and salt together. Set aside. Just before serving, toss lettuce, onion, celery, and mandarin oranges together. Put dressing on salad when ready to serve. Salad will be soft if it sits too long.

Ruth Nesbitt, Buncombe County

ORIENTAL CRUNCH SALAD
and
CHINESE CABBAGE SALAD

2 packages Beef or Chicken
** Ramen Noodles**
1 package cole slaw *or* 1
** small head cabbage**
** shredded, with carrots or**
** mixed with white and**
** purple cabbage**
1 bunch green onions
1/2 cup sliced almonds

1/2 to 1 cup sunflower seeds
Dressing:
1 cup oil
1/2 cup sugar
1/3 to 1/2 cup vinegar
2 beef or chicken seasoning
** packets (from the Ramen**
** Noodles)**

Mix salad together 4 or 5 hours before serving time, and refrigerate. Mix dressing together, and refrigerate. Toss together when ready to serve.

Sarah Lee, Stanly County
Hilda Ray, Columbus County

Sarah Lee uses beef-flavored noodles for her Oriental Crunch Salad. Hilda Ray uses either beef or chicken to prepare her Chinese Cabbage Salad.

—

LAYERED CABBAGE SALAD

1 large head green cabbage, shredded	1 cup sugar
1 large sweet onion, chopped	3/4 cup vegetable oil
	1 cup white vinegar
1 large sweet green pepper, chopped	1 teaspoon salt
	1/2 teaspoon celery seed

Shred cabbage, placing half of it in a bowl. Reserve the other half. Sprinkle chopped onion over cabbage. Sprinkle chopped green pepper over onion. Top with remaining cabbage. Sprinkle sugar over the top of cabbage. *Do not stir.* Bring oil, vinegar, salt, and celery seed to a full boil, and pour this hot mixture over the cabbage mixture. *Do not stir!* Cover container, and place in refrigerator overnight. Next day, stir well. This will keep for 10 days or longer in the refrigerator.

Juanita Fisher Lagg, Rowan County

Every month, for our Primetimers' luncheon, I make this slaw. They would not let me in the door if I did not bring this dish. One member said his late mother made slaw just like that, and he never knew how she made it, but it reminded him so much of his early childhood days in Pennsylvania. The lack of mayonnaise is pleasing to older adults.

HOPPIN' JOHN SALAD

2 15-ounce cans blackeyed
  peas, rinsed
2 15-ounce cans whole
  kernel corn, rinsed
2 cups cooked white rice
1 small red onion, chopped

1 2-ounce jar pimientos,
  rinsed
1 16-ounce bottle Italian
  dressing
1/4 cup granulated sugar
Salt and pepper to taste

Drain all rinsed items very well. Mix all ingredients together, and marinate 8 hours before serving. This recipe will last in refrigerator for 7 to 10 days. May top with sliced green onions just before serving.

Shirley B. Wright, Cleveland County

This is a fairly new recipe. It is especially good with meats, very colorful and tasty. It can be made low-calorie by using fat-free dressing and artificial sweetener.

PICKLED VEGETABLE SALAD

1 cup sugar
3/4 cup vinegar
1 tablespoon water
1/2 cup salad oil
1/2 teaspoon black pepper
1 16-ounce can white shoe
  peg corn, drained

1 16-ounce can small early
  peas, drained
1 16-ounce can French-style
  green beans, drained
1 cup chopped green pepper
1 cup chopped onion
2/3 cup celery, diced

Combine sugar, vinegar, water, salad oil, and pepper in saucepan; bring to a boil. Set aside to cool. In a bowl, combine remaining ingredients. After sauce has cooled, pour over vegetables. Refrigerate.

Desma Young, Buncombe County

PICNIC SALAD IN WINTER

1 cup seedless grapes
1 15-ounce can small white
  beans, drained
1/2 cup diced celery
1/4 cup minced green
  onions

2 tablespoons chopped
  parsley
Lemon mustard dressing
Lettuce leaves

Combine all ingredients except lettuce; mix well. Serve on lettuce leaves with Lemon Mustard Dressing (recipe follows). Serves 4.

Melinda M. Houser, Lincoln County

LEMON MUSTARD DRESSING

2 tablespoons vegetable oil
1 teaspoon Dijon-style
  mustard

1/4 teaspoon salt
2 tablespoons lemon juice
1/4 teaspoon pepper

Combine all ingredients and mix well. Makes 1/4 cup.

Melinda M. Houser, Lincoln County

APRICOT SALAD

1 16- to 22-ounce can
  crushed pineapple
2 boxes apricot Jell-O

2 cups buttermilk
12-ounce container Cool
  Whip

Mix pineapple with boxes of Jell-O. Bring to a boil. Let cool. Mix buttermilk and Cool Whip, and spoon into 9 x 12-inch serving dish. Fold in pineapple and Jell-O. Refrigerate and let set. Serves 12.

Betty Jones, Rockingham County

BLUEBERRY SALAD

Salad:
2 packages grape Jell-O
2 cups boiling water
1 16-ounce can crushed
  pineapple, not drained
1 16-ounce can blueberry
  pie filling

Topping:
1 8-ounce package cream
  cheese
1/2 pint sour cream
1 teaspoon vanilla
1/2 cup sugar
Nuts (optional)

Dissolve the Jell-O in hot water. Stir in undrained pineapple and pie filling. Let congeal in a 9 x 13-inch serving dish. *Prepare topping:* Mix cream cheese, sour cream, vanilla, and sugar together. Smooth topping over base. Top with nuts, if desired. Refrigerate.

Ann Lowder, Stanly County

This is my family's favorite congealed salad.

BUTTERMILK SALAD

1 large can crushed
  pineapple
6 ounces Jell-O, any flavor

2 cups buttermilk
1 9-ounce carton Cool Whip

Place pineapple in bowl that can be heated. Sprinkle on Jell-O, and heat for 4 to 5 minutes but not to boiling. Remove from heat, and cool. Stir in buttermilk and Cool Whip. Store in covered container in refrigerator until ready to serve.

Kappa Extension Homemakers, Davie County

This recipe is in memory of Louise G. Cartner, a charter member of our club, who always served this Buttermilk Salad at the meetings and at her Stanley parties.

BUTTERMILK SALAD

1 20-ounce can pineapple
  tidbits, drained well;
  reserve juice
2 3-ounce packages lemon
  gelatin
1 package plain Knox
  gelatin

1/2 cup cold water
2 cups buttermilk
1 pint whipping cream,
  whipped, *or* 9-ounce
  carton whipped topping,
  thawed
3/4 cup chopped pecans

Drain pineapple tidbits. Heat juice to boiling. Dissolve lemon gelatin in juice. Dissolve plain gelatin in cold water. Combine gelatins. Cool slightly. Add buttermilk. Stir in whipped cream or whipped topping. Add nuts and pineapple. Pour into 9 x 13-inch container, and chill. Serves 15.

Patsy H. McNeill, Stanly County

This recipe came from a 1965 bulletin called Favorite Dairy Recipes *by Miss York Kiker. It was before whipped topping was on the market!*

CHERRY JELL-O SALAD

1 can tart cherries
1 cup sugar
1 3-ounce box cherry Jell-O
1/3 cup cold water
1 package plain gelatin

1 8-ounce can crushed
  pineapple
3 oranges, peeled and cut in
  sections
1/2 cup pecans, chopped

Bring cherries and juice and sugar to a boil. Remove from heat. Add Jell-O. Stir to dissolve. Dissolve gelatin in 1/3 cup water. Add to cherry mixture. Put in refrigerator to cool. When cool, add undrained pineapple, oranges, and pecans. Place in 9 x 13-inch serving dish and refrigerate.

Mildred M. Harper, Edgecombe County

This Jell-O salad is very refreshing and good served on lettuce.

CRANBERRY SALAD

1 package gelatin, plain
1 cup cold water
1 3-ounce box cherry Jell-O
1 3-ounce box lemon Jell-O
1 large can whole cranberry
  sauce
2 1/4 cups water, cold
1 large can crushed
  pineapple in juice
Almonds or pecans,
  chopped (optional)

Add 1 package plain gelatin to 1 cup cold water. Add cherry and lemon Jell-O, and heat until dissolved. Add large can of whole cranberry sauce, and stir to mix. Add 2 1/4 cups cold water and large can pineapple with juice. Add nuts if desired. Pour into mold or 9 x 12-inch dish, and refrigerate until set.

Sandra Vann, Northampton County

CRANBERRY SALAD

1 3-ounce box raspberry
  gelatin
1 3-ounce box cherry
  gelatin
1 cup boiling water
1 cup cold water
1 large can crushed
  pineapple, juice included
1 can whole cranberry
  sauce
1 cup chopped pecans

Dissolve both gelatins in boiling water. Add cold water. Mix in pineapple with juice and cranberry sauce. Stir in nuts. Pour into 9 x 13-inch dish. Congeal, stirring once or twice while setting to distribute nuts.

Betty Mosley, Union County

CRANBERRY SALAD

1 cup ground cranberries
1 cup sugar
1 cup (8 1/2-ounce can)
  crushed pineapple,
  drained, retain juice
1 package cherry Jell-O

1/2 cup boiling water
1/4 cup orange juice and
  grated rind
1 cup chopped celery
1 cup chopped pecans

Combine cranberries and sugar. Let stand. Drain juice from pineapple, retaining juice. Dissolve Jell-O in boiling water. Add orange juice and pineapple juice. Chill until slightly thickened. Add cranberries, pineapple, celery, and pecans. Chill until firm.

Elizabeth Harper, Edgecombe County

FESTIVE CRANBERRY SALAD

1 14-ounce can sweetened
  condensed milk
1/4 cup lemon juice
1 20-ounce can crushed
  pineapple, drained
1 16-ounce can whole-berry
  cranberry sauce

2 cups miniature
  marshmallows
1/2 cup chopped pecans
Red food coloring (optional)
1 8-ounce carton frozen
  whipped topping, thawed

In a bowl, combine milk and lemon juice. Mix well. Stir in the pineapple, cranberry sauce, marshmallows, pecans, and food coloring. Fold in whipped topping. Spoon into a 13 x 9 x 2-inch baking dish. Freeze until firm, about 4 hours, or overnight. Cut into squares. Serves 12 to 16.

Glenda Beavers, Duplin County

This salad is so good that one of the cookbook judges asked for a sheet of paper so she could copy it down. "I don't want to wait for the cookbook to come out!"

Create Your Own Layered Salad

To modify a layered congealed salad so that it includes your family's favorite fruit, remember that ingredients can be divided into two categories: those that sink and those that float.

Ingredients that float include fresh Bing cherries, apples, grapefruit, oranges, cantaloupe, honeydew, raspberries, strawberries, fresh

*peaches, pears, bananas, grapes, nuts, and marshmallows.
Ingredients that sink include canned pineapple, pears, apricots,
canned peaches, mandarin oranges, Royal Anne cherries, and dark
sweet cherries.*

*Use the recipes in this section and create your own congealed salad
full of healthy fruits. Your family will welcome it on a hot, humid
North Carolina summer day.*

PINEAPPLE-STRAWBERRY FROZEN SALAD

1 14-ounce can Eagle Brand
   sweetened condensed milk
2 or 3 large (or 4 small)
   bananas, sliced
1 medium can crushed
   pineapple, drained

1 pint frozen, sliced
   strawberries (or fresh); do
   not drain, thaw slightly
1 8-ounce container Cool
   Whip

Mix ingredients together, folding in Cool Whip last. Put in 9 x 13-
inch container (Tupperware works well); cover and freeze. Cut into
squares and serve. Salad also may be served as a dessert.

Nancy R. Wilson, Granville County

*This recipe has been enjoyed by everyone in my family, especially
on special occasions.*

PINEAPPLE-STRAWBERRY FROZEN SALAD

1/2 cup chopped pecans
3/4 cup sugar
1 10-ounce package frozen
   strawberries, thawed
2 bananas, diced

1 cup chunk or tidbit
   pineapple, drained
1 8-ounce package cream
   cheese, softened
1 large container Cool
   Whip

Mix pecans, sugar, strawberries, bananas, and pineapple. Add cream
cheese. Fold in Cool Whip. Pour into 9 x 13-inch serving dish.
Cover with foil and freeze.

Joyce Ann McFail, Granville County

*I make this for most of my club's special dinners and have shared
the recipe with many friends.*

PINEAPPLE-CHERRY FROZEN FRUIT SALAD

2 envelopes Dream Whip
2 3-ounce packages cream
  cheese, softened
1/4 cup lemon juice
1 14-ounce can Eagle Brand
  condensed milk

1 cup pecans, chopped
1 15 1/4-ounce can crushed
  pineapple, drained
1 21-ounce can cherry pie
  filling

Prepare Dream Whip according to package directions. Set aside. In large bowl, combine cream cheese and lemon juice. Beat until smooth. Stir in milk, pecans, and pineapple. Fold in Dream Whip and pie filling. Pour mixture into paper baking cups set in muffin tins; freeze. Transfer to plastic freezer bags. Individual servings keep well in freezer until needed. Mixture also may be frozen in two 9-inch-square casserole dishes and sliced as needed.

Susan Harper Britt, Nash County

This cool and refreshing fruit salad adds to any meal.

MANDARIN ORANGE SALAD

6 ounces orange Jell-O
2 cups hot water
1 cup orange juice
1 20-ounce can crushed
  pineapple in juice
1 cup sour cream

1 15-ounce can mandarin
  orange sections, drained
  and cut into pieces
1 cup chopped pecans
  (optional)

Dissolve Jell-O in hot water. Add orange juice. Place in refrigerator and let gel slightly. In a separate bowl, mix pineapple with juice and sour cream. Add mandarin orange pieces and nuts. Stir into slightly gelled Jell-O, and pour into mold. Congeal completely. Serves 10.

Sandra Vann, Northampton County

ORANGE SALAD

1 8-ounce container Cool
  Whip, thawed
1 4-ounce package orange
  Jell-O

1 8-ounce carton sour
  cream
1 15-ounce can pineapple
  tidbits, drained
1 small can mandarin
  oranges, drained

35

Combine all ingredients in a medium-sized bowl. Cover, and store in the refrigerator until ready to serve.

Vicki Heath, Craven County

ORANGE JELL-O SALAD

1 15 1/2-ounce can crushed
  pineapple in juice
1 6-ounce package orange
  Jell-O (or any gelatin)
1 cup coconut

2 cups buttermilk
1 cup pecan pieces, if
  desired
1 12-ounce container
  whipped topping

Pour pineapple with juice into saucepan and bring to a boil. Remove from heat and stir in Jell-O until dissolved. Allow to cool but not set. Mix in coconut and buttermilk. Add pecans. Fold in whipped topping. Pour into bundt pan or ring mold that has been sprayed lightly with cooking spray. Refrigerate until congealed.

Brenda Hefner, Alexander County

This salad serves a lot of people, and it's great to take to family gatherings, church meals, and socials.

PINEAPPLE, CARROT, APPLE SALAD

1 3.4-ounce box lemon Jell-O
1 cup boiling water
1 cup reserved pineapple
  juice plus water
1 large carrot, grated
1 8-ounce can crushed
  pineapple, drained
1/2 cup chopped pecans

1/2 cup chopped celery
1/4 cup golden raisins
1 tablespoon lemon juice
1 medium red onion, finely
  chopped
1/4 cup grated cheddar
  cheese

Dissolve Jell-O in boiling water in a large bowl. Add enough water to the reserved pineapple juice to make 1 cup liquid; add to dissolved Jell-O. Chill until it begins to gel. Add all other ingredients, mixing well. Pour into a 9 x 3-inch pan. Return to refrigerator to set. Serves 12.

Carolyn Lackey, Wake County

PINEAPPLE LIME COTTAGE CHEESE SALAD

1 3.4 ounce package lime
Jell-O
1 3.4-ounce package lemon
Jell-O
2 cups boiling water
1 20-ounce can crushed
pineapple, undrained

1/2 cup "lite" mayonnaise
1 cup evaporated milk
12 ounces "lite" cottage
cheese
1/2 cup chopped pecans

In a large bowl, dissolve Jell-O in boiling water. Add undrained
pineapple. Put into refrigerator until Jell-O begins to set. Combine
mayonnaise, evaporated milk, cottage cheese, and nuts. Add to
Jell-O. Pour into 9 x 13-inch pan. Refrigerate until set. Serves 12.

Fuchsia Yelton, Gaston County

PISTACHIO SALAD

1 box pistachio instant
pudding
1/2 cup nuts, chopped
1 cup miniature
marshmallows

1 small container Cool
Whip
1 large can crushed
pineapple

Mix ingredients, and chill. Spoon onto lettuce leaves to serve.

Jessica Herring, Duplin County

SAWDUST SALAD

1 3-ounce package orange
gelatin
1 3-ounce package lemon
gelatin
2 cups hot water
1 1/4 cups cold water
1 16-ounce can crushed
pineapple, drained and
liquid saved
3 or 4 bananas, sliced
Miniature marshmallows

Topping:
2 eggs, well beaten
1 cup sugar
6 tablespoons all-purpose
flour
1 3/4 cups pineapple juice
(add water to saved juice
to get 1 3/4 cups liquid)
1 8-ounce package cream
cheese, softened
1 8-ounce container Cool
Whip
Crushed pecans (optional)

Dissolve gelatins with 2 cups of hot water in a 9 x 13-inch dish or large serving container. Add 1 1/4 cups cold water. Drain pineapple juice; refrigerate juice. Add pineapple and sliced bananas to gelatin. Sprinkle entire top with miniature marshmallows. Let stand until firm in refrigerator. *Prepare topping:* Use a double boiler saucepan. Mix eggs, sugar, flour, and pineapple juice (add water to juice to get 1 3/4 cups). Cook until thick. Let cool and spread on top of gelatin mixture. Blend cream cheese and Cool Whip together. Spread on top of cooked mixture. Sprinkle with crushed pecans, if desired.

Nancy R. Wilson, Granville County

My family enjoys this salad, especially on special occasions.

—

STRAWBERRY SALAD

1 6-ounce package
  strawberry Jell-O
2 cups boiling water
1 20-ounce package frozen
  strawberries

1 16-ounce can crushed
  pineapple
1 cup mashed bananas
2/3 cup chopped pecans
1/2 pint sour cream

Dissolve Jell-O in hot water. Stir in strawberries, pineapple, bananas, and pecans. Pour half of mixture into oblong pan. Allow to set in refrigerator. Spread set mixture with sour cream. Cover with remaining Jell-O mixture and return to refrigerator.

Della Stephens, Forsyth County

Della Stephens was assistant fair director for the Dixie Classic Fair. She retired at the end of 2002 after serving 40 years in the Dixie Classic Fair Administrative Office.

STRAWBERRY PRETZEL SALAD

2 cups coarsely chopped
  pretzels
3/4 cup melted butter
3 tablespoons sugar
1 8-ounce package cream
  cheese, softened
1 cup sugar

1 8-ounce container frozen
  non-dairy whipped
  topping
1 6-ounce package
  strawberry gelatin
2 cups boiling water
2 10-ounce packages frozen
  strawberries

Mix chopped pretzels, melted butter, and 3 tablespoons sugar together. Press into the bottom of a 9 x 13-inch pan. Bake 8 to 10 minutes at 400° F. Cool. Blend cream cheese and 1 cup sugar. Fold in whipped topping and spread on cooled crust. Dissolve strawberry gelatin in boiling water, and stir in frozen strawberries. When partially set, pour over cream cheese layer. Refrigerate. Must be prepared ahead of time.

Pearl Ange, Craven County

SWEET PASTA SALAD

1 16-ounce box rainbow rotini noodles
1/2 cup chopped celery
1 cup chopped purple onion
1/4 cup chopped red bell pepper
1/4 cup chopped green bell pepper
1 cup coarsely grated carrots
Sauce:
1 can Eagle Brand sweetened condensed milk
2 cups mayonnaise
1 cup sugar
1 cup apple cider vinegar

Prepare sauce first: Mix milk, mayonnaise, sugar, and vinegar together, and set aside. Prepare noodles as directed on box. Rinse in hot water, drain, and add chopped celery, onion, bell pepper, and carrots. Pour sauce over vegetables and noodles, and stir. Refrigerate overnight in a sealed container. Stir well before serving. Serves approximately 15.

Ella R. Richardson, Randolph County

This salad is enjoyed by all.

TOMATO-GRAPEFRUIT SALAD

1 15-ounce can grapefruit sections
1 15-ounce can cut up tomatoes
1/2 8-ounce bottle Italian dressing

Mix ingredients together in a non-metal mixing bowl. Chill before serving. Serve in a salad bowl. Serves 6.

Pam Riemer, Scotland County

This recipe is from my friend Wilma Andrews, who now lives in Independence, Kansas.

BLUE CHEESE DRESSING

1 small onion, cut up
1 cup mayonnaise or salad
  dressing
1/3 cup salad oil
1/4 cup catsup
2 tablespoons sugar
2 tablespoons vinegar

1 teaspoon prepared
  mustard
1/2 teaspoon salt
1/2 teaspoon paprika
1/4 teaspoon celery seed
Dash of pepper
1 cup (4 ounces) crumbled
  blue cheese

Combine all ingredients except the blue cheese in a blender. Cover container, and blend until smooth. Remove the dressing from the blender container, and stir in the blue cheese. Cover and chill. Garnish with additional blue cheese. Serve over your favorite tossed vegetable salad. Makes 2 1/2 cups salad dressing.

Hannah Cox, Craven County

FRENCH DRESSING

1 can tomato soup
3/4 cup vinegar
1 teaspoon black pepper
1 teaspoon dry mustard
1 teaspoon onion salt

1 teaspoon Worcestershire
  sauce
2 teaspoons salt
1 cup sugar
1 1/2 cups vegetable oil

Place all ingredients except oil in blender. Begin blending and slowly add oil to other ingredients. Store in refrigerator. Makes about 1 quart, or 32 servings.

Sandra Vann, Northampton County

GREEN GODDESS DRESSING

1/2 cup parsley, minced
3 tablespoons chives,
  minced
1/2 cup low-fat mayonnaise
1/2 cup low-fat yogurt

1/2 cup low-fat sour cream
2 tablespoons tarragon
  vinegar
1/2 teaspoon salt
1/2 teaspoon sugar

Place ingredients in blender, and process on low for 30 seconds. Refrigerate.

Fay Driver, Nash County

BBQ CHICKEN SAUCE

2 large onions
1/2 gallon vinegar
1 cup sugar

1 12-ounce bottle Carolina
Treat Sauce
1 12-ounce bottle Kraft
Hickory BBQ Sauce

Boil the onions in the vinegar for 5 minutes. Add sugar and bottled sauces. To serve, pour over grilled or baked chicken.

Charles Martin, Tim Martin, Wayne County

BBQ SAUCE

32 ounces ketchup
2 cups water
1/2 cup brown sugar
2 teaspoons chili powder
2 cups vinegar
2 cups sugar

2 teaspoons dry mustard
1/4 bottle Worcestershire
sauce
Red pepper and Texas Pete
hot sauce to taste

Mix all ingredients, and heat to boiling to blend flavors. Sauce keeps 2 to 3 weeks in the refrigerator, and is good on all kinds of meat.

Sandra Vann, Northampton County

DARRELL'S HOMEMADE BARBECUE SAUCE
(good on pork, chicken, turkey, and beef)

1/2 gallon apple cider
vinegar
1 ounce Texas Pete hot
sauce
1 tablespoon black pepper

1 24-ounce bottle ketchup
1 2-ounce jar crushed red
pepper
1 20-ounce Coke

Put all ingredients except Coke in a pot, and bring to a boil. Reduce heat, and slow boil for about 30 minutes. Add Coke to sauce, and bring to a full boil. Cook 3 to 5 minutes, and then reduce heat and simmer for 15 minutes. Take off heat, and let cool. Store *cooled* sauce in a glass jar. Reduce or increase the amounts of hot sauce and pepper, based on your taste.

Darrell Lee Jones, Duplin County

It's best when cooked outdoors.

EASTERN CAROLINA CHOPPED BBQ SAUCE

1 gallon vinegar
5 pounds sugar
1 3-ounce jar crushed red
  pepper

1 3-ounce jar ground
  cayenne pepper
1 2-ounce container black
  pepper

Combine ingredients in a large cooking pot. Cook 1 hour over medium heat. Add more of above ingredients to adjust taste.

Charles Martin, Timothy Martin, Wayne County

This recipe has been passed down through the Martin family for over 70 years. It is especially enjoyed at the family's annual reunion and other family gatherings. This recipe has been made by the oldest Martin family member—80-plus Elizabeth Martin of Wayne County—to the youngest cooking member—9-year-old Wesley Martin of Wake County.

CHILI SAUCE

18 ripe tomatoes, peeled
  and quartered
3 green peppers, chopped
2 large onions, chopped
1 tablespoon cinnamon

1/2 tablespoon cloves
1 tablespoon salt
3/4 cup sugar
1/2 cup vinegar

Cook over slow heat, stirring occasionally. Cook to desired thickness. Best started in the morning.

Sandy Shultz Smith, Wake County

QUICK AND EASY HOT SAUCE
AKA PETE'S PUCKER UP!

1 Bottle Heinz Chili Sauce
  (no other)
1 Bottle Heinz Ketchup
  (same size)

Fresh horseradish sauce to
  taste (or until eyes water)
Juice from 1/2 lemon

Mix all ingredients and enjoy.

Pete and Gael Jaeger, Chatham County

DARRELL'S HOMEMADE ITALIAN SAUCE

32 ounces tomato sauce
16 ounces stewed tomatoes
1/2 tablespoon basil
1/2 tablespoon oregano
1 teaspoon parsley
Salt and pepper to taste
1 medium onion, diced

1 small green bell pepper,
  diced
1 package fresh
  mushrooms, diced
2 cloves garlic
1 package Italian sausage
1 pound hamburger

Put tomato sauce, tomatoes, basil, oregano, parsley, salt, and pepper in a large pot, and simmer over medium heat. While sauce is simmering, dice onion, green pepper, mushrooms, and garlic. In a frying pan, cook the Italian sausage completely. When sausage is finished, drain on paper towels. Using the same pan, drain all but a small layer of grease, and sauté onion, green pepper, mushrooms, and garlic until tender. Drain grease and put mixture into sauce. Cook hamburger until brown, and drain off grease. Put hamburger into sauce. Cut up the sausage, and put into sauce. Cover pot and simmer on low-medium heat for 30 to 35 minutes. Serves 4 to 6 adults.

Darrell Lee Jones, Duplin County

HEAVENLY CHOCOLATE SAUCE

1 14 1/2-ounce can
  evaporated milk
2 cups sugar

3 squares (3 ounces)
  unsweetened chocolate
1 teaspoon vanilla

Combine milk, sugar, and chocolate in a double boiler. Cook over water for 15 minutes, stirring occasionally until chocolate is melted. Be careful not to get any water in the mixture. Remove from heat. Add vanilla. Beat with rotary beater until smooth and thick. Serve over ice cream, angel food cake, or other dessert.

Debby McGilvery, Guilford County

This recipe came from the cookbook put out by Hope United Methodist Church.

SPAGHETTI SAUCE WITH SAUSAGE
(for a crowd)

3 pounds lean ground beef
1 pound hot Italian sausage
1 pound mild Italian
  sausage
4 28-ounce jars of spaghetti
  sauce (we like chunky
  style)

1 onion, chopped
2 cloves garlic, minced
3 soup-sized cans beef broth
Italian seasoning to taste, if
  desired

Cook hamburger and sausage until done. I use a dutch oven so the
fat doesn't spatter, and cook the meat in three batches. Drain away
fat, retaining two tablespoons. Put retained fat back in pan, and
sauté onion and garlic. Combine meat, onion, garlic, spaghetti
sauce, and broth in a large pot. Cook for an hour over low heat. Stir
occasionally so that it doesn't stick to the bottom of the pan, and
add water if the sauce is too thick. Taste and add Italian seasoning
15 minutes before the sauce is done. You can use 2 pounds hot
sausage or 2 pounds mild sausage, depending on how spicy your
family likes its food. Freezes well and is also good in lasagna.

Janet Singleton, Wake County

This sauce tastes like you spent the day in the kitchen.

Fruits & Vegetables

Apples
Cranberries
Figs
Pears
Pineapple
Asparagus
Beans
Beets
Broccoli

Cabbage
Carrots
Collards
Corn
Creasy Greens
Cucumbers
Onions
Peas
Peppers

Poke Greens
Potatoes
Pumpkin
Rice
Squash
Sweet Potatoes
Tomatoes
Turnips

A Taste of North Carolina's Heritage

Food . . . For Thought?

Did you know that . . .

- Through the Expanded Food and Nutrition Education Program (EFNEP), North Carolina Cooperative Extension has been improving nutrition for the state's citizens for 30 years?

- Compared to 10 years ago, pork has 31 percent less fat, 14 percent fewer calories, and 10 percent less cholesterol, making its lean cuts comparable to skinless chicken breasts?

- One cup of muscadine grapes has only 90 calories and no fat or cholesterol. One egg has 69 nutrients. A tomato is a great source for Vitamin A, Vitamin C, potassium, phosphorus, and other minerals, and is low in calories?

- Sweet potatoes contain more fiber than oatmeal and offer 23 times more cancer-fighting beta carotene than broccoli?

- 25 grams of soy protein included in a daily diet low in saturated fat and cholesterol may reduce the risk of heart disease?

- A new system for rapidly cooling eggs with carbon dioxide, developed at NC State University, will help reduce consumers' risk of contracting *Salmonella enteritidis* from eggs?

- Eating small, frequent servings of peanuts can reduce the risk of heart disease?

APPLE-CRANBERRY CASSEROLE
(or Apple-Blueberry Casserole)

2 cups fresh cranberries (or blueberries)
3 cups apples, peeled and chopped
1 1/4 cups sugar
1/3 cup flour

1 1/2 cups oatmeal, uncooked
1/2 cup pecans, chopped
2/3 cup brown sugar
1 stick margarine

Mix cranberries (or blueberries), apples, and sugar. Put in greased 2-quart casserole dish. Mix flour, oatmeal, pecans, and brown sugar, and spread over fruit mixture. Pour melted butter over topping. Bake at 350° F. for 1 hour. Serves 8.

Vicki Walton, Wake County

This is great as a dessert or fruit dish with main meal.

APPLE-CRANBERRY DISH

2 cups raw cranberries
1 cup sugar
3 cups apples, unpeeled and diced

Topping:
1 stick margarine
1 cup uncooked oatmeal (quick, 1-minute-type)
1/2 cup brown sugar

Combine cranberries, sugar, and apples. Put in 9 x 12-inch casserole dish that has been lightly sprayed with cooking spray. Mix margarine, oatmeal, and brown sugar. Sprinkle on top of fruit mixture. Bake at 350° F. for 40 minutes. Serves 8 to 10.

Sylvia S. Burgess, Vance County

I take this dish to our church homecomings, and the dish always returns empty. It's good with turkey, pork, and chicken.

North Carolina Apples

According to the Blue Ridge Apple Growers Association, Henderson County ranks seventh in production among all the counties in the United States. The county's 200 apple growers produce about 65 percent of all the apples grown in the state.

CRANBERRY-APPLE CASSEROLE

4 apples, peeled and
  chopped
2 cups fresh cranberries
2 tablespoons all-purpose
  flour
1 cup sugar
Cinnamon to taste

Topping:
3/4 cup chopped pecans
5 ounces oatmeal, uncooked
1/2 cup all-purpose flour
1/2 cup brown sugar
1/2 cup margarine, melted

Combine apples, cranberries, and 2 tablespoons flour, tossing to coat fruit. Add sugar and cinnamon. Mix well, and pour in a greased 9 1/2 x 13-inch casserole dish. Combine pecans, oatmeal, 1/2 cup flour, brown sugar, and melted margarine. Stir well; spoon over fruit mixture. Bake uncovered at 350° F. for 45 minutes. Serves 6 to 8.

Sarah Ray, Harnett County

This recipe was given to me by Nancy Guy, a wonderful cook from Erwin. It is one of my family's favorites.

CRANBERRY-APPLE RELISH

1 orange, unpeeled
5 or 6 red apples, unpeeled
1 pound fresh cranberries
2 cups sugar

1 20-ounce can crushed
  pineapple, drained
1/2 cup chopped pecans

Remove seeds from orange and apples. Put in blender or food processor with cranberries, and chop coarsely. Mix with sugar, pineapple, and nuts. Refrigerate overnight. Makes 2 quarts.

Ann Lowder, Stanly County

This is good with turkey and dressing.

MEXICAN CRANBERRY RELISH

1/2 cup orange juice
1 cup dark raisins
1 15-ounce can whole berry
  cranberry sauce
1 Gala or Golden Delicious
  apple, peeled and chopped
1 cup chopped pecans

Juice of 1/2 lemon
Zest of 1/2 lemon
1/2 teaspoon Texas Pete hot
  sauce
Cilantro, chopped
  (optional)

Heat orange juice in microwave for 1 to 2 minutes. Add raisins, and let cool. Break up cranberry sauce, and add all ingredients. Refrigerate for 1 to 2 hours so flavors have a chance to blend. You can add more hot sauce and some chopped cilantro, if desired.

Shirley B. Wright, Cleveland County

The relish keeps 2 to 3 weeks in the refrigerator, and it gets better the longer it sits. It's delicious with ham, turkey, or chicken.

—

DRIED FIGS

2 cups sugar　　　　　　**2 quarts fresh figs**
2 cups water

Boil sugar and water about 10 minutes. Add figs and cook 45 minutes, stirring often. Let mixture remain in pot overnight. Then cook 30 minutes, stirring often. Let mixture remain in pot a second night. Cook 30 minutes, stirring constantly. Let stand overnight a third night. Place figs on cookie sheet and place in oven for about half a day on low temperature. When dry, roll in white sugar. Pack in container and refrigerate or freeze. Note: Smaller figs hold their shape better than larger figs.

Juanita Fisher Lagg, Rowan County

My mother had an abundance of fresh figs, and she used this recipe so that she would have figs to use in her fruit cake at Christmas. She dried them in the sun, but I use the oven. The dried figs taste like candy, and everyone on my Christmas list looks forward to this special treat.

HOT FRUIT

1 15-ounce can sliced peaches, drained
1 15-ounce can pineapple chunks, drained
1 15-ounce can apricots, drained

1 14-ounce jar of apple rings, retain juice
1/2 cup sugar
1/4 cup all-purpose flour
1 stack Ritz crackers, crushed
1 stick margarine, melted

Layer fruit in 9 x 12-inch casserole dish. Sprinkle sugar and flour over fruit. Pour 6 tablespoons retained juice from apple rings over fruit. Mix melted margarine and crushed Ritz crackers. Sprinkle cracker mixture on top. Bake at 350° F. until bubbly, about 30 minutes. Serves 12.

Pearl Freedman, Columbus County

This makes a pretty addition to a buffet table.

—

PICKLED PEARS

6 medium pears
1/2 box whole cloves
1 cup cider vinegar

1 cup granulated sugar
3 sticks cinnamon

Select firm pickling pears. Peel, quarter, and remove core. Stick two whole cloves into each quartered pear. Combine vinegar, sugar, and cinnamon sticks in a large saucepan. Bring to a boil. Add pears. Simmer until pears are tender, about 10 minutes. Serve warm or chilled.

Helen Mae Hilliard King, Warren County

Martha Elizabeth Stallings Paschall and her husband, John William Henry Paschall, planted a pickling pear tree in the backyard so that she could make this pickle each year in Warren County. This tree is still standing. These pears are hard as a rock before they are cooked. The recipe submitted was halved for family use.

CHEESY PINEAPPLE

2 tablespoons flour
3/4 cup sugar
2 large cans pineapple
   chunks, drained (retain
   juice)

2 cups grated cheddar
   cheese
1/2 cup Ritz crackers,
   crushed
1/4 cup butter or
   margarine, melted

Combine flour and sugar with 6 tablespoons pineapple juice. Mix with cheese. Place in greased 9 x 11-inch casserole dish. Top with cracker crumbs. Pour melted butter over top. Bake uncovered for 20 minutes at 375° F. Serves 8 to 10.

Billie Walker, Orange County

This dish is good with meats. Take it to church suppers and reunions.

ASPARAGUS TOAST

1 cup medium thick white sauce	2 boiled eggs
1 can asparagus spears, drained (retain liquid)	4 slices toasted bread
	Salt and pepper

While making white sauce, add 4 tablespoons of asparagus juice.
Slice boiled eggs cross-ways. Layer toast, asparagus, egg slice, and
white sauce. Salt and pepper to taste. Serves 4.

Pam Riemer, Scotland County

This was a family favorite and the only way the children would eat asparagus.

OVEN-BAKED ASPARAGUS

Fresh asparagus	Garlic salt, to taste
Olive oil-flavored Pam cooking spray	Pepper, to taste

Line a baking sheet with heavy-duty aluminum foil. Put in oven and
set temperature for 500° F. When oven reaches 500° F., set timer for
10 minutes. Meanwhile, wash and trim asparagus. When pan has
heated for 10 minutes, remove from oven and quickly spray foil
with cooking spray. Place one layer of asparagus on pan. Spray
asparagus with cooking spray. Sprinkle with garlic salt and pepper.
Return to oven. Cook until crisp-tender. Cooking time varies with
size of asparagus and personal taste, but ranges from 5 to 15
minutes.

Laura B. Wooten, Wake County

The asparagus has a grilled flavor.

ASPARAGUS CASSEROLE

4 15-ounce cans cut asparagus, drained (reserve liquid)	1 pound sharp cheddar cheese, grated
4 tablespoons butter	1 2-ounce jar sliced pimientos, drained
4 tablespoons flour	30 Ritz crackers
Salt and pepper, to taste	1/4 cup slivered almonds

Preheat oven. Place drained asparagus in 13 x 9-inch baking dish.
Melt butter in a saucepan; blend in flour. Gradually stir in half the

reserved asparagus liquid. Bring sauce to a boil; stir constantly until thickened. Season to taste with salt and pepper. Then add cheese, pimientos, and remaining asparagus liquid. Pour sauce over asparagus. Mix lightly and carefully. Sprinkle with cracker crumbs and almonds. Bake in a 350° F. oven for 20 to 30 minutes. Serves 10 to 12. Note: This dish may be prepared ahead of time, but do not add almonds until just before baking.

Elizabeth Harper, Edgecombe County

LEBANESE-STYLE GREEN BEANS

1/2 cup chopped onion	1 4-ounce can tomato sauce
1 tablespoon oil	1 teaspoon salt
2 cups water	1 teaspoon pepper
2 pounds fresh green beans	1/2 teaspoon ground allspice

In large cooking pot on top of the stove, combine chopped onion and oil, and cook on medium heat until slightly browned. Add water and green beans, and continue cooking on medium heat for about 20 minutes. Add tomato sauce, salt, pepper, and allspice. Cover and turn heat down to low; cook an additional 20 to 30 minutes or until beans are done and tender. This dish can be stored in the refrigerator for several days. It always tastes good, even re-heated. Serves 6.

Cecilia Wilson, Pamlico County

My grandmother and mother cooked these beans with every major meal for as long as I remember. I don't think I ever ate green beans seasoned any other way until I was married and had a family of my own. I still prefer this recipe to today's seasoned green bean recipes.

MARINATED BEAN SALAD

1 can cut green beans	1 jar pimiento, sliced
2 cans lima beans	1 bunch green onions,
1 can kidney beans	chopped
1 can wax beans	2 cups vinegar
1 can garbanzo beans	2 cups sugar
1 large green pepper,	1/2 cup water
chopped	1 teaspoon salt
3 stalks celery, sliced	

Drain all cans of beans. Rinse lima and kidney beans. Place in a large bowl. Add green pepper, celery, pimiento, and onions; set aside. Bring remaining ingredients to a boil in a saucepan; boil for 5 minutes. Remove from heat and immediately pour over vegetables. Refrigerate several hours or overnight. Serves 15.

Sandra Vann, Northampton County

BAKED BEANS

**2 15-ounce cans baked
 beans with pork
1/2 cup packed brown sugar
1/2 onion, chopped
1/2 cup ketchup
1 tablespoon prepared
 mustard**

**1 teaspoon Worcestershire
 sauce
Salt and pepper to taste
2 slices raw bacon, cut into
 1-inch pieces**

In a 9 x 9-inch baking dish, combine the pork and beans, sugar, onion, ketchup, mustard, and Worcestershire sauce. Add salt and pepper to taste. Top with bacon pieces. Bake in 350° F. oven about 1 hour, until sauce is thickened and bacon is cooked. Serves 6.

Tina Brown, Cabarrus County

These baked beans are great with hot dogs and hamburgers.

BUTTERED BEETS

**2 tablespoons butter
1 tablespoon cornstarch
3 cups cooked beets
1 cup liquid from cooked
 beets**

**1 small onion
2 tablespoons cider vinegar
1/4 teaspoon salt
Black pepper to taste
1 1/2 teaspoons sugar**

Melt butter; blend in cornstarch. Add beets and 1 cup beet liquid. Stir constantly over direct heat until sauce boils and thickens. Add remaining ingredients, and heat slowly until beets are hot through. Serves 5.

Betty Jean King, Warren County

Malaha Green Paschall and her husband, Thomas Paschall, are remembered for planting a beautiful garden. This is one of the recipes used for the vegetables they harvested. They had only two children and shared vegetables with neighbors and friends.

GRANDMOTHER'S PICKLED BEETS

1/2 cup white vinegar	1/8 teaspoon black pepper
1/2 cup sugar	1 large onion, thinly sliced
1/2 cup water	2 cups sliced, canned beets,
1 teaspoon salt	with juice

In a 1 1/2 quart saucepan, combine vinegar, sugar, water, salt, pepper, and sliced onion. Bring to boil. Simmer for 5 minutes. Meanwhile, place the sliced beets with juice in serving bowl. Pour hot marinade over beets, and let cool to room temperature. Cover the bowl with plastic wrap, and refrigerate for at least 6 hours, stirring every few hours to keep the slices moist. Makes 2 cups.

Shirley A. Pendergrass, Franklin County

PICKLED BEETS

1 cup sugar	1 cup plus 3 tablespoons
1 quart beets	vinegar
1/2 teaspoon salt	1/2 cup water

Combine all ingredients in large pan, and simmer 15 minutes. Refrigerate before eating.

Evelyn Stevens, Wake County

The original recipe is for 3 quarts, but we've scaled it down for family use.

BROCCOLI BAKE

2 packages frozen broccoli,	8 ounces Velveeta cheese
cooked and drained	2/3 stack Ritz crackers,
1 stick butter, divided	crushed

Cook broccoli as directed on package. Drain well. Place broccoli in a shallow casserole dish; set aside. Melt 1/2 stick butter and Velveeta over low heat or in microwave. Pour over broccoli. Melt remaining half stick of butter, and mix with crushed crackers. Sprinkle over broccoli-cheese mixture. Bake in 350° F. oven for 20 to 30 minutes. Serves 6 to 8.

Becky Davis, Vance County

I have to make this every time my son comes home for a visit. It's simple and delicious.

BROCCOLI CASSEROLE

2 packages chopped
 broccoli
1 can cream of mushroom
 soup
2 eggs, slightly beaten

2 tablespoons minced onion
1 cup salad dressing
1 cup grated cheese
Ritz crackers, crushed

Cook broccoli according to package instructions. Drain well. Put in buttered 9 x 11-inch buttered casserole. Spoon mushroom soup over broccoli. In a separate bowl, blend together eggs, onion, salad dressing, and cheese. Pour over soup. Cover with crushed cracker crumbs. Bake 45 minutes in a 350° F. oven. Serves 8 to 10.

Carolyn Hinnant, Johnston County

My sister passed this recipe on to me. It is so good, I serve it on special occasions.

BROCCOLI-RICE CASSEROLE

1 medium onion, chopped
3 tablespoons butter
2 10-ounce packages frozen,
 chopped broccoli
1 5-ounce jar processed
 cheese

2 1/2 cups cooked rice
1 can cream of chicken
 soup, *or* 1 can cream of
 mushroom soup
1 cup herb-seasoned
 stuffing mix, if desired

Cook onion in butter until transparent; add frozen broccoli. Cook over low heat, uncovered, until broccoli thaws. Add jar of cheese, rice, and soup. Pour into 2-quart casserole. Cover with herb-seasoned stuffing mix. Bake 20 to 30 minutes at 350° F. until bubbly. Serves 8.

Sandra Calhoun, Surry County
Georgia Kight, Currituck County

Georgia Kight uses cream of chicken soup and tops the casserole with stuffing mix when she makes this recipe each year for her family reunion. Sandra Calhoun prefers cream of mushroom soup and no topping.

CRUNCHY BROCCOLI AND CAULIFLOWER TOSS

1 small head cauliflower,
  broken into florets
1/2 pound fresh broccoli,
  broken into florets

1/2 pint cherry tomatoes,
  halved
1/2 cup Italian reduced-
  calorie dressing

Wash broccoli, cauliflower, and cherry tomatoes, and combine all ingredients in a medium-sized bowl. Pour dressing over vegetables, and toss lightly to coat. Cover and chill overnight. Serves 6.

Johnsie C. Cunningham, Granville County

My reputation as a cook is based on what is fast, easy, and GOOD...but does not require cooking. This vegetable dish is not just a pretty dish, it's a family favorite.

CABBAGE CASSEROLE

1 stick margarine, melted
1 can celery soup
1/4 cup mayonnaise
1 1/2 cups corn flakes,
  crushed, divided

4 to 5 cups cabbage,
  shredded
1 1/2 cups grated cheese,
  divided
Salt and pepper, if desired

Mix margarine, soup, and mayonnaise. Take 1 cup of crushed corn flakes, and put in bottom of greased baking dish. Put cabbage on top of corn flakes. Mix 3/4 cup cheese with soup mixture. Pour over cabbage, and sprinkle 1/2 cup corn flakes over the top. Bake at 350° F. for 40 to 45 minutes. Put remainder of cheese on top and cook 10 minutes longer. Serves 8 to 10.

Witt Fogleman, Alamance County

PEANUT SLAW

Salad:
2 cups green cabbage,
  shredded
1 cup red cabbage,
  shredded
1 cup celery, chopped
1 cup mayonnaise
1 teaspoon sugar
1 teaspoon salt

1/2 teaspoon black pepper
  (to taste)
Topping:
1 tablespoon margarine,
  melted
1 cup dry-roasted peanuts
2 tablespoons grated
  Parmesan cheese

Mix salad ingredients, and place in a shallow dish. *Prepare topping:* In a saucepan, mix margarine and peanuts, stirring and watching closely. Sprinkle cheese over peanuts. Heat for an additional 30 seconds, stirring often. Sprinkle topping over slaw just before serving. Serves 8.

Shirley B. Wright, Cleveland County

STANLY COUNTY SLAW

1 large green cabbage, shredded or chopped fine
1 4-ounce jar pimiento pieces
1 large green pepper, chopped

1 15-ounce can tomatoes
Dash hot sauce
1 tablespoon sugar
1 tablespoon salt
1/2 cup vinegar

Mix all ingredients well. May be served immediately or chilled and served cold.

Patsy A. McNeill, Stanly County

This is a barbeque type of slaw, as opposed to mayonnaise-based slaw. It's what we serve with barbeque in Stanly County. Any leftover slaw stores well in the refrigerator.

SWEET AND SOUR SLAW

1 large head green cabbage, coarsely shredded
1 green pepper, finely chopped
1 onion, finely chopped
1 cup sugar

1 cup vinegar
3/4 cup vegetable oil
1 tablespoon salt
1 teaspoon celery salt
1 teaspoon mustard seeds

Combine cabbage, green pepper, and onion in bowl. Combine remaining ingredients in saucepan. Bring to a boil. Boil 3 minutes. Pour over cabbage. Cover and refrigerate about 4 hours. Toss before serving. Refrigerate any leftovers. Serves 8.

Juanita L. Guthrie, Onslow County

Instant Vegetable Platter

Buy cut-up vegetables from the salad bar in the supermarket. Serve with low- or non-fat ranch dressing in a separate bowl.

CARROT SOUFFLE

1 pound baby carrots,
cooked, drained, and
mashed
1 stick butter, melted
2 tablespoons all-purpose
flour

1 teaspoon vanilla
1 teaspoon baking powder
1 cup sugar
3 eggs

Add butter to hot, mashed carrots. Add all other ingredients and
blend with mixer. Pour into buttered casserole dish. Bake at 350° F.
for 45 minutes. Serves 4 to 6.

Elizabeth Parrish, Chowan County

*The dish looks like sweet potato pudding. It's good at Thanksgiving
or any time with meats and vegetables.*

COLLARDS

2 large-headed collards

3 pounds fresh pork with
salt added, *or* 1 1/2 pounds
ham hocks

Separate leaves and discard wilted ones. Wash collards well. Cook
seasoned meat until tender (test with a fork). Remove meat from
broth. Put collards in broth, and cook until tender, not mushy. When
tender, remove from broth and chop. Season to taste.

Lula Mae Tyndall, Sampson County

*If you pick collards in early fall, they take longer to cook. If you
pick them after a frost, it doesn't take as long to cook, maybe only
15 minutes.*

BAKED COLLARDS

2 pounds fresh collards
1 pound sliced bacon
2 Vidalia onions, chopped

1 cup water
Salt and pepper to taste
Apple cider vinegar to taste

Prepare collards by removing the leafy part from the stem. Wash
thoroughly and drain. Tear leaves into bite-sized pieces. Fry bacon
until crisp. Save drippings. Sauté chopped onion and collards
together in the bacon drippings until tender. Season with salt and
pepper. Put in a 2 1/2-quart casserole dish (I use a dish with a lid).

Add water. Cover, and bake at 350° F. for 30 minutes. Crumble bacon, and stir into collards. Add vinegar to taste. Serves 6.

Shawn Poe, Chatham County

NASH COUNTY CABBAGE COLLARD GREENS

3 to 5 pounds cabbage
collards
1 1/2 pounds ham hock, *or*
1/2 pound fatback, washed
and thinly sliced

Water
Salt to taste

Remove large stems from collards. Wash well through 3 or 4 rinses. Fill a large pot (10- to 12-quart) two-thirds full of water, and place seasoning meat in pot. Add collards. Add salt to taste. Cook about 2 hours or until stems will cut with fork. Take up greens and strain broth. Chop, and serve with hush puppies.

Marie Joyner, Nash County

I take these to church homecomings, family dinners, Thanksgiving, Christmas, and any time you want good greens. Your serving dish will always be left empty.

CORN FRITTERS

2 eggs
1 cup all-purpose flour
1 cup fresh corn (can be
canned or frozen)

1/2 cup milk
2 tablespoons vegetable oil
1 tablespoon sugar
Oil for frying

Mix eggs, flour, corn, milk, 2 tablespoons vegetable oil, and sugar into a batter. Cover bottom of frying pan with vegetable oil. Heat on medium-high heat until oil is hot. Place a large serving spoon of batter in hot grease, and cook until browned. Turn and brown the other side. Remove fritter to paper towel to remove excess oil. Serves 6.

Georgia Kight, Currituck County

This is a family recipe that was passed down from another family and is a favorite year 'round, but especially during fresh corn season.

FRIED CORN

12 ears of corn (about 5
  cups of corn cut off the
  cob)
1/3 cup butter

Salt to taste
Black pepper to taste
Pinch of white sugar

Husk, silk, and wash corn. Cut corn from the cob using very sharp
knife, cutting about half the depth of the kernels. Using the back of
the knife, scrape remaining pulp downward. Melt butter in skillet.
Add corn and enough water to make a thin gravy. Season with salt,
pepper, and sugar. Cook, stirring constantly for 5 minutes, reduce
heat. Cover and simmer for 20 minutes. Stir occasionally.

Betty Jean King, Granville County

*This recipe was used by Mary Jane Currin King in Granville
County. When Mary Jane died, she had been helping her husband,
William Henry King, Sr., replant corn and had corn kernels in her
apron pocket.*

FRIED CORN

6 strips bacon
1/3 cup chopped onion
1/3 cup chopped green bell
  peppers
2 cups fresh corn (frozen
  can be used)

1 large tomato, skinned and
  diced
1/2 teaspoon salt
Dash pepper
1 teaspoon cumin

Fry and crumble bacon; reserve 1/4 cup bacon drippings. Sauté
onion and bell pepper in 1/4 cup bacon drippings. Add corn, tomato,
salt, pepper, and cumin. Cook slowly over medium heat for about
10 minutes, stirring frequently. Sprinkle bacon pieces over top and
serve. Makes 4 to 6 servings.

Shirley Pendergrass, Franklin County

Corn on the Cob

*Have you heard that you should get five servings of fruits
and vegetables every day? An ear of corn on the cob fresh
from a North Carolina farm makes a delicious serving,
and corn is a good source of fiber and vitamin C.*

Here are eight variations on a North Carolina favorite: Fresh Corn Pudding.

THE COMMISSIONER'S CORN PUDDING

2 cups corn
2 tablespoons flour
1 tablespoon sugar
1 cup milk

2 tablespoons butter or
   margarine
2 teaspoons salt
Red or white pepper to taste
3 eggs

Cut corn from cob or use leftover stewed corn. In a separate bowl, mix flour and sugar together. Add milk, butter, flour-sugar mixture, and seasonings to corn. Beat eggs together until light; add to mixture. Pour into a buttered baking dish and bake at 350° F. for 1 hour or until firm like custard. If you prefer a more custard-like texture, place the dish with pudding in it in a pan of boiling water. Bake at 350° F. for 1 hour and 15 minutes, or until custard is set.

Commissioner Jim Graham

BULLARD'S FRESH CORN PUDDING

2 cups fresh corn
2 eggs
2/3 cup milk
4 tablespoons sugar

1/4 teaspoon baking powder
Salt and pepper to taste
1/2 stick butter

Combine corn, eggs, and milk in a medium bowl. In a separate bowl, mix sugar, baking powder, salt, and pepper. Add to corn mixture. Pour into 1-quart baking dish. Dot with butter. Cook in 350° F. oven until lightly brown on top and set like a custard, about 45 minutes. Serves 4 to 6.

Lois Bullard, Wake County

This recipe has been passed down through several Bullard generations.

ONSLOW COUNTY FRESH CORN PUDDING

6 eggs
2 cups milk
1 cup sugar
1 stick margarine
Fresh corn cut from 6 to 8
  cobs

Dash of nutmeg
Pinch of salt
2 tablespoons self-rising
  flour

Beat eggs until light and fluffy. Add milk and sugar, and blend thoroughly. Add remaining ingredients and stir well. Pour mixture into a 9 x 12-inch baking dish. Bake at 350° F. for 45 minutes.

Ada Macon Sanders, Onslow County

My dad was born and raised on a Wake County farm and always had fresh corn. After moving from the farm, we always had a big garden, and we always had fresh corn pudding when corn was in season. After raising corn all his life, he wouldn't eat it in anything but pudding. You can make this recipe using just half a cup of sugar; Mom always put in a whole cup because Daddy loved sweets.

NASH COUNTY FRESH CORN PUDDING

2 cups fresh corn, cut from
  cob
1 cup milk
2 tablespoons butter or
  margarine, melted

2 tablespoons all-purpose
  flour
1 scant teaspoon salt
2 tablespoons sugar
3 eggs

Preheat oven to 350° F. Place cut corn in large bowl. In smaller bowl mix milk, butter, flour, salt, and sugar. Pour this mixture into bowl with corn. Beat eggs together until light; add to corn mixture. Stir. Pour into buttered 1 1/2 quart baking dish. Cook 45 to 60 minutes until golden brown.

Jennifer Britt Crumley, Nash County

AUNT DORIS' CORN PUDDING

2 cups canned corn
3 eggs, beaten
1/2 cup sugar
1 teaspoon vanilla

1 tablespoon flour
Dash salt and pepper
3/4 cup milk
1/2 stick butter

Grease an 8 x 8 x 2-inch dish. Preheat oven to 350° F. Mix corn, beaten eggs, sugar, vanilla, flour, salt, pepper, and milk together. Pour into baking dish. Cut butter in pieces, and place on top of pudding. Bake for 20 minutes; remove from oven and stir. Cook an additional 45 minutes until done. Serves 8.

Brenda Morris, Guilford County

When I was growing up, my aunt, Doris Allen, used to make this every time we had family get-togethers. It has been a favorite for more than 60 years.

—

CORN PUDDING

3 cups fresh corn
1 cup milk
4 tablespoons sugar
3 eggs

2 tablespoons all-purpose flour
1/2 cup butter, melted
Salt and pepper to taste

Mix all ingredients together. Pour into greased 8 x 8-inch casserole dish. Bake 45 minutes at 325° F. Serves 6.

Ruth M. Phipps, Ashe County

This was my mother-in-law's favorite. She grew her own corn and had 12 children.

CORN PUDDING

2 16-ounce cans creamed corn
2 cups whole or skim milk
1 tablespoon butter or margarine

1/4 cup all-purpose flour
1 teaspoon salt
2 tablespoons sugar
2 eggs, beaten

In a large mixing bowl, combine corn, milk, butter, flour, salt, and sugar. Add eggs. Pour into a buttered 9 x 13-inch casserole dish. Bake at 350° F. After 30 minutes, stir. Bake for another 30 minutes or until firm like a custard. Serves 8 to 10.

Jean S. Rawls, New Hanover County

Mother carried this dish to many church dinners and family reunions.

GRANDMOTHER'S CORN PUDDING

2 tablespoons all-purpose
  flour
1 cup sugar
2 eggs
1 cup whole milk

1 teaspoon vanilla
1 pint corn (fresh, frozen, or
  canned)
1/2 stick margarine

Add flour to sugar. Mix in eggs. Add milk, vanilla, and corn. Pour into greased 2-quart casserole dish. Dot with margarine. Place in 325° F. oven. Remove and stir after 15 minutes and again after 30 minutes. Pudding will be set after about 45 minutes total baking time.

Vicki Walton, Wake County

This was my grandmother's recipe. She served it with fresh butterbeans at all family gatherings.

MARINATED CORN

1 16-ounce can white corn,
  drained
1 16-ounce can yellow corn,
  drained

3 medium tomatoes, diced
1 cup celery, diced
1 small bottle Zesty Italian
  dressing

Mix all ingredients together. Cover. Refrigerate overnight. Drain before serving.

Becky Davis, Vance County

This is my son-in-law's favorite! It's a very colorful side dish for holidays.

CREASY GREENS SALAD

The salad greens are harvested in the early spring and fall in fields that have been harvested. A large butcher knife is used to cut the top of the flat-growing green plants. Boil in water, and season to taste with oil, salt, pepper, and pinch of sugar.

Betty Jean King, Warren County

Tabitha Jordan White is remembered for her good cooking. Her husband, Jim, would help to cut creasy salad so she could make this recipe.

CUCUMBERS AND SOUR CREAM

8 ounces sour cream
1/4 cup milk
4 large cucumbers, peeled,
  sliced thick, and quartered

1/4 cup fresh dill weed,
  chopped
2 tablespoons wine vinegar

In a plastic container with a lid, mix sour cream and milk until smooth. Add cucumbers, dill, and vinegar. Mix well. Cover and chill at least 1 hour in the refrigerator. Stir well before serving. Serves 6 to 8.

Shawn Poe, Chatham County

FROZEN CUCUMBERS

1/2 cup vinegar
1 cup sugar
8 cups sliced cucumbers

1 1/2 tablespoons salt
1 medium onion, sliced thin

Mix vinegar and sugar together. Pour over remaining ingredients. Refrigerate in a covered container for 2 hours. Drain well but do not rinse. Place into freezer containers and freeze.

Vivian Chappell Merrill, Perquimans County

I made up these easy, yummy cucumbers because there were so many in the garden! They are great for a mid-winter snack.

ONION CASSEROLE

8 to 10 onions, sliced
2 cups potato chips, crushed
1 cup sharp cheddar cheese,
  shredded

2 cans cream of mushroom
  soup
1/2 cup milk
Dash red pepper

In a large baking dish, layer onions, potato chips, and cheese. Mix soup, milk, and red pepper. Pour soup mixture over layers. Bake at 350° F. for 1 hour. Serves 10 to 12.

Bee Simpson, Union County

Leftover Vegetable Salad

Mix leftover corn, peas, or green beans with sliced tomato, some grated carrot, and sliced green onion. Add non-fat Italian salad dressing, and toss lightly.

DILLY ONIONS AND CUCUMBERS

1/2 cup white vinegar	1 teaspoon dried dill weed
1/4 cup water	1 mild, sweet onion, thinly
2 teaspoons salt	sliced
1/3 cup sugar	1 cucumber, thinly sliced

Combine vinegar, water, salt, sugar, and dill. Stir until salt and sugar dissolve. Pour over onions and cucumbers, and refrigerate for at least 5 hours, stirring occasionally. Serve with slotted spoon.

Laura B. Wooten, Wake County

Makes an excellent accompaniment for potato salad. We use English cucumbers.

STEWART'S ONIONS

4 large sweet onions, sliced	1/2 cup vinegar
2 cups boiling water	2 teaspoons celery seed
1 cup sugar	1/2 cup mayonnaise

Slice onions; separate rings. Put in deep bowl. Bring water, sugar, vinegar, and celery seed to a boil, and boil for 1 minute. Pour hot mixture over onions. Let stand for 20 minutes. Drain; add mayonnaise. Mix. Cover. Refrigerate.

Juanita Fisher Lagg, Rowan County

My fisherman friend, Stewart Cuthrell, came home with this recipe after it was served to him in a boarding house on the coast. The onions are crisp and have a wonderful flavor. They give a dull meal zip, and they will keep for several days.

ENGLISH PEA CASSEROLE

2 cans English peas (reserve 1/2 cup liquid)	18 round crackers, crumbled
1 can cream of chicken soup	2 teaspoons butter or
2 teaspoons grated onion	margarine, melted
1/4 teaspoon pepper	1/2 cup shredded cheese

Drain peas, reserving 1/2 cup liquid. Combine liquid and soup; add peas, onion, and pepper. Coarsely crush crackers; add butter. Spoon half of pea mixture into lightly greased baking dish. Sprinkle with half the cracker crumbs. Add remaining pea mixture, and then remaining cracker crumbs. Sprinkle cheese over top. Bake uncovered at 350° F. for 25 minutes. Serves 6.

Bee Simpson, Union County

PEPPER RELISH CHOW CHOW

1 cup sugar
1 1/2 cups vinegar
1 tablespoon salt
3 red bell peppers, chopped
   very fine

3 green bell peppers,
   chopped very fine
1 1/2 large onions, chopped
   very fine
1/4 large cabbage, chopped
   very fine

Combine sugar, vinegar, and salt in a medium saucepan. Bring to a boil. Add bell peppers, onions, and cabbage. Heat until mixture boils. Remove from heat. Cool and store covered in refrigerator.

Nancy Beck, Burke County

Nancy Beck's original recipe was for a large amount of canned Chow Chow. We have scaled it down so it can be kept in the refrigerator for several weeks. This dish is good with pinto beans any winter day.

POKE GREENS

Poke greens
Water
Chopped onions

Bacon grease (I add some
   corn oil to ours)
Salt to taste

Pick very young leaves from the poke plant when they first appear in the spring. Wash the leaves very well, and boil them in water. Cook until they are very tender. Drain the leaves. With two knives, cut the leaves into small pieces. Sauté them with chopped onion in bacon drippings or oil. Serve as a green vegetable with country ham and corn bread. They are healthy and delicious.

Othola Thompson, Rockingham County

My sister-in-law gave this recipe to me. She lived in Oneida, Tennessee, and cooked poke greens every spring in her 67 years of marriage.

HASH BROWN POTATO CASSEROLE

1 10 1/4-ounce can cream of
chicken soup, undiluted
1 8-ounce carton sour
cream
1/2 cup butter or
margarine, melted
1/2 cup chopped onion

1 teaspoon salt
1 teaspoon pepper
1 2-pound package frozen
hash brown potatoes,
thawed
2 cups shredded cheese

Combine soup, sour cream, butter, onion, salt, and pepper in a large
bowl, and mix well. Carefully fold in thawed potatoes. Spoon
mixture into a lightly greased 13 x 9 x 2-inch baking dish. Bake at
350° F. for 40 minutes. Sprinkle with cheese, and bake an additional
5 minutes. Serves 8 to 10.

Mildred M. Harper, Edgecombe County

Everyone enjoys these potatoes. They are very good with beef roast.

HASH BROWN CASSEROLE

Use the above recipe, substituting a can of cream of mushroom and
a can of cream of celery soup for the cream of chicken soup. Mix
cheese into casserole instead of using it as a topping, and top
casserole with bread crumbs or crushed corn flakes.

Nancy Johnston, Buncombe County

IRISH POTATO CASSEROLE

6 to 8 potatoes, cooked,
drained, and diced
1 stick margarine
1 onion, chopped
1 2-ounce jar pimiento

2 1/2 tablespoons flour
2 cups milk
1 3/4 cup grated cheese,
divided
Salt and pepper to taste

Prepare potatoes. In a saucepan, melt margarine, and sauté chopped
onion and pimientos. Sprinkle flour into saucepan and stir. When
this starts to thicken, add milk and 1 cup of cheese. Add salt and
pepper to taste. Pour over cooked potatoes. Bake at 350° F. for 25
minutes. Sprinkle an additional 3/4 cup cheese over top to melt.
Serves 8 to 10.

Witt Fogleman, Alamance County

IRISH POTATO CASSEROLE

8 to 10 medium potatoes
1 8-ounce package cream
  cheese, softened
1 8-ounce carton sour
  cream

1/2 cup margarine
1 teaspoon chopped chives
Pinch of garlic powder
Paprika

Peel, cook, and mash potatoes. Beat cream cheese until smooth.
Add potatoes and remaining ingredients except paprika. Beat well.
Spoon into lightly buttered 2-quart casserole dish. Sprinkle with
paprika, cover, and refrigerate overnight. Remove from refrigerator
15 minutes before baking. Uncover and bake 30 minutes in a 350° F.
oven. Serves 8 to 10.

Donna Edsel, Wilkes County

*My husband's aunt, Bessie Brock, fixes this favorite recipe for all
family gatherings. Everyone just loves it, and it can be made ahead
of time.*

OVERNIGHT POTATO CASSEROLE

Use the recipe above, but use 1/4 cup chopped chives or green
onion tops and 1/4 teaspoon garlic powder. Omit the paprika. Bake
at 350° F. for 25 minutes. Serves 12.

Barbara Ross, Haywood County

*This is a great recipe because it can be put together the day before
and baked just before serving.*

OVEN-FRIED POTATOES

3 medium potatoes
1 tablespoon grated
  Parmesan cheese
1/2 teaspoon salt

1/4 teaspoon paprika
1/4 cup vegetable oil
1/4 teaspoon garlic powder
1/4 teaspoon pepper

Scrub and cut potatoes into eight wedges. Place wedges, slightly
overlapping, in a single layer in a 13 x 9 x 2-inch baking pan.
Combine remaining ingredients, stirring well. Brush potatoes with
half of this mixture. Bake uncovered at 375° F. for 45 minutes,
basting occasionally with remaining seasoned oil mixture.

Margaret Clark, Wake County

PARSLIED POTATOES

1 1/2 pounds small new
  potatoes, scrubbed
1 tablespoon vegetable oil
1 medium onion, chopped
1 small clove garlic, crushed

1 cup chicken broth
1 cup chopped fresh
  parsley, divided
1/2 teaspoon pepper

Peel a strip of skin from around the middle of each potato. Place potatoes in cold water and set aside. Heat oil in a large skillet over medium high heat. Sauté onion and garlic for 5 minutes until tender. Add broth and 3/4 cup parsley; mix well. Bring to a boil. Place potatoes in a single layer in skillet; return to a boil. Reduce heat. Simmer, covered for 10 minutes or until potatoes are tender. Remove potatoes with a slotted spoon to a serving bowl. Add pepper to skillet. Stir. Pour sauce over potatoes. Sprinkle with remaining parsley.

Velma McClure Poe, Ashe County

My mother always made these potatoes for Sunday dinner. They are very good.

POTATO PIE

8 medium potatoes
Strained bacon fat or other
  collected fat (or butter)

Salt and pepper to taste

Peel 8 medium potatoes. Place about 1/4 inch of strained bacon fat or other collected fat in a cast iron skillet. Melt fat over medium heat. As soon as the fat is melted, use a potato peeler and rapidly peel potatoes into the pan. You must have paper-thin slices; a paring knife will not do. And you have to peel very quickly. Once the pan has been filled, salt and pepper the top of the potato pie and cover the skillet. When the bottom and sides of the potato pie have browned, carefully flip the potato pie. You may have to add another scoop of fat. Cover the pan again, and cook until the bottom is browned. Remove from the pan and slice into wedges. Serves 8.

Debby McGilvery, Guilford County

Mom served potatoes every night, and this was our favorite potato dish. There were eight in our family, and there were never any leftovers.

POTATO SUPREME

9 medium baking potatoes
1/2 cup butter
1 1/2 teaspoons salt
1/4 teaspoon pepper
2/3 cup warm milk

1 1/2 cups shredded
cheddar cheese
1 cup heavy cream,
whipped

Peel and boil potatoes until tender; drain. In a large bowl, beat potatoes, butter, seasonings, and milk with electric mixer until fluffy. Check seasonings for taste. Turn into buttered shallow casserole dish. Fold cheese into whipped cream, and spread over potatoes. Bake at 350° F. for about 25 minutes, only until golden brown. Casserole may be prepared ahead of time and the topping added just before baking.

Carol Cox, Wake County

I make this for my family at Thanksgiving and Christmas. It is a special treat that they would like all year 'round.

POTATO-TOMATO SCALLOP

1/2 cup chopped onion
2 tablespoons butter or
  margarine
2 tablespoons flour
1 teaspoon paprika
1/2 teaspoon salt

1/4 teaspoon pepper
1 cup water
1 cup chopped tomatoes
2 chicken bouillon cubes
5 cups thinly sliced raw
  potatoes

Cook onion in butter until tender but not brown. Blend in flour, paprika, salt, and pepper. Add 1 cup water, tomatoes, and bouillon cubes. Cook and stir over medium heat until bouillon cubes dissolve and mixture thickens and bubbles. Place potato slices in a 2-quart casserole dish. Pour tomato sauce over potato slices. Cover and bake at 400° F. for 60 to 75 minutes. Serves 6 to 8.

Lizzie Mock, Forsyth County

PUMPKIN

Wash pumpkin and cut off stem. Cut in half. Remove seeds and scrape the pulp out. Place the pumpkin halves in a roasting pan or broiler pan, cut side up. Bake at 350° F. until tender. (A fork will easily slide into the outside of the pumpkin.) Cool. Drain water. Scrape out pumpkin. Put pumpkin in a food processor or blender, or mash with a fork. Drain excess water. Use in cooking, or place in containers in 1 to 2 cup quantities, and freeze for later use.

Dorothy C. Fisher, Nash County

BAKED RICE

4 2/3 cups water
2 cups long-grain rice
1 stick margarine

4 heaping teaspoons beef
  bouillon granules, *or* 4
  beef bouillon cubes
4 tablespoons onion, finely
  chopped

Preheat oven to 350° F. Mix all ingredients in a 4-quart casserole dish, and cover. Bake for 45 minutes. Serves 6.

Juanita McKnight, Wayne County

This recipe for busy or working housewives takes very little preparation time and brings many compliments.

CHRISTMAS RICE

1 cup uncooked rice
2 10.75-ounce cans chicken
  and rice soup
1 1/4 cups water
1 teaspoon salt
1 stick margarine

1 large onion, chopped
1 3-ounce jar chopped
  pimiento
1 4-ounce can sliced
  mushrooms

Mix all ingredients in a bowl. Pour into a 9 x 13-inch casserole dish. Put in 350° F. oven for 50 minutes; stir two or three times while cooking. Serves 12.

Jane H. Ross, Bladen County

RICE CASSEROLE

2 tablespoons margarine
1 cup uncooked rice
2 cups any flavored broth

1 2.8-ounce can French
  fried onions
1 can mushrooms, optional

Melt margarine in frying pan. Add rice, stir, and cook until golden. Put in greased 2-quart casserole. Stir in broth, onions, and mushrooms. Cover. Bake at 350° F. for about 35 minutes.

Laura B. Wooten, Wake County

Our favorite broth flavor is beef. This casserole is great with meatloaf, and it offers a nice change with steak.

—

PINEAPPLE RICE

1 cup uncooked rice	Sugar to taste
1/2 teaspoon salt	1 small can crushed
1 cup whipping cream	pineapple

Cook rice with salt according to package directions. Place in colander and rinse with cold water until rice cools. Drain well. Whip cream and add sugar to taste. Fold crushed pineapple and sweetened whipped cream into rice, and chill.

Dorothy Fender, Alleghany County

I can remember my mother, Lillie Edwards, serving Pineapple Rice often. It was always a favorite.

FRIED SQUASH

2 or 3 medium squash	Bacon drippings
2 small onions, sliced or	Salt and pepper to taste
chopped	

Boil squash until tender. Drain off water, and mash very lightly with fork; set aside. Fry onions in bacon drippings. Add squash to onions, and fry until brown, stirring occasionally. Season with salt and pepper to taste.

Lizzie Mock, Forsyth County

BUTTERNUT SQUASH CASSEROLE

2 cups cooked mashed	2 beaten eggs
squash (see directions	3/4 teaspoon salt
below)	Buttered bread crumbs *or*
1/2 stick margarine, melted	crushed crackers to top
1 cup grated sharp cheddar	casserole
cheese	Green pepper rings for
1/4 cup chopped onion	garnish (optional)
4 teaspoons sugar	

To cook squash, split in half, and put in microwave-safe dish face down with a little bit of water. Cover with Saran wrap and vent.

Cook on high for 10 minutes. Pierce skin with knife for tenderness. Scoop out seeds and discard. Scrape out squash meat. Mix squash, margarine, cheese, onion, sugar, eggs, and salt; pour into quart casserole. Top with buttered bread crumbs or crushed crackers. Decorate the top when the casserole is almost done with green pepper rings. Bake casserole 20 minutes at 350° F.

Lou Roberts, Lee County

EASY SQUASH CASSEROLE

5 medium yellow squash,
  sliced or diced
1 medium onion, sliced or
  diced
1 tablespoon sugar
1/2 cup milk

2 eggs, beaten
1 teaspoon salt
9 or 10 Ritz crackers,
  crushed
1 stick margarine
Cheese for topping

Cook squash and onions until done. Mix in remaining ingredients except cheese. Pour into 8 x 13-inch casserole dish. Top with cheese of choice, and bake at 350° F. until cheese melts, about 10 minutes.

Lula Mae Tyndall, Sampson County

Easy to make and very good.

HOLIDAY SQUASH CASSEROLE

3 1/2 pounds yellow squash,
  cooked and mashed
1/2 stick margarine, melted
1 pint sour cream

Salt and pepper to taste
2 eggs, well beaten
1 onion, chopped
Cracker crumbs

Mix first six ingredients together, and pour into a 9 x 13-inch Pyrex dish. Bake at 350° F. for 20 minutes. Add cracker crumbs, and bake an additional 7 minutes.

Mary Porter Brown, Wake County

This casserole is great for all that good summer squash, and I have served it at many reunions, Thanksgiving, Christmas, and other occasions.

ONSLOW COUNTY SQUASH CASSEROLE

2 cups cooked squash
1/4 cup butter or margarine
1/2 cup onion, finely
  chopped
1/4 teaspoon salt
1/4 teaspoon black pepper

1 egg, beaten
1/2 cup milk
1 cup cracker crumbs
1 cup herb-seasoned
  stuffing mix
1 cup grated cheese

Mash squash, and blend in all ingredients except cheese. Place in greased casserole dish; top with grated cheese. Bake at 350° F. for 30 minutes. Serves 6.

Juanita L. Guthrie, Onslow County

SQUASH CASSEROLE

3 cups yellow squash,
  grated
1/2 cup oil
1/2 onion, diced

3 eggs, beaten
1 cup cheese, grated
1 cup Bisquick baking mix

Mix all ingredients. Bake at 400° F. for 20 minutes, or until casserole is sufficiently browned. Cut into squares and serve.

Sandra Vann, Northampton County

YELLOW SQUASH CASSEROLE

2 1/2 cups mashed yellow
  squash (6 to 8 squash
  cooked until tender)
1 1/2 tablespoons finely
  chopped onion
2 tablespoons butter,
  divided

1 can cream of potato soup
10 Ritz crackers, crushed
1 1/2 teaspoons salt
Pepper to taste
1 cup grated cheese

Mix all ingredients except crackers, cheese, and 1 tablespoon butter. Pour into greased 2-quart casserole dish. Top with crushed crackers, cheese, and 1 tablespoon butter. Bake at 350° F. for 30 minutes. Serves 8.

Vicki Walton, Wake County

SWEET POTATO PONE

2 cups grated raw sweet
  potatoes
1 cup sugar
1 cup milk or cream
1/2 cup nuts, chopped

2 eggs, well beaten
1 teaspoon nutmeg
Pinch salt
2 tablespoons melted butter

Peel raw potatoes, and grate. Blend with sugar, milk, nuts, eggs, nutmeg, and salt. Pour into baking dish. Dot with melted butter. Bake at 350° F. until brown.

Lizzie Mock, Forsyth County

Here are three variations of a North Carolina favorite: Candied Sweet Potatoes.

DIXIE CLASSIC CANDIED SWEET POTATOES

8 to 10 medium sweet
  potatoes, peeled, cooked,
  cooled, and sliced
1 1/2 sticks margarine,
  divided

1 1/2 cups brown sugar,
  divided
1 1/2 teaspoons cinnamon,
  divided
1/2 cup flour

Boil potatoes. Allow to cool, then slice. Melt 1 stick margarine in a long casserole dish. Sprinkle 1 cup brown sugar and 1 teaspoon cinnamon over margarine. Arrange sliced potatoes in baking dish. Mix 1/2 stick margarine, 1/2 cup flour, 1/2 cup brown sugar, and 1/2 teaspoon cinnamon; makes moist crumbles. Sprinkle across top of potatoes. Bake at 350° F. for 25 to 30 minutes or until crumble mixture melts and makes a soft topping. Serves 10 to 12.

Della Stephens, Forsyth County

Della Stephens was assistant fair director of the Dixie Classic Fair in Winston-Salem until her retirement.

SAMPSON COUNTY CANDIED SWEET POTATOES

6 medium sweet potatoes
1 1/2 cups water
2/3 cup white sugar

2/3 cup light brown sugar
1 stick margarine
1/2 teaspoon salt

Slice uncooked potatoes into 1/2-inch wedges. Arrange in a buttered 9 x 13-inch baking dish. Make syrup of the remaining ingredients, and pour over potatoes. Cover and bake at 350° F. until tender.

Remove cover for last 10 minutes and allow to brown. If desired, just before removing dish from oven, add a layer of marshmallows and allow it to brown.

Lula Mae Tyndall, Sampson County

Very good and easy to make.

—

WAYNE COUNTY CANDIED SWEET POTATOES

6 medium sweet potatoes
1/2 cup white sugar
1/2 cup brown sugar
1 cup light Karo syrup

1 teaspoon cinnamon
1/4 cup water
1 teaspoon vanilla extract
1/2 stick margarine

Wash and cook sweet potatoes until about half done (can just stick a fork into them). Peel, cut into serving-sized pieces, and place in a 9 x 13-inch baking dish. Mix sugars, syrup, cinnamon, water, vanilla, and margarine. Pour over potatoes. Bake at 350° F. until potatoes are done and syrup is thick. Serves 12.

Debby Smith, Wayne County

These sweet potatoes have a delicious flavor. The cinnamon and vanilla add so much to the taste. I get a lot of compliments on this home-grown vegetable.

MICROWAVED SWEET POTATOES

3 or 4 sweet potatoes, peeled
2 tablespoons cornstarch
1/2 cup water
1 1/2 cups sugar

1 stick margarine
1 teaspoon vanilla flavoring
Pinch of salt

Slice peeled potatoes into 9 x 13-inch dish. Mix cornstarch and water, and pour over potatoes. Pour sugar over potatoes. Dot margarine over the top of potatoes. Add vanilla flavoring and salt. Cover with microwave-safe plastic wrap. Microwave on high for 30 minutes.

Mona Scism, Cleveland County

This recipe always turns out perfectly. It's great for covered-dish suppers at church.

GRATED SWEET POTATO PUDDING

3 cups grated sweet
  potatoes
2 1/2 cups milk
1/2 cup soft butter or
  margarine

1 1/2 cups sugar
2 eggs
1 teaspoon salt
2 teaspoons vanilla extract
1 cup coconut

Grate sweet potatoes into milk, which keeps the potatoes from turning dark. Blend butter, sugar, eggs, salt, and vanilla extract together. Add sweet potatoes-milk mixture and coconut. Mix well. Pour mixture into a greased, oblong pan, and bake at 350° F. for approximately 1 hour, or until potatoes are tender when tested. Serves 6 to 8.

Emily Clapp, Guilford County

This recipe has been a favorite in our farm family for more than 60 years.

You know you've got a winner when people send in the same casserole. Reba Adams of Cove City and Faye Kennedy of Richlands both make the following Sweet Potato Casserole. Faye Kennedy, who specifies pecans for her dish, says, "My family looks forward to this special dish every Christmas."

SWEET POTATO CASSEROLE

6 cups cooked, mashed
  sweet potatoes
1 cup sugar
1 stick margarine, melted
2 eggs, beaten
1/2 cup milk

1 teaspoon vanilla
Topping:
1 cup brown sugar
1/3 to 1/2 cup flour
1/3 cup margarine
1 cup chopped nuts

Mix sweet potatoes, sugar, margarine, eggs, milk, and vanilla together, and pour into 3-quart casserole dish. To make top crust, mix sugar, flour, and margarine until coarse. Add chopped nuts. Spread over sweet potato mixture. Bake at 375° F. for 30 minutes or until golden brown. Serves 12.

Reba Adams, Craven County
Faye Kennedy, Onslow County

If you have fewer people sitting down at the table, try the Sweet Potato Casserole submitted by Dolores Benthall of Hertford County, Margaret Helton of Rutherford County, Jennifer Mitchell of Harnett County, and Vicki Pettit of Lee County. Margaret Helton adds 1/4 cup of evaporated milk when she makes her casserole. Dolores Benthall leaves the butter out of the topping.

SWEET POTATO CASSEROLE

3 cups cooked and mashed
  sweet potatoes
1 cup granulated sugar
1 stick butter or margarine,
  melted
1 teaspoon vanilla extract
1/4 cup evaporated milk
  (Margaret Helton's
  recipe)

2 eggs
Topping:
1 cup light brown sugar
1/2 stick butter or
  margarine, melted
1/3 cup all-purpose flour
1 cup chopped pecans

Mix mashed sweet potatoes, granulated sugar, melted butter, vanilla, and eggs (and milk, if desired) in a large bowl until well blended. Pour into a buttered 9 x 12-inch baking dish. *Prepare topping:* Mix 1 cup of light brown sugar, 1/2 stick melted butter, 1/3 cup all-purpose flour, and chopped pecans in a medium mixing bowl with a fork until well blended. Spread topping evenly over sweet potato mixture. Bake at 350° F. for 30 minutes. Serves 8 to 10.

Dolores Benthall, Hertford County
Margaret Helton, Rutherford County
Jennifer Mitchell, Harnett County
Vicki Pettit, Lee County

APPLE-SWEET POTATO CASSEROLE

4 cups sweet potatoes, raw,
  sliced
2 cups apples, peeled, sliced

3/4 cup maple syrup
1/4 cup melted butter
1 teaspoon salt

Place potatoes in a greased 12 x 8 x 2-inch baking dish. Arrange apple slices on top of potatoes. Combine syrup, butter, and salt, and pour over potatoes and apples. Cover, and bake at 350° F. for 45 minutes. Bake another 30 minutes uncovered. Can be made the day before. Raw sweet potatoes can be hard to slice, so I recommend using an electric slicer or food processor.

Connie B. Greene, Avery County

This recipe was given to me by a dear friend, Frances Louise Eller Brown.

—

THE NORTH CAROLINA SWEET POTATO PEEL

6 medium sweet potatoes
1 cup butter, softened
1 cup sugar
1/2 cup canned evaporated milk
2 eggs, beaten

1 teaspoon vanilla flavoring
1/8 teaspoon (or less) cinnamon
2 cups mini-marshmallows (enough to completely cover potatoes)

Preheat oven to 400° F. Scrub potatoes and pierce in several places with a fork. Bake potatoes until barely soft, about 1 hour. Let cool enough to handle. Cut 1/3 slice lengthwise from top of potato; discard slice. Carefully scoop out inside of potato, leaving about 1/3 inch of potato next to skin. Cream butter and sugar, and mix with scooped-out potato. Add milk, eggs, vanilla flavoring, and cinnamon to potato mixture. Spoon mixture into potato shells. Push marshmallows lightly into potatoes to hold in place. Bake until marshmallows are nicely browned. Be sure to watch carefully so marshmallows don't burn.

Mary Ellen Causby, Johnston County

When I was a little girl, my mother made sweet potato souffle using the above mixture. I thought stuffing the potatoes would bring this old recipe up to date.

North Carolina Sweet Potatoes

North Carolina is the leader in sweet potato production. Is 2001 our state supplied 39 percent of our nation's production of sweet potatoes, according to the North Carolina Department of Agriculture and Consumer Services.

One cup of cooked sweet potatoes provides 30 mg (50,000 IU) of beta carotene (Vitamin A).

SWEET POTATO ROLL-UPS

1 10-count can Hungry Jack
  Biscuits
2 cups sugar
2 cups water

2 sticks margarine
2 medium sweet potatoes,
  raw

Divide biscuits and roll out flat; you will have 20 pieces. Mix sugar, water, and margarine together in a large dish. Place in oven until margarine is melted and stir. Peel potatoes and cut 10 strips about 3/4 by 1 1/2-inch long. Roll each strip inside two biscuit pieces, and put in melted butter solution. Sprinkle with nutmeg. Bake at 350° F. for 30 minutes. Turn oven back to 325° F., cover dish with foil, and bake 20 minutes longer.

Cynthia Burton, Surry County

SWEET POTATO SOUFFLE

8 medium sweet potatoes,
  cooked and mashed
Pinch of salt
Butter, size of an egg
1/2 cup brown sugar

1/2 cup maple syrup
Handful of coconut
1/2 cup chopped pecans
Dash of nutmeg
1 teaspoon vanilla

Mix ingredients together. Spoon into a 9 x 13-inch baking dish. Bake at 350° F. for 15 to 20 minutes.

Nancy Johnston, Buncombe County

FRIED GREEN TOMATOES

1 medium green tomato per
  person
Flour

Salt and pepper
Cooking oil

Wash, core, and slice tomatoes in 1/3-inch slices. Do not peel them. Dip each slice in flour, season to taste with salt and pepper, and fry until golden in hot oil. Drain on paper towels, then serve hot with butter.

Eva S. Pridgen, Wilson County

Tomatoes in a Hurry

Wash, slice, serve, and enjoy!

GRANDMOTHER HICKS' GREEN TOMATO PIE

6 to 8 green tomatoes
Juice of 1 small lemon *or* 2
 tablespoons vinegar
1 cup brown sugar
1/4 cup white sugar
4 heaping tablespoons flour
4 tablespoons butter

1 teaspoon salt
9-inch pie shell, unbaked
Additional unbaked pie
 crust, cut into strips
3 tablespoons butter (for
 top of pie)

Slice tomatoes thinly; lightly toss with lemon juice. Crumble together the sugars, flour, butter, and salt. Layer tomatoes and crumbled mixture in unbaked 9-inch pie shell. Lattice top of pie with pastry strips. Dot top with butter. Bake at 425° F. for 25 to 30 minutes. Serves 6.

Othola Thompson, Rockingham County

My great-grandmother gave this recipe to my mother, who enjoyed it. My sister gave it to me, and I serve it to my family in the summer.

GREEN TOMATO CASSEROLE

4 large or 5 medium green
 tomatoes
2 medium onions, thinly
 sliced

1/2 cup Parmesan cheese,
 grated
1/2 cup Romano cheese,
 grated

Slice tomatoes and onions. Layer half of each in a greased 1 1/2-quart casserole dish. Sprinkle half of the cheese over this layer. Repeat layers with remaining tomatoes and onions, ending with cheese. Bake at 350° F., covered, for 30 minutes. Then bake uncovered for 10 minutes. Serves 6.

Othola Thompson, Rockingham County

We have a garden, raise plenty of tomatoes, and enjoy this recipe.

TOMATO PIE

Pam cooking spray
1 can Hungry Jack flaky
 biscuits
1 large tomato, peeled and
 sliced

1 Vidalia onion, chopped
2/3 cup mayonnaise
1 cup shredded mozzarella
 cheese

Spray a 9-inch pie pan with Pam. Flatten biscuits, and place in pan to make bottom piecrust. Sauté onion in Pam cooking spray until tender. Place tomato slices in pie pan. Put sautéed onion on top of the tomato slices. Mix the mayonnaise and cheese together, and spread on top of the onion. Bake uncovered for 30 minutes at 350° F. Let stand 10 minutes before serving. Serves 8.

Shawn Poe, Chatham County

TOMATOES AND CABBAGE

1 pint canned tomatoes with juice
1 cup shredded cabbage
1/2 cup diced onion
1/2 cup diced celery
1 1/2 tablespoons sugar
1 1/2 tablespoons vinegar

Mix all ingredients together. Can be stored in an airtight container in refrigerator for 2 to 3 days.

Mary Alice Brooks, Union County

ONION-STUFFED TOMATOES

6 large firm, ripe tomatoes
Salt
3/4 cup chopped onion
2 tablespoons bacon grease
1 tablespoon honey
3/4 teaspoon salt
1 tablespoon celery seed
Milk, if desired
Dry bread crumbs or stuffing mix
6 pats butter
Grated Parmesan cheese

Remove tomato stems, and scoop out pulp, leaving 1/4-inch-thick shell. Sprinkle with salt, and drain. Sauté onion in bacon grease. Finely chop tomato pulp. Add to sautéed onion along with honey, salt, and celery seed. Simmer 10 minutes. If desired, thin with milk. Add just enough bread crumbs or stuffing mix to consume extra liquid. Stuff tomato shells. Dot with butter and sprinkle with cheese. Bake at 350° F. for 10 to 12 minutes. Serves 6.

Karen DeBord, Wake County

I once won a cooking contest with my recipe for Onion-Stuffed Tomatoes.

HASHED TURNIPS

1 large yellow turnip, *or* 6
  purple top turnips
2 level tablespoons butter

1 level teaspoon salt
1/4 level teaspoon pepper
1/4 cup light cream

Peel and dice turnip(s). Cook in boiling water until tender. Drain and add butter, seasoning, and cream. Let mixture start to boil, and then serve.

Betty Jean King, Warren County

VEG-ALL CASSEROLE

1 large can Veg-All, drained
1 can whole kernel corn,
  drained
1 can French-style green
  beans, drained
1 can cream of chicken
  soup, undiluted
1 cup grated sharp cheddar
  cheese

1/2 cup onion, chopped
1/2 cup celery, chopped
1/2 cup mayonnaise
1/2 stick margarine, melted
Topping:
1/2 stick margarine, melted
1 stack (sleeve) Ritz
  crackers, crumbled

Mix first 9 ingredients together and place in a 13 x 9-inch baking dish. Mix topping ingredients, and place on top of vegetable mixture. Bake at 350° F. for 35 minutes. Can be made ahead and refrigerated. Serves 8 to 10.

Patricia Herring, Wayne County

Great for covered-dish meals at church.

VEGETABLE CASSEROLE

1 can cream of chicken soup
2 cans Veg-All
1 cup water chestnuts,
  drained and chopped
1 cup onions, chopped
1 cup mayonnaise

1 cup grated sharp cheese
Topping:
1 cup grated cheese
1/4 pound Ritz crackers,
  crushed

Mix soup, Veg-All, water chestnuts, onion, mayonnaise, and cheese together. Pour in a greased casserole dish. Top with Ritz crackers and cheese. Cook at 350° F. for 45 minutes.

Lula Mae Tyndall, Sampson County

This is good for homecoming or family get-togethers.

—

VEGGIE BARS

2 packages crescent dinner
  rolls
2 8-ounce packages cream
  cheese, softened
1 cup mayonnaise
1 package Hidden Valley
  dry salad dressing

1 cup tomatoes, cut in small
  pieces
1 cup broccoli florets
1 cup cauliflower, cut in
  small pieces
1 cup grated cheese

Press rolls onto cookie sheet to form crust. Bake as directed on package. Cool crust. Mix cream cheese, mayonnaise, and dressing mix until smooth. Spread on cooled crust. Sprinkle raw vegetables over cream cheese mixture. Top with cheese. Chill, slice, and serve. Serves 10 to 15.

Anne W. Harper, Edgecombe County

A quick and easy family favorite. Good for parties because it's colorful and an easy-to-eat, delicious finger food.

WILD RICE SUPREME

1 pound hot sausage
1 cup onions, chopped
1 10-ounce can cream of
  celery soup
2 4-ounce cans mushrooms

1 box wild brown rice,
  cooked to package
  directions
1/4 cup milk

Brown sausage 10 minutes, and drain. Add onions to grease, and cook until done. Drain; do not use grease. Add soup, mushrooms, prepared rice, and milk. Put mixture in baking dish, and bake at 350° F. until bubbly, about 20 minutes.

Ruth Nesbitt, Buncombe County

Wild Rice

Wild rice is not actually a rice. It's a grain. There are different types of wild rice, which require different amounts of water and cooking times, so follow package instructions.

FRIED ZUCCHINI

6 medium zucchini   **1/2 teaspoon salt**
1 cup fine bread crumbs   **1/4 teaspoon pepper**

Wash each zucchini. Dry thoroughly. Cut into 1/2-inch slices.
Combine bread crumbs, slat, and pepper. Dip each zucchini slice in
bread crumb mixture. Fry in oil for 5 minutes on each side.

Debby McGilvery, Guilford County

Poultry, Meat, & Main Dishes

Chicken
Turkey
Brunswick Stew
Beef

Pork
Sausage
Lamb
Seafood

Game
Cheese

A Taste of North Carolina's Heritage

Food ... For Thought!

According to the North Carolina Department of Agriculture and Consumer Services, in 2001 North Carolina ranked:

No. 1 in Sweet Potato production

No. 2 in Hogs & Pigs
Cucumbers for Pickles
Lima Beans
Trout sold
Turkeys raised

No. 3 in Turnip Greens
Collard Greens
Poultry & Egg products cash receipts

Based on cash receipts received by farmers in 2000, here's how the food commodities ranked:

1. Hogs
2. Broilers
5. Turkeys
7. Cattle & Calves
8. Chicken Eggs
9. Soybeans
10. Dairy Products
11. Corn

13. Peanuts
14. Wheat
15. Sweet Potatoes
16. Cucumbers
17. Irish Potatoes
18. Tomatoes
19. Apples
20. Blueberries

(Tobacco was 4, cotton was 6, Christmas trees & greenery was 12)

FRIED CHICKEN

4 eggs
2 cups buttermilk
12 chicken pieces
4 cups flour
2 tablespoons kosher salt
1 tablespoon black pepper

1 tablespoon granulated
garlic
1 tablespoon granulated
onion
1 teaspoon cayenne pepper

Mix eggs and buttermilk. Add chicken pieces, and let soak for 15 to
20 minutes. Drain chicken. Mix flour, salt, pepper, garlic, onion,
and cayenne. Dredge chicken in flour mixture. Deep fry in oil for 15
minutes. Put in oven at 150° F. on a drip pan until ready to serve.

Barbara Braswell, Union County

DIXIE GRILLED CHICKEN

6 broilers, halved and
washed
Olive or vegetable oil
Salt and pepper to taste
2 tablespoons butter
1 tablespoon pepper
2 1/2 cups vinegar

1 tablespoon chili powder
2 tablespoons smooth
peanut butter
2 teaspoons celery seed,
optional
2 tablespoons salt
1/2 to 3/4 cup lemon juice

Prepare grill. Rub chicken with oil; lightly sprinkle with salt and
pepper. In a saucepan, combine butter, pepper, vinegar, chili
powder, peanut butter, celery seed, salt, and lemon juice. Heat
thoroughly. When coals are glowing, place chicken on the grill. Use
vinegar mixture to frequently baste chicken. Grill for 1 1/2 hours, or
until done. Serves 12.

Dayle Oakley, Wake County

Grilling Safely

*Thaw poultry thoroughly before grilling
and then cook it thoroughly. Use a clean
plate when retrieving the cooked food
from the grill, not the plate that held the
raw chicken.*

CHICKEN GUMBO

1 1/2 pounds smoked
   sausage
1/2 cup flour
1 large cooked and deboned
   chicken
1 large onion, cut in chunks
1 cup celery, chopped
1 cup green onions, chopped

1 cup green bell pepper,
   chopped
1 teaspoon filé (ground
   sassafras leaves)
Salt, pepper, and cayenne
   pepper to taste
2 quarts water

Cook sausage. Brown flour in sausage drippings in an iron skillet
until penny-colored. Cook all ingredients together, and serve over
steamed rice. Serves 8 to 12.

Vernon Tyndall, Duplin County

INDIVIDUAL CHICKEN PIES

Homemade pastry for 2-
   crust pie
1/2 cup chopped onion
6 tablespoons butter
1/2 cup all-purpose flour
1 teaspoon salt
3 cups boiled chicken,
   cubed (reserve broth)

3 cups reserved chicken
   broth
1 10-ounce package frozen
   peas and carrots, cooked
   and drained
1/4 cup chopped pimiento

Roll prepared pastry 1/4-inch thick. Cut to fit tops of six individual
casseroles (or one large casserole). Bake on ungreased baking sheet
at 450° F. for 10 to 12 minutes. Meanwhile, cook onion in butter
until tender but not brown. Blend in flour and salt. Add broth all at
once. Cook and stir until thick and bubbly; add chicken, peas,
carrots, and pimiento. Heat until bubbling. Pour into six heated
individual casseroles (or one large casserole). Place pastry over hot
filling just before serving. Serves 6.

Elizabeth Harper, Edgecombe County

This is a family favorite.

CHICKEN PIE

1 box Pillsbury pie crust
1 cup boiled chicken, cut up
   (retain broth)
1 1/2 cups chicken broth
4 tablespoons butter

3 tablespoons flour
1 teaspoon salt
Pepper to taste
2/3 cup milk

Prepare pie crust according to directions for two pie crusts. Place bottom crust in a 9-inch round pie pan. Boil chicken (retain broth), and debone. Place chicken in pie crust. In a saucepan, combine broth, butter, flour, salt, and pepper. Bring to a boil. Remove from heat, and stir in milk; mixture will be thick. Pour over chicken. Put on top crust. Bake at 375° F. for 30 minutes or until golden brown. Serves 4. Note: Drained, canned vegetables may be added.

Linda Dalton, Stokes County

CHICKEN SQUARES

1 3-ounce package cream
   cheese and chives
2 tablespoons butter or
   margarine, melted
2 cups cooked chicken,
   diced
2 teaspoons milk
1/4 teaspoon salt

1/8 teaspoon pepper
1 tablespoon pimiento,
   chopped
1 tablespoon onions, minced
1 8-ounce can crescent rolls
Melted margarine
3/4 cup crushed croutons or
   herb stuffing crumbs

In a bowl, blend cream cheese and butter until smooth. Add chicken, milk, salt and pepper, pimiento, and onions. Separate crescent rolls into eight parts and spoon equal amounts of chicken mixture onto each roll. Wrap the rolls around the chicken mixture to form balls. Seal all edges. Roll each ball in melted margarine and then in crushed croutons. Bake on a greased cookie sheet at 350° F. for 20 to 25 minutes. Serves 8.

Dennis Furr, Cabarrus County

Poultry Is Big in North Carolina

Based on cash receipts in 2000, production of broilers is North Carolina's No. 2 food commodity. Turkeys rank fifth, and chicken eggs are eighth, according to the North Carolina Department of Agriculture.

GOLDEN CHICKEN NUGGETS

4 to 6 boneless chicken
  breasts
1 egg
1/2 cup water
3/4 teaspoon salt

2 teaspoons sesame seeds
  (optional)
1/2 cup all-purpose flour
Vegetable oil

Cut chicken breasts into 1 x 1 1/2-inch pieces. Break egg into bowl. Beat slightly. Add water, salt, sesame seeds (if desired), and flour. Pour 2 to 3 inches of vegetable oil into deep, heavy sauce pan. Heat oil over medium heat until hot enough to fry chicken pieces (about 375° F.). Dip chicken pieces into batter, and carefully drop into hot oil. Fry one layer of chicken at a time, separating pieces as they cook. Cook 3 to 5 minutes until golden brown. Transfer chicken to paper towels to drain.

Kristen Elizabeth Britt, Nash County

AUNT NELL'S CHICKEN 'N' DUMPLIN'S

1 whole chicken (about 3
  pounds), cut into pieces
1 large onion, quartered
2 large carrots, cut into 2-
  to 3-inch pieces
2 celery stalks, cut into 2- to
  3-inch pieces
Water
3 teaspoons salt
1 teaspoon pepper
1/2 teaspoon dried thyme

1/4 teaspoon cayenne
  pepper
1 cube chicken bouillon
  (optional)
Dumplings:
3 cups self-rising flour
1/2 teaspoon poultry
  seasoning
1/3 cup shortening
2 teaspoons bacon
  drippings–no substitute
1 cup whole milk

Place chicken pieces, quartered onions, carrots, and celery in large covered roasting pan. Cover with water, and bring to a boil. While chicken is boiling, add 1 1/2 teaspoons salt, 1/2 teaspoon black pepper, thyme, and cayenne pepper. Cover chicken again, reduce the heat, and simmer 1 hour. Remove chicken and vegetables, reserving broth in pan. Cool chicken, and skim fat from broth. Discard vegetables or save to use in soup. Place broth on stove again, and bring to a simmer. Remove chicken skin and bone, and coarsely chop chicken. Add chicken, 1 cube chicken bouillon, and remaining 1 1/2 teaspoons salt and 1/2 teaspoon pepper to simmering broth. Return to simmer if the temperature drops.

Prepare dumplings: Stir flour and poultry seasoning in a bowl; mix well. Cut in shortening and bacon drippings with a pastry blender or using two knives until mixture is crumbly. Add milk, stirring until dry ingredients are moistened. Lightly flour the board or counter. Turn out dough onto lightly floured surface. Roll dough out to about 1/8-inch to 1/4-inch thickness and cut into 2-inch circles or small squares. Bring broth-chicken mixture to a boil. Drop dumplings, a few at a time, into the boiling broth, stirring ever so gently so as not to break up the dumplings. Reduce the heat, cover, and simmer for about 30 minutes, stirring often. Serves 8.

Linda Reasor, Durham County

Aunt Nell had a farm in Johnston County, and the most memorable Sundays in our young lives were spent there after church with relatives and friends, listening to the grownups tell stories and, of course, eating Sunday dinner. Weather permitting, Aunt Nell would set up huge tables out under the oak trees, and we would play quietly (it was Sunday, you know) while the grownups talked. Then, after we'd all gathered around for prayer, we would eat until we thought we would surely bust. Chicken 'n' Dumplin's was a favorite during the winter months, and it was often warm enough at midday to eat outdoors. Sometimes Aunt Nell would cut a few of the dumplings into small hearts for the kids. She would always make sure that the children got the heart-shaped dumplings in their servings. It was such a treat to see one on your plate! We kids saved it to eat last, scraping up the last bit of broth with it. Yum!

—

CHICKEN 'N' DUMPLINGS

1 whole chicken (or 5 or 6 chicken breasts)	**1 teaspoon salt**
2 cups flour	**1/3 cup shortening**
1 teaspoon baking powder	**Enough milk to make a dough**

Place chicken in pan, and cover with water. Boil about 45 minutes or until done. Remove chicken, retaining chicken broth. Debone. Place chicken back into chicken broth. *Make dumplings*: Mix flour, baking powder, and salt in a bowl. Cut in shortening. Add enough milk to make a sticky dough. Let rest a few minutes. Place dough on floured surface, and roll it out very thin; cut into squares. Bring broth with chicken to a boil. Drop dumplings in one at a time. Cover and simmer for 12 minutes. Remove cover, and thicken broth, if you like. To thicken, pour off 1 cup of broth, and replace it with 1 cup of milk with 2 tablespoons flour dissolved in it. Serves 5 to 6.

Della Stephens, Forsyth County

OLD-TIMEY BYNUM-STYLE CHICKEN CRACKER STEW

1 fat hen, cut up	1 pound butter
Water to cover hen	1 15-ounce box of saltine
1 tablespoon red pepper	crackers
flakes	Black pepper to taste

Put cut-up hen in a large pot with water to cover and a tablespoon of red pepper flakes. Simmer until very tender and the meat falls off the bone. Remove all the gristle and bone, and return the well-cooked meat pieces to the stew. Add 1 pound of butter and one box of saltine crackers, and reheat thoroughly. Some of the crackers will be broken—that is OK ... but otherwise leave them whole. They aren't stirred in either—they just sit on top and soak up the chicken juice. When hot, cover the entire top surface with freshly ground black pepper. Serve and enjoy—if possible, while sitting on the porch of the Bynum General Store on a perfect spring day, or on the banks of the Haw River at dusk. Best when consumed in the presence of good friends. Garnish when possible with exuberant spirits, freshly played country music, and good old-timey songs. Serves 12.

Cynthia Raxter, Chatham County

Cynthia Raxter submitted this recipe for Jerry Partin, owner of Bynum General Store. She says he sells groceries, fishing supplies, and soft drinks, and works on lawn mowers outside between customers. The post office is in the back of the store, so he is the postmaster, too. The U.S. Postal Service has proposed canceling the contract for the post office, and the General Store will have to close if the post office closes. "Needless to say, everyone in town is trying to persuade them to change their minds!"

"On Saturday nights, musicians come play on the porch at the General Store, and they pass the hat. And if we're lucky, Jerry makes a giant pot of chicken cracker stew."

TASTY CHICKEN CASSEROLE

1 1/2 cups grated sharp
  cheddar cheese, divided
4 cups stuffing mix, crushed
  finely, divided
4 cups cooked, diced hen
3 cups broth
1 1/2 cups diced celery

3 large eggs, slightly beaten
1 large onion, diced
1 large carrot, grated
1 can cream of mushroom
  soup
1 teaspoon pepper
3 teaspoons salt

Set 1/2 cup cheddar cheese and 1 cup stuffing mix aside. Combine
the rest of the ingredients in a large bowl. Stir well. Bake in a
9 x 13-inch baking dish for 1 hour at 350° F. After about 45
minutes, sprinkle the reserved stuffing mix over the casserole, and
top with the reserved cheese. Bake for 15 minutes longer. This dish
may be frozen before or after baking. Serves 12 to 15.

LaRue P. Cunningham, Forsyth County

*A dear family friend, now deceased, shared this recipe with my
mom. For large family gatherings, it is great and always receives
rave reviews. I have used the recipe for covered-dish meals and for
sick friends. It is extra good with a chicken plucked fresh from the
barnyard, and sometimes I can do this when visiting the farm. I
made this dish for my parents' 55th wedding anniversary in March
2002.*

CHICKEN AND DRESSING CASSEROLE

1 package Pepperidge Farm
  Herb Dressing
1 stick butter, melted
4 chicken breasts, boiled,
  and cut into chunks

1 can cream of celery soup
1 can cream of chicken soup
2 cans chicken broth
  retained from boiling
  chicken

Add butter to stuffing mix. Put half of stuffing mix in 9 x 13-inch
baking dish. Add layer of chicken. Mix retained warm chicken broth
with the cans of soup. Pour over chicken. Add other half of stuffing
mix. Bake in 400° F. oven until stuffing browns. Serves 12.

Nancy Plummer, Brunswick County

This is good for a potluck supper or a large family gathering.

CHICKEN AND DRESSING CASSEROLE

Eva S. Pridgen uses the same recipe as above, but she uses cream of mushroom soup instead of cream of celery soup. She also layers her casserole as follows: 1/3 dressing, 1/2 chicken, 1/2 can mushroom and chicken soups, 1 can chicken broth; repeat layers, then top with remaining dressing. Bake at 350° F. for 45 minutes.

Eva S. Pridgen, Wilson County

CHICKEN CASSEROLE

1 stick butter or margarine, melted	1 small carton sour cream
	Slivered almonds
1 package Pepperidge Farm Dressing mix	2 to 3 cups cooked, diced chicken, reserve chicken
1 can cream of chicken soup	stock

Mix melted butter with stuffing. Cover the bottom of an 8 x 10-inch baking dish with half the stuffing mix. Arrange cut-up chicken over stuffing. Mix chicken soup with sour cream and pour over chicken. Top with remaining stuffing mix, and sprinkle with almonds. Dribble 1 3/4 cups chicken stock over top. The casserole needs to be rather moist. Bake at 350° F. for 30 minutes. Serves 8.

Juanita Cannon, Gaston County

It is easy to make, and with a salad you have a full meal with little effort.

CHICKEN CASSEROLE WITH CORN BREAD DRESSING

6 to 8 small boneless, skinless chicken breasts	1 large can evaporated milk
	1 small onion, chopped
1 can cream of chicken soup, undiluted	1 package corn bread dressing mix
1 can cream of mushroom soup, undiluted	1 stick margarine, melted

Boil chicken, and cut into small pieces. Place chicken in bottom of 9 x 13-inch baking dish. Combine soups, milk, and onion, and pour over chicken. Mix dressing mix with melted margarine, and sprinkle over the top of the casserole. Bake at 350° F. for 35 to 40 minutes.

Patricia Herring, Wayne County

This is great for Sunday dinners.

CHICKEN WITH SWISS CHEESE AND STUFFING

8 boneless chicken breasts
8 4 x 4-inch slices Swiss
  cheese
1 can cream of chicken soup

1/2 cup water
1 cup herb-seasoned
  stuffing mix
1 stick melted margarine

Arrange chicken in a greased 9 x 13-inch baking dish. Top with cheese slices. Combine soup and water, and stir well. Spoon over chicken. Sprinkle with stuffing mix. Drizzle margarine over crumbs. Bake at 350° F. for 45 to 55 minutes. Serves 8.

Linda H. Harris, Vance County

CHICKEN AND DRESSING FOR ONE

3 ounces cooked chicken
  breast
4 ounce can mushroom
  pieces
1 piece bread, toasted and
  crumbled in blender

1/2 cup skim milk
1 tablespoon parsley
Dash of garlic powder
1/2 teaspoon poultry
  seasoning
Paprika for garnish

Combine all ingredients, reserving some bread crumbs. Place in a small baking dish. Top with reserved crumbs and paprika. Bake at 425° F. for 35 minutes. Serves 1.

Jennifer Mitchell, Harnett County

CHICKEN AND EGG CASSEROLE

4 boiled chicken breast
  halves
1/2 cup reserved chicken
  broth

3 hard-boiled eggs, chopped
1 can cream of chicken soup
1 can cream of celery soup
15 Ritz crackers, crushed

Cut chicken into bite-sized pieces. Mix all ingredients together. Pour into greased casserole dish. Sprinkle top of casserole with as many additional crushed Ritz crackers as desired. Bake at 350° F. for 30 to 40 minutes or until the casserole bubbles. Note: This is better if the casserole is mixed the night before and left in the refrigerator until it is time to bake it.

Pearl Freedman, Columbus County

This is an ideal dish to take a sick friend, or to serve just about any time.

CHICKEN SUPREME

6 strips bacon
6 boneless chicken breasts
1 can cream of mushroom
    soup

1 8-ounce container sour
    cream
1 small jar mushrooms
1 bay leaf
Salt and pepper to taste

Wrap a strip of bacon around each chicken breast. Arrange chicken in 9 x 12-inch baking dish. Mix together soup, sour cream, mushrooms, bay leaf, salt, and pepper. Pour mixture over chicken, and cook uncovered for 2 1/2 hours at 250° F.

Pearl Ange, Craven County

FIESTA CHICKEN LASAGNA

2 16-ounce jars thick-and-
    chunky salsa
9 cooked lasagna noodles
1 9-ounce package frozen
    Southwest chicken breast
    strips, thawed

1 15-ounce can black beans,
    drained and rinsed
1/4 cup chopped fresh
    cilantro
3 cups (12 ounces) shredded
    Monterey Jack cheese

Heat oven to 375° F. Spread 1/4 cup of salsa in ungreased 9 x 13-inch baking dish. Layer with three noodles and one third each of the chicken, beans, cilantro, remaining salsa, and cheese. Repeat layers twice more. Cover and bake 20 minutes. Uncover and bake 15 to 20 minutes longer, or until lasagna is hot in the center. Let stand 10 minutes before cutting. Serves 8.

Jean Richardson, Wake County

Serve this hearty, filling dish when your family comes in after a long, cold day working outside.

CHICKEN-RICE CASSEROLE

1 cup long-grain rice,
    uncooked
1 can onion soup
1 chicken, cut up

Salt and pepper to taste
1 can cream of mushroom
    soup
1 soup can of water

Spray 9 x 12-inch casserole dish with Pam cooking spray. Pour in rice, and cover with onion soup. Season chicken with salt and pepper, and place on top of rice and onion soup. Mix cream of mushroom soup with water, and pour over chicken. Cover, and bake 2 hours at 375° F.

Eva S. Pridgen, Wilson County

CHICKEN PUFFS

3 ounces cream cheese,
  softened
2 tablespoons margarine,
  melted
2 cups chicken breast,
  cooked and cubed
1/4 teaspoon salt
1/8 teaspoon pepper
2 tablespoons 1% milk

1 tablespoon onion,
  chopped
1 tablespoon pimiento,
  chopped
1 can crescent rolls
3 tablespoons margarine,
  melted
Sauce:
1 can cream of celery soup
1/2 cup 1% milk

Blend cream cheese and 2 tablespoons melted margarine. Add chicken, salt, pepper, milk, onion, and pimiento; mix well. Separate crescent rolls into four rectangles. Seal lines. Place 1/2 cup chicken mixture in center of each rectangle, and pull four corners to center; seal lines. Brush top with 3 tablespoons melted margarine. Bake at 300° F. for 20 to 25 minutes. *Prepare sauce:* While puffs are baking, combine cream of celery soup and 1/2 cup milk; heat. To serve, spoon sauce over puffs. Any leftovers reheat well in the microwave. Serves 4.

Sandra Vann, Northampton County

SALISBURY ANTIQUE SHOW CHICKEN SALAD
(for a large crowd)

14 pints cooked chicken
  breast, cut into rather
  large pieces
7 pints celery, chopped
1 1/2 quarts mayonnaise
15 hard-cooked eggs,
  chopped

1/2 cup fresh lemon juice
2 tablespoons Durkee's
  Famous Sauce
Salt and white pepper to
  taste

Mix all ingredients thoroughly but gently. If chicken appears to be too dry, moisten it with a little chicken broth. Mix the day before serving, if possible, so the flavors can meld. Serve on a lettuce leaf. Serves 60.

Juanita Fisher Lagg, Rowan County

Juanita Lagg credits the late Arline Crawford for coming up with this recipe about 25 years ago. It's been used every year since at the annual Salisbury Antique Show. It is such a hit that people come to the show just to eat lunch, which consists of homemade chicken salad and vegetable soup.

—

CURRY CHICKEN SALAD

2 1/2 cups cubed cooked chicken
1/2 cup chopped walnuts
1/3 cup finely chopped celery
2 tablespoons grated onion
1/2 cup mayonnaise
2 tablespoons sour cream
1/8 teaspoon Cajun seasoning
3/4 teaspoon curry powder

In a food processor, process chicken until finely chopped. Transfer to a large bowl. Add walnuts, celery, and onion. In a small bowl, combine mayonnaise, sour cream, and dry seasonings. Mix well. Pour over chicken mixture, and stir well. Refrigerate for at least 1 hour.

Nancy Johnston, Buncombe County

ELEGANT CHICKEN SALAD

1 package long-grain and wild rice, prepared
2 cups cut-up chicken
1 8-ounce can water chestnuts, drained and slivered
1 cup toasted slivered almonds
2/3 cup mayonnaise
1/3 cup milk
1/3 cup lemon juice
2 tablespoons grated onion
1 teaspoon seasoned salt

Cook rice according to package instructions. Mix in chicken, water chestnuts, and almonds. Combine mayonnaise, milk, lemon juice, onion, and seasoned salt. Pour over rice mixture, and mix thoroughly. Chill. Serves 6 to 8. Recipe can be doubled.

Laura B. Wooten, Wake County

HOT CHICKEN SALAD

4 cups boned, cooked
chicken (or turkey) diced
in fairly large, bite-sized
pieces
6 hard-boiled eggs, coarsely
chopped
1 cup sliced fresh
mushrooms
1 cup sliced water chestnuts
2 cups celery, chopped
1/2 cup onion, chopped

1 coarsely chopped green
pepper, sautéed slightly
1/2 pound cheddar cheese,
cubed
3 cups Hellman's
mayonnaise
1 teaspoon prepared
mustard
1 cup pecans, chopped
Salt and pepper to taste

Preheat oven to 350° F. Mix all the ingredients lightly, and place in
a 2-quart casserole. Bake for 20 minutes. Serves 10.

Mrs. Kathryn Ort, Wake County

*This recipe was given to me by one of my favorite childhood friends.
I frequently prepare this for my Church Circle brunch. It is
excellent for brunch, served with tossed salad and fresh fruit.*

TROPICAL CHICKEN SALAD

2 cups cooked chicken,
cubed
1 cup celery, chopped
1 cup mayonnaise
1/2 to 1 teaspoon curry
powder
1 20-ounce can chunked
pineapple, drained

2 large firm bananas, sliced
1 11-ounce can mandarin
oranges, drained
1/2 cup flaked coconut
Salad greens, optional
3/4 cup salted peanuts or
cashew halves

Place chicken and celery in a large bowl. In a separate bowl,
combine mayonnaise and curry powder. Add to chicken mixture and
mix well. Cover and chill for at least 30 minutes. Before serving,
add pineapple, bananas, oranges, and coconut. Toss gently. Serve on
salad greens, and sprinkle with nuts. Serves 4 to 6.

Witt Fogleman, Alamance County

YANCEY COUNTY HOT CHICKEN SALAD

3 cups chicken, cooked, diced
1 cup celery, chopped fine
2 teaspoons onion, chopped
1/2 cup sliced almonds
1 10-ounce can cream of chicken soup, undiluted
1 1/2 cups rice, cooked
1 tablespoon lemon juice
1/2 teaspoon salt
1/4 teaspoon pepper
3/4 cup mayonnaise
1/4 cup water
3 hard-cooked eggs, sliced
2 cups crushed potato chips
3/4 cup shredded cheddar cheese

Combine chicken, celery, onion, almonds, cream of chicken soup, rice, lemon juice, salt, and pepper. Toss gently, and set aside. Combine mayonnaise and water. Beat with wire whisk until smooth. Pour over chicken mixture; stir well. Add sliced eggs to the chicken mixture, and toss lightly. Spoon into a greased 2-quart, shallow baking dish, cover and refrigerate 8 hours or overnight.

Bake at 450° F. for 10 to 15 minutes or until thoroughly heated. Sprinkle with potato chips and cheese. Bake an additional 5 minutes. Serves 6 to 8.

Eloise McIntosh, Yancey County

This recipe has been a favorite of my family and friends for a long time. I make it for holiday meals and special occasions, and it is always a big hit.

Handle Chicken Safely

When shopping, buy perishables last. Never leave chicken in a hot car. Refrigerate raw poultry promptly, and freeze uncooked chicken if it's not going to be used within 2 days

Properly packaged frozen chicken will maintain top quality in a home freezer for up to 1 year. Thaw chicken in the refrigerator, not on the countertop.

WHITE CHILI WITH SALSA VERDE

Chili:
2 1/2 cups water
1 teaspoon lemon juice
1 teaspoon black pepper
1 teaspoon cumin seed,
    ground
4 chicken breast halves,
    cubed
1 teaspoon garlic, minced
1 cup chopped onion,
    sautéed

2 9-ounce packages frozen
    white shoe peg corn,
    thawed
1 4- or 5-ounce can green
    chilies
2 15.5-ounce cans Great
    Northern Beans, drained
Topping:
1 12- to 14-ounce can Salsa
    Verde
Sour cream

In a large saucepan, combine water, lemon juice, pepper, and cumin seed. Bring to a boil. Add chicken. Reduce heat to low. Cover and simmer 20 to 30 minutes or until chicken is fork-tender. Add minced garlic and sautéed onion to chicken mixture. Cook and stir until tender. Add corn and chilies to mixture. Bring to a boil, and add beans. Cook until thoroughly heated. Top each serving of chili with sour cream and Salsa Verde. Serves 4 to 6.

Nancy Lilley, Onslow County

TURKEY AND OYSTER DRESSING

1 pint turkey broth
3 8-ounce cans broth
1 can water
2 sticks margarine
16 ounces herb stuffing mix

1 1/2 packages cornbread
    stuffing mix
1 1/2 pint North Carolina
    oysters, chopped

Heat turkey broth, canned broth, water, and margarine until warm and combined. Add mixture to combined stuffings. Add oysters last, and mix thoroughly. Make into patties. Lightly grease a pan to prevent sticking. Bake patties at 375° F. until set and brown. Makes 25 to 30 patties.

Emily Clapp, Guilford County

This dressing has become a tradition at our Thanksgiving and Christmas dinners and was our grandmother's original recipe.

TURKEY AND WILD RICE CASSEROLE

1 6-ounce package long-
grain and wild rice mix
1/2 pound bulk pork
sausage
1 cup fresh mushrooms,
sliced
1/2 cup celery, sliced

1 tablespoon cornstarch
1 cup milk
1 tablespoon
Worcestershire sauce
3 cups turkey, cooked,
chopped
1 cup dried cranberries

Prepare rice mix according to package instructions and set aside.
Brown sausage, mushrooms, and celery in a large skillet, stirring to
crumble meat. Drain sausage, and set aside. Add cornstarch to
drippings in skillet, stirring until smooth. Cook for 1 minute.
Gradually add milk and Worcestershire sauce. Cook until mixture is
thickened. Combine everything together, and spoon into a greased
11 x 7 x 1 1/2-inch baking dish. Cover and refrigerate up to 2 days
or freeze up to 2 weeks. Thaw in refrigerator. Bake uncovered at
375° F. for 40 to 45 minutes.

Mildred Moxley, Alleghany County

WHITE TURKEY CHILI

1 1/2 cups chopped onion
2 tablespoons olive oil
1/2 cup chopped celery
1/2 cup chopped red bell
pepper
1 garlic clove, minced
3 cups (about 15 ounces)
chopped cooked turkey
2 15-ounce cans of any
white beans (I use Great
Northern beans)
2 16-ounce cans fat-free
chicken broth

1 4.5-ounce can chopped
green chilies, undrained
1 cup frozen whole kernel
corn (I use white shoe peg)
1 1/2 teaspoons ground
cumin
1 teaspoon chili powder
1/2 teaspoon salt
1/4 teaspoon white pepper
1 cup 1% milk
1/2 cup chopped fresh
cilantro (must be fresh)

Over medium heat in a large Dutch oven, sauté onions for 1 or 2
minutes in olive oil. Add celery, peppers, and garlic. Continue to
cook and stir for 5 minutes. Add turkey, beans, broth, chiles, corn,
cumin, chili powder, salt, and pepper. Bring mixture to a boil.
Cover, reduce heat, and simmer for 15 minutes. Mash remaining
beans. Add mashed beans and milk to turkey mixture. Simmer

uncovered for 20 minutes, stirring occasionally, until mixture is thick. Several minutes before serving, stir in fresh cilantro. The cilantro makes the chili wonderful! Makes 6 to 8 bowl servings and 10 to 12 cup servings.

Zoe C. McKay-Tucker, Wake County

Who says chili has to have tomatoes and beef? Make a pot of this anytime in less than 1 hour, and your family or guests will think you've been cooking all day.

—

Brunswick County, Va., claims that the original Brunswick stew was a squirrel stew created in 1828 by Jimmy Matthews, camp cook for Dr. Creed Haskins, a member of the state legislature. Only one of our eight Brunswick stew recipes calls for squirrel. Brunswick stew is now most commonly made with chicken, or a combination of several meats. Give one of the following recipes a try, and modify it to suit your family's tastes. That's a North Carolina tradition.

JIM GRAHAM'S TAR HEEL BRUNSWICK STEW

1 large stewing chicken	2 8-ounce cans tomato sauce
1 pound veal, beef, goat, or	or canned tomatoes
squirrel	Salt
2 large potatoes, diced	Pepper
1 large onion, diced	Hot pepper sauce
4 cups fresh or canned corn	Worcestershire sauce
4 cups lima beans	Butter

Stew chicken and other meat together until chicken is ready to fall from bones. Cook and shred chicken and other meat with fingers, discarding skin and fat. Put meat back in broth. Skim off excess fat and continue to simmer. Cook potatoes with onion, corn, lima beans, and tomato sauce. When potatoes are tender, combine with chicken and other meats. The mixture will be thin like soup. Simmer for several hours to thicken. Season to taste with salt, pepper, hot pepper sauce, Worcestershire sauce, and butter. Serves 10 to 12. May be frozen.

Commissioner Jim Graham

My mamma always served this with pickles or slaw.

1940 BRUNSWICK STEW

1 old hen	1/2 pound pork
4 quarts tomatoes	1 bottle Worcestershire
2 quarts corn	sauce
2 quarts butter beans	2 sticks margarine
12 Irish potatoes	Salt and pepper to taste
1 pound ground beef	

Mix all ingredients. Cook over slow heat for 4 hours. Makes 6 quarts.

Sarah Odom, Harnett County

My grandmother taught me this recipe around 1940, and it has been a family favorite ever since. We even use this recipe for our yearly barbeque and Brunswick stew sale at my church.

BRUNSWICK STEW

1 large hen, cooked, skin pulled off, and deboned	1 large cabbage, chopped into chunks
5 pounds stew beef, cooked until tender	1 gallon butter beans
5 pounds hamburger	2 gallons stewed tomatoes
1 big onion, cut in small pieces	2 small cans tomato paste
4 or 5 potatoes, cut up small, as for potato salad	Salt and pepper to taste
	1 gallon corn
	2 cans corned beef

Cook the hen and stew beef separately. Get a 20-quart pot or washtub for the stove. (We cook ours in a washtub over gas heat.) While the hen and beef are cooking, brown hamburger in a big pot. Then add onion, potatoes, cabbage, butter beans, stewed tomatoes, tomato paste, and salt and pepper to taste. Once hen and stew beef are done, add the meat to the pot. After 2 or 3 hours, add 1 gallon corn and the corned beef, making sure to stir frequently so that the stew doesn't stick to the bottom of the pan. Cook for 1 more hour. Makes 17 to 18 quarts.

Judy Wheeless Cogdell, Harnett County

Every year when our father was alive we would make a big pot of Brunswick stew for the freezer. We cooked the stew as a family, and we all enjoyed the results for the entire winter. We continue this tradition whenever we can. It is always a good time for family to be together.

—

GRANNY RITA'S BRUNSWICK STEW

10 pounds chicken
5 quarts canned tomatoes
2 1/2 pounds onions
4 16-ounce cans butter
  beans

4 16-ounce cans corn
1 bottle Worcestershire
  sauce
1 stick butter
Instant potatoes

Boil chicken; tear meat off bones. Return meat to broth. Add tomatoes and onions. Cook about 1 1/2 hours until stew begins to thicken. Cook slowly, and stir often. Add butter beans, corn, Worcestershire sauce, and butter. Thicken to desired consistency by adding instant potatoes.

Jennifer Tysinger Mitchell, Harnett County

This recipe is from my father's mother, who was born just outside Buies Creek and later moved to Sanford.

GREENE COUNTY BRUNSWICK STEW

2 pounds ground beef
2 pounds hot sausage
1 medium onion
2 fryers, cooked, deboned,
  and chopped
1 32-ounce bottle ketchup
2 or 3 ounces
  Worcestershire sauce
4 quarts chopped tomatoes

4 16-ounce cans garden
  peas
4 16-ounce cans butter
  beans (if substituting
  frozen butter beans,
  precook)
4 cans cream-style corn
2 cups potato flakes
Chicken broth, if needed

Brown ground beef, sausage, and onion in a large pot. Add all other ingredients, leaving potato flakes for last. Potato flakes will thicken broth. I always add chicken broth. Simmer.

Elizabeth Cunningham, Greene County

This recipe was given to me by a friend. It's excellent to take to a sick friend and good for cold winter days. It also freezes well.

HEART-HEALTHY BRUNSWICK STEW

1 large fryer (or 2 pounds
chicken breasts)
2 pounds stew beef
1 quart canned tomatoes (or
fresh)
5 pounds Irish potatoes
1 pound carrots
6 stalks celery
1 quart green lima beans
2 cups yellow corn
1/2 cup diced onions
1/2 cup ketchup

1/2 to 1 cup vinegar
1 to 1 1/2 cup sugar (you
may substitute Splenda or
sugar substitute for part
of the sugar)
1 tablespoon or less salt (or
use a salt substitute)
1/2 teaspoon black pepper
1/4 teaspoon cayenne
pepper
1 tablespoon prepared
mustard

You may want to prepare meats a day before assembling the stew.
Place chicken and beef in separate pots with enough water to cover
and cook until tender. Remove chicken and beef and place broth in
containers in refrigerator; when broth cools, skim off and discard
congealed fat. Remove skin and bones from chicken and dice lean
meat. Remove visible fat from beef and dice meat. When fat has
been removed from broths, place both broths and tomatoes in a
large pan and heat. Dice potatoes and gradually add, stirring gently.
Slice carrot rounds, dice celery, and add both to the pot. Add lima
beans, corn, and onions. Stir often, making sure you stir the bottom
of the pot to prevent sticking and scorching. Blend meats and
vegetables and continue cooking until thickened. Vegetables should
retain their shape and color and not be mushy and gray. Add
ketchup, vinegar, sugar, salt, peppers, and mustard, and cook an
additional 5 minutes.

Virginia Bailey Harris, Columbus County

*My family has enjoyed variations of Mrs. Durant's Brunswick Stew
from Marion Brown's cookbook, which was published in 1951. In
1992, I entered Columbus Stew in our county's anniversary
celebration and won. I've made it more heart healthy for the 21st
century.*

MOM'S BRUNSWICK STEW

1 large hen
2 pounds stew beef
2 pounds pork
6 16-ounce cans tomatoes
6 cans vegetable soup
2 pints corn
2 pints butter beans

1 stick margarine
1/2 box oatmeal
Dash salt
Dash black pepper
Dash red pepper
1 quart mashed potatoes

Cook hen and pull meat off bone. Cook beef and pork. Combine three meats and all other ingredients. Simmer slowly in a large stock pot for 6 or more hours, stirring occasionally and making sure the stew is not sticking to the bottom of the pan. Serves 12 to 15.

Evelyn Stevens, Wake County

This was my mother's recipe, and it is great to cook on a cold, rainy day.

ST. LEWIS BRUNSWICK STEW

28 to 30 pounds chicken
4 pounds ground pork
(Boston butt or side meat)
2 gallons canned tomatoes
2 gallons butter beans

4 gallons cream-style corn
1/3 cup salt
1/3 cup black pepper
1 cup sugar

Put chicken and pork in a 35-quart or larger gas-fired wash pot, and cover with water. When boiling well (after about 1/2 hour), add tomatoes. When chicken begins to come off the bone, remove from pot and debone. Return meat to broth, and add butter beans. *It is very important to stir frequently all the time the stew is cooking.*

When chicken is done, add the corn, and cook until the desired consistency. Add salt, pepper, and sugar. Cook a few minutes longer, then cut off the heat. Stew gets thicker after it sets for a while. Approximate cooking time is 5 hours.

Elbert Ray Pitt, Edgecombe County

This recipe was used as a fund-raiser for St. Lewis Ruritan Club for years. Today, Elbert Ray cooks a pot, divides it among two sons' families and his own, freezing the stew in quart-sized containers. Brunswick Stew is great on cold, rainy days.

PEPPER STEAK

1 1/2 pounds cube steak cut
   into strips
Sauer's steak seasoning
Flour
2 tablespoons butter or
   margarine

1 beef bouillon cube
2 cups water, divided
1 cup chopped onions
1 can cream of mushroom
   soup

Sprinkle meat with steak seasoning on both sides, and flour lightly.
Brown on both sides in margarine in a large pan. Dissolve the
bouillon cube in 1 cup water, and add to meat. Pour in onions, and
simmer for 10 minutes. Mix the soup and 1 cup water. Pour in pan,
and simmer until steak is tender. Serve with rice or potatoes. Serves
4 to 5.

Wanda H. Powell, Nash County

FILET MIGNONS WITH SHIITAKE MADEIRA SAUCE

1/2 pound shiitake
   mushrooms
1 tablespoon olive oil
2 cloves garlic, minced
1 teaspoon dried thyme
1/2 teaspoon black pepper
4 5- to 6-ounce filet mignon
   (beef tenderloin) steaks, 1
   to 1 1/2 inches thick

2 shallots, finely chopped
2 cloves garlic, minced
1 cup Madeira wine
1/2 cup beef broth
1/4 cup whipping cream
Chopped parsley
Salt to taste

Remove stems from mushrooms. Cut into thin slices. Combine oil,
two cloves garlic, thyme, and pepper. Coat steaks with mixture.
Place in a preheated nonstick skillet. Cook for 12 minutes over
medium-high heat, turning once. Remove from pan and keep warm.
Cook shallots, remaining garlic, and mushrooms until tender. Add
Madeira and broth. Bring to a boil. Reduce heat and simmer for 10
minutes or until reduced to 1/2 cup. Remove from heat. Stir in
whipping cream, salt, and parsley. Spoon over steaks. Serves 4.

Nancy Johnston, Buncombe County

TENDERLOIN MEAT PIE

1 pint canned tenderloin or
  2 cups cooked pork
  tenderloin

1 cup water
1/3 cup butter
Prepared biscuit dough

Place tenderloin, water, and butter in a 9-by-13-inch baking dish. Top with biscuit squares. Bake at 425° F. until biscuits are browned.

Dorothy E. Fender, Alleghany County

My Grandmother Crouse always canned a lot of vegetables, meats, and fruits. This dish was especially good and easy to fix.

BEEF STEW

1 1/2 to 2 pounds stew beef
1 can tomatoes
2 onions
1 pound carrots, cut in
  large pieces

Potatoes, 5 large or 8 small,
  cut in bite-sized pieces
4 tablespoons tapioca
1 package frozen peas
Salt and pepper to taste

Put all ingredients in a roaster in the above order. Bake at 250° F. for 3 to 4 hours.

Dixie Porter, Wake County

This is a quick, delicious, hearty meal that feeds lots of hungry folks! It's also a great Sunday meal. Put it on before Sunday school, and it's ready when the family comes home.

ESTHER'S CORNED BEEF HASH

2 cups water
Salt and pepper to taste
6 Irish potatoes, diced

1 large onion, chopped
1 12-ounce can corned beef

Place water, salt, pepper, and diced potatoes in a saucepan. Sprinkle chopped onion over top. Open can of corned beef, and put contents on top of onion; do not mix, just place on top of potatoes and onion. Cook for 20 minutes. Stir and serve.

Esther Hickman Collier, Columbus County

This recipe has been passed down for four generations and has always been a hit.

TEXAS SHORT RIBS

3 to 4 pounds beef short
   ribs
2 teaspoons salt
1/4 teaspoon pepper
1 8-ounce can tomato sauce
1/3 cup brown sugar
1/4 cup ketchup

1/4 cup vinegar
2 tablespoons prepared
   mustard
1/2 cup chopped onion
1 clove garlic, minced
1 tablespoon chili powder

Place short ribs in large frying pan or Dutch oven, cover tightly, and cook slowly in oven for 1 1/4 hours, turning occasionally. Season with salt and pepper. Combine tomato sauce, brown sugar, ketchup, vinegar, mustard, onion, garlic, and chili powder in a saucepan and simmer for 5 minutes, stirring to blend. Remove each short rib from the pan, dip it in the sauce to coat all sides, and place it on rack in broiler pan (4 to 5 inches from heat) or on grill top over ash-covered coals. Cook at moderate temperature, brushing with sauce and turning occasionally, for 20 to 30 minutes or until done. Serves 4.

Eva Pridgen, Wilson County

KOREAN BEEF

1 1/2 pounds lean round
   steak, sliced thin
1/4 cup soy sauce
1/4 cup water
1 teaspoon garlic, minced

2 teaspoons sugar
1 tablespoon chopped chives
2 tablespoons cooking
   sherry (optional)

Mix all ingredients well, and marinate beef overnight or for a few hours. Remove steak from marinade, and place in a pan with a small amount of oil. Cook on the stove to desired doneness. The steak takes only a few minutes to cook.

Eva Ketelsleger, Duplin County

Home Grown

Based on cash receipts in 2000, cattle and calves rank seventh among agricultural commodities raised by North Carolina farmers, according to the North Carolina Department of Agriculture.

HAMBURGERS

1 1/4 pounds ground beef
1/4 cup applesauce
1/4 cup Ritz crackers, crumbled
1/2 teaspoon Worcestershire sauce

1 1/2 tablespoons Accent (MSG)
1/2 tablespoon Tabasco sauce
1/2 package Lipton soup mix
Salt and pepper to taste

Mix, and form into patties. Grill.

Thelma Blake, Columbus County

I made these for a child development center benefit cookout at Southeastern Community College.

WILMA'S EASY MEAT LOAF

1 8-ounce can tomato sauce, divided
1 1/2 pounds lean ground beef
1 cup bread crumbs
1 egg
1 medium onion, finely chopped

2 teaspoons Worcestershire sauce
1/2 teaspoon garlic powder
1/4 teaspoon pepper
1 tablespoon packed brown sugar
1 teaspoon prepared mustard

Reserve 1/4 cup tomato sauce. Combine the remaining tomato sauce with ground beef. Add bread crumbs, egg, onion, Worcestershire sauce, garlic powder, and pepper. Mix lightly but thoroughly. Shape mixture into 8 x 4 1/2-inch loaf pan. Place pan on rack in shallow roasting pan. Combine reserved tomato sauce, brown sugar, and mustard. Spread on top of meat loaf. Bake at 350° F. for about 1 hour or until done.

Wilma B. McCollum, Union County

Leftover Meat or Poultry

Cut up leftover meat or poultry, and add it to a tossed salad. Dice it and use it in an omelette, scrambled eggs, quiche, or macaroni and cheese. Chop it and heat it up with canned tomatoes, and serve over rice. Chop it and mix with mayonnaise; serve on lettuce or as a filling for sandwich.

MEAT LOAF WITH TOMATO TOPPING

1 pound ground beef
1 egg, slightly beaten
2 slices bread, broken into
  small pieces
1/2 can tomato soup
1 onion, chopped
Salt and pepper to taste

Sauce:
1/2 can tomato soup
1/2 can water
2 tablespoons mustard
2 tablespoons vinegar
2 tablespoons brown sugar

Mix meat loaf ingredients, shape, and place loaf in 6 x 9½ x 2-inch pan. Mix sauce ingredients, and pour over meat loaf. Bake for 1 1/2 hours at 350° F. Serves 6.

Janet Turner, Forsyth County

This was one of my mother's and sister's favorites for family gatherings.

HAMBURGER CASSEROLE

1 pound lean hamburger
3 to 4 medium potatoes
1 medium onion

Salt and pepper to taste
Cheddar cheese (optional)

Lightly press hamburger into bottom of 7 x 11-inch baking dish. Place thinly sliced potatoes and thinly sliced onion on top of hamburger. Sprinkle with salt and pepper. It is best not to use extra lean hamburger because some fat is needed for baking. Cover, and bake at 350° F. for 1 hour. Sprinkle loaf with cheese the last few minutes of baking. Serves 6.

Sylvia I. Pate, Robeson County

This quick supper was often prepared after a hard day barning tobacco. Served with sliced tomatoes and cucumbers from our garden along with bread and sweet tea, this meal was always eagerly anticipated.

MEAT LOAF

2 pounds ground chuck
1 teaspoon garlic powder
1 teaspoon onion powder
1 1/2 teaspoons black
  pepper

1 cup bread crumbs
1 egg
1 10.75-ounce can tomato
  soup
1/2 teaspoon salt

Mix ingredients, and place in loaf pan. Bake at 350° F. for 1 hour.
You may add chopped green pepper and onion if desired.

Sarah Lee, Beaufort County

JACKPOT CASSEROLE

1 pound ground beef
1/2 cup chopped onion
1 10.75-ounce can tomato
  soup
1 1/2 cups water
4 ounces small noodles

Salt and pepper to taste
1 14-ounce can creamed-
  style corn
1/4 cup green olives
1 cup grated cheese, divided

Brown meat and onion. Add soup, water, and noodles. Simmer until
noodles are tender. Season with salt and pepper. Add corn, olives,
and half of cheese. Pour into a casserole dish. Top with remaining
cheese. Bake at 350° F. for 35 to 40 minutes.

Karen DeBord, Wake County

I was raised on this casserole and still love it.

STUFFED CABBAGE CASSEROLE

1 pound ground beef
1 onion, chopped
1/2 cup uncooked rice
1 teaspoon salt
1/2 cup water

1 medium head cabbage,
  chopped
1 10 3/4-ounce can tomato
  soup
1/2 soup can water

Sauté ground beef and onion lightly. Do not brown beef. Drain
excess fat. Remove from heat, add rice, salt, and water, and mix
well. Place half of cabbage into ungreased 9 x 13-inch baking dish.
Cover with meat mixture. Put remaining cabbage over meat. Mix
soup and water. Pour over meat mixture. Cover and bake at 350° F.
for 1 1/2 hours. Serves 6 to 8.

Shirley A. Pendergrass, Franklin County

ONE-DISH MEAL

1 pound hamburger
1 package taco seasoning
  mix, prepared
1 small onion
1/2 cup chopped bell pepper
1 can kernel corn, drained

1 can kidney beans, drained
1 can mild salsa
Sour cream
Cheese, grated
Taco chips

Brown meat and drain. Prepare taco mix according to package directions. Sauté onion and pepper in taco mix in pan used to cook meat. Add meat, corn, beans, and salsa. Simmer for 1/2 hour. Serve with sour cream, cheese, and taco chips.

Wanda H. Powell, Nash County

GROUND MEAT CORN BREAD

1 pound ground beef
1 large onion, chopped
1 cup cornmeal
1 cup milk
1/2 teaspoon baking soda

3/4 teaspoon salt
2 eggs, beaten
1 16-ounce can cream-style
  corn

Cook ground beef and onion together in a skillet. Drain excess fat and set aside. Combine all other ingredients in a large bowl. Pour half of corn bread mixture into large rectangular baking pan. Top with meat mixture. Pour remaining corn bread mixture over meat. Bake at 450° F. for about 45 minutes or until corn bread is done. Serves 6.

Shirley A. Pendergrass, Franklin County

BABE'S BEST SWEET AND SOUR MEATBALLS

1 pound ground round
  steak
1 pound ground pork
2 cups soft bread crumbs
2 tablespoons onion, finely
  chopped
2 eggs, beaten
1 teaspoon salt
1/4 teaspoon pepper
1 tablespoon margarine

3 tablespoons cornstarch
1 cup vinegar
3/4 cup sugar
3 drops hot sauce
1 tablespoon
  Worcestershire sauce
1 green pepper, diced
1 20-ounce can pineapple
  chunks, drained
1 8-ounce can tomato sauce

Combine first seven ingredients, mixing well. Shape into 1-inch meatballs. Brown in margarine over medium heat, then drain. Place meatballs in a 13 x 9 x 2-inch baking dish. Combine cornstarch, vinegar, and sugar in a medium saucepan. Cook over low heat, stirring constantly, until clear and thickened. Stir in remaining ingredients; pour over meatballs. Bake at 300° F. for 40 minutes. Makes about six dozen.

Bobby Joe Fisher, Nash County

This dish is good any time, especially over rice.

SPANISH RICE SUPPER

1 pound lean ground beef	1 6-ounce can tomato paste
1 onion, chopped	1 cup water
1/2 green pepper, chopped	1/2 teaspoon ground cumin
1 cup uncooked converted rice	1/4 cup canned diced green chilies
1 28-ounce can cut up and peeled tomatoes, undrained	1/2 teaspoon salt
	1/4 teaspoon pepper

Cook beef, onion, and green pepper over medium-high heat in a 10-inch skillet, stirring often, until beef is browned, about 8 to 10 minutes. Drain excess fat. Stir in rice, tomatoes with their liquid, tomato paste, water, cumin, and chilies. Heat to boiling, stirring occasionally. Reduce heat to low. Cover pan and simmer over low heat for 30 to 35 minutes or until rice is tender. Stir in salt and pepper. Serves 5.

Jeanelle Bumgardner, Gaston County

This dish is one that I have kept in the family and everyone loves it!

MAMA'S CHILI

2 tablespoons bacon drippings	1 pint canned kidney beans, drained and rinsed
1/2 cup chopped onion	2 tablespoons chili powder
1 pound ground beef	1 16-ounce can stewed tomatoes
1 can condensed tomato soup	

Sauté onion in bacon drippings, then add and sauté ground beef. Add soup, kidney beans, chili powder, and stewed tomatoes. Cover and simmer for 1 hour.

Sandy Smith, Wake County

This is my husband's mother's recipe. Her name is Annella Smith, and she lives in Granville County.

FOUR ALARM CHILI

2 pounds ground beef
1 teaspoon ground onion
1 large green pepper, diced
2 cloves garlic, minced
1 16-ounce can tomatoes, undrained
1 8-ounce can tomato sauce
1 cup water
1/4 cup chili powder
1 teaspoon salt
1 teaspoon paprika
1 teaspoon oregano
2 to 3 teaspoons Tabasco pepper sauce
1 teaspoon instant coffee powder
2 16-ounce cans red kidney beans, drained and rinsed

In a large heavy pot brown beef with onion, green pepper, and garlic. Drain off fat. Add remaining ingredients except kidney beans. Simmer uncovered at least 45 minutes, stirring occasionally. When thickened, stir in drained kidney beans, heat through, and serve.

Chip Braswell, Rowan County

Have plenty of ice water handy!

North Carolina Beef

Beef (and pork) is leaner and more flavorful, thanks to research efforts by NC State animal scientists. Programs and research have improved meat products over the years.

30-MINUTE STEW

1 pound ground beef	1 cup water
2 10.75-ounce cans	2 cups Minute Rice,
vegetable beef soup	prepared

Brown ground beef, and drain off grease. Add soup and 1 cup of water to beef. Stir and let simmer. While beef mixture is simmering, prepare Minute Rice according to package directions. When rice is ready, place rice in oblong serving dish, and spoon beef mixture over rice.

Alice Allred, Cabarrus County

This is quick, simple, and inexpensive. Serve it with a salad and hot biscuits, and you've got a complete meal.

CABBAGE PATCH STEW

1 1/2 pounds ground beef	2 soup cans water
1 onion, chopped	1 1/2 cups coarsely chopped
1 16-ounce can pinto beans,	cabbage
drained and rinsed	1 to 2 teaspoons chili
2 16-ounce cans tomatoes,	powder
with liquid	1 teaspoon salt
1 10 3/4-ounce can tomato	1/4 teaspoon pepper
soup	

Brown ground beef and onion in large Dutch oven. Drain excess fat. Add pinto beans, tomatoes, tomato soup, and water. Bring mixture to a boil. Add cabbage, chili powder, salt, and pepper. Simmer 30 to 45 minutes. Serves 6.

Della Stephens, Forsyth County

Barbeque is another North Carolina favorite with as many variations as there are regions of the state. Here are two recipes for beef and two recipes that may be used with beef or with pork. For additional barbeque sauce recipes, look under Soups, Salads, and Sauces.

BAR-B-QUE BEEF
(for 3 to 4 pounds of meat)

1/2 cup vinegar	Dash garlic salt
2/3 cup ketchup	1/8 teaspoon salt
1/4 cup molasses	1 teaspoon sugar
1 teaspoon dry mustard	2 teaspoons orange juice
1 teaspoon Worcestershire sauce	Crushed red pepper to taste

Combine all ingredients together, and mix well. Adjust seasonings to taste; I usually add more salt. Use sauce to barbeque 3 to 4 pounds of beef. I use rib eye or sirloin for smaller amounts of barbeque beef because I can cook the smaller amounts much faster. I chop or slice the meat.

Billy Knowles, Duplin County

BAR-B-QUE BEEF
(for 20 pounds of meat)

20 ounces vinegar	5 dashes garlic salt
26 ounces ketchup	1 teaspoon salt
10 ounces molasses	5 teaspoons sugar
5 teaspoons dry mustard	10 teaspoons orange juice
5 teaspoons Worcestershire sauce	Crushed red pepper to taste

Combine all ingredients together, and mix well. Adjust seasonings to taste; I usually add more salt. Use sauce to barbeque beef. I use brisket or boneless chuck and usually cook the meat for 6 to 8 hours. Heat the meat over the fire on all sides and then move the meat away from the fire and let it smoke. Take it up when it is about medium-rare. Chop the meat if it's sirloin or slice it if it's brisket.

Billy Knowles, Duplin County

MARGARET'S BARBECUE
(pork or beef)

3 to 4 pounds pork or beef
  roast
1 1/2 cups water
1/2 cup tomato ketchup
1 cup vinegar
1/2 cup Worcestershire
  sauce

1 cup chopped onion
3 teaspoons brown sugar
3 tablespoons dry mustard
1/4 teaspoon red pepper
1/4 teaspoon black pepper
1 teaspoon salt

Place roast in large pan. Mix remaining ingredients, and pour over roast. Bake at 325° F. for 3 hours (or cook on top of stove). Serves about 15.

Margaret H. Spencer, Gaston County

I couldn't cook much when I got married 50 years ago, but this is one of the recipes that I could make, and it's very good. I serve it with slaw and a vegetable, but you could put it in a bun.

SLOW COOKER BARBEQUE

Lean beef brisket *or* pork
  roast *or* half beef brisket
Half a pork roast

Equal parts of white
  vinegar, ketchup, and
  brown sugar, enough to
  nearly cover meat in slow
  cooker

Set the cooker on low. Cook for 8 to 10 hours (until meat shreds easily with a fork). Shred meat in sauce, and serve with vegetables of your choice or on a bun.

Byron Simonds, Hertford County

This recipe also works well using deer shoulder roast.

PORK CHOPS AND RICE

6 pork chops
1 can chicken and rice soup
2 soup cans milk

1 soup can long-grained rice
(not instant rice)

Brown pork chops in electric frying pan. Pour soup over chops.
Pour rice over chops. Pour milk over rice. Mix until rice is covered.
Cover pan and simmer slowly until rice is done.

Vicki Walton, Wake County

SMOTHERED PORK CHOPS

4 1-inch-thick center-cut
  pork chops
1 large clove garlic, halved
1 1/2 teaspoons salt
1 teaspoon freshly ground
  pepper
2 teaspoons dried basil
1/2 teaspoon dried thyme

1/2 teaspoon dried
  rosemary
1/2 cup flour
1/3 cup vegetable oil
1 cup yellow onion, diced
1 medium green pepper,
  sliced
1 1/2 cups water

Rub the chops on both sides with the cut sides of the halved garlic
clove. Mix the salt, pepper, basil, thyme, and rosemary together.
Generously sprinkle both sides of the chops with the herb mixture,
pressing it into the meat. Cover loosely with waxed paper or plastic
wrap, and let stand in the refrigerator for 30 minutes. Remove and
dredge the chops in flour. Heat the oil in a skillet large enough to
hold all the chops. Brown both sides, approximately 6 minutes on
each side. Remove the chops to a warmed platter. Add the onion
and bell pepper to the skillet and cook until soft, approximately 2
minutes. Add 2 tablespoons of the flour used for dredging and the
water. Stir until the flour is completely dissolved. Return the chops
to the pan and bring to a boil. Cover, reduce the heat, and simmer
for 30 to 40 minutes. The pork will be very tender and the gravy
delicious. Serve with rice. Serves 4.

Linda Braswell, Rowan County

BAKED CHILI PORK STEAKS

3/4 cup corn flake crumbs
1 tablespoon chili powder
3/4 teaspoon garlic salt
1/8 teaspoon pepper

1/4 cup chili sauce
4 pork blade steaks, cut 1/2-
to 3/4-inch thick

Combine crumbs, chili powder, garlic salt, and pepper. Spread chili sauce on both sides of pork steaks, and dredge steaks in crumb mixture. Place steaks on rack in roasting pan and bake at 350° F for 60 minutes. Place pan in broiler 3 to 4 inches from heat for 5 minutes to brown, if desired. Serves 4 to 6.

Eva S. Pridgen, Wilson County

ITALIAN PORK ROAST

4- to 5-pound pork roast
1 12 to 16-ounce bottle
Pepperoncini

1 package dry Italian
dressing seasoning

Combine all ingredients in Crock-Pot. Cook on high for 2 to 3 hours, then slow cook on low until pork is done.

Jean Richardson, Beaufort County

Pepperoncini is pickled pepper. You'll find it near olives in the grocery store.

LEMON-ROSEMARY PORK TENDERLOIN

1 medium onion, finely
chopped
2 tablespoons olive or
canola oil
1 tablespoon lemon juice
1 teaspoon minced fresh
rosemary, *or* 1/4 teaspoon
dried rosemary, crushed

1 teaspoon minced fresh
thyme, *or* 1/4 teaspoon
dried thyme
1 teaspoon grated lemon
peel
1 garlic clove, minced
1/2 teaspoon salt
1/2 teaspoon pepper
2 pork tenderloins (1 pound
each)

Combine ingredients, and rub over tenderloins. Place on a rack in a shallow roasting pan. Bake uncovered at 400° F. for 45 to 50 minutes, or until a meat thermometer reads 160° F.. Cover with foil and let stand for 10 minutes before slicing. Serves 8.

Linda H. Harris, Vance County

GRILLED STUFFED PORK TENDERLOIN

1 cup water
2 tablespoons cornstarch
1/2 teaspoon salt
1/4 cup brown sugar
1/4 cup vinegar
1/2 cup pineapple juice
1 tablespoon soy sauce
1 tablespoon green pepper
1 tablespoon dry onion
  flakes
1/3 cup chopped apple

1/3 cup raisins
2 1/2 tablespoons brown
  sugar
1 tablespoon vinegar
1/4 teaspoon salt
1/4 teaspoon sage
3 tenderloins
  (approximately 1 pound
  each)
3 slices bacon

Combine water, cornstarch, salt, 1/4 cup brown sugar, vinegar, pineapple juice, soy sauce, green pepper, and dry onion flakes. Cook sauce over medium heat 10 minutes. Set aside. In a separate bowl, combine chopped apple, raisins, 2 1/2 tablespoons brown sugar, 1 tablespoon vinegar, 1/4 teaspoon salt, and sage. Stuff pork tenderloins with this mixture. Wrap tenderloin in bacon, and skewer together. Brush sauce over tenderloin tips as they cook over gray white coals for approximately 50 minutes. Serves 8.

Frances S. Voliva, Tyrrell County

This recipe was Dee Voliva Furlough's award-winning presentation in the 4-H Pork Cookery Contest in the mid-1970s. It has been a family favorite ever since.

Pork in North Carolina

North Carolina ranks second in the nation in production of hogs and pigs. Based on cash receipts, hog farming brings in more money in this state than any other food commodity except broilers.

SWEET AND SOUR PORK

1 1/2 pounds pork
2 tablespoons shortening
1 cup water
1 chicken bouillon cube
1/4 teaspoon salt
1 20-ounce can pineapple
  chunks (reserve syrup)
1/4 cup brown sugar

2 tablespoons cornstarch
1/4 cup vinegar
1 tablespoon soy sauce
1/2 teaspoon salt
1 medium bell pepper
1/4 cup *or* 1 small onion,
  chopped

Cut pork into strips; brown in shortening. Stir in water, bouillon cube, and salt. Cover and simmer for about 1 hour. Drain pineapple, saving syrup. Combine brown sugar and cornstarch in saucepan. Add pineapple syrup, vinegar, soy sauce, and salt. Cook and stir until bubbly. Add sauce to pork; mix well. Stir in pineapple, bell pepper, and onion. Cook for 2 to 3 minutes. Serve over hot rice.

Eva S. Pridgen, Wilson County

SWEET AND SOUR SPARERIBS

3 1/2 pounds lean pork
  spareribs, cut into two-rib
  pieces
Salt and pepper to taste
2 large onions, sliced
1/2 cup brown sugar
1/2 cup vinegar
1 tablespoon soy sauce

2/3 cup pineapple juice
1/3 cup water
1/2 teaspoon salt
1/8 teaspoon pepper
1 tablespoon water
1 tablespoon cornstarch
1 cup pineapple chunks

Arrange cut spareribs on oven broiler pan, and sprinkle with salt and pepper. Broil, turning once, until spareribs are deep brown on both sides. Sauté onions in large Dutch oven with 2 tablespoons pork drippings from broiler pan. Add brown sugar, vinegar, soy sauce, pineapple juice, 1/3 cup water, salt, pepper, and ribs. Cover and simmer over low heat for 2 hours. Remove ribs. Combine 1 tablespoon water and cornstarch to make a paste. Thicken sauce with cornstarch. Return ribs to sauce, and add pineapple chunks. Simmer until thoroughly warmed. Serve with cooked rice. Serves 6.

Shirley Pendergrass, Franklin County

HAM, BROCCOLI, 'N' CHEESE POT PIE

1 16-ounce package frozen
  broccoli, thawed
2 cups cut-up cooked ham
2 10 3/4-ounce cans
  condensed cheddar soup

1/4 cup milk
2 cups baking mix
1 cup milk
2 eggs
2 tablespoons mustard

Mix broccoli, ham, soup, and 1/4 cup milk in ungreased
13 x 9 x 2-inch baking dish. Stir remaining ingredients until
blended. Pour over ham mixture. Bake at 400° F for 35 minutes, or
until golden brown. Serves 6.

Jeanelle Bumgardner, Gaston County

LIVER MUSH

Take one liver, including lights, and one-half of head. Put liver and
the lights in one pot and the head in another. Cook until meat falls to
pieces. Drain separately. Remove bones from head and grind all
meat in chopper. Put water that you cooked liver and lights and
meats in together in a large pot. Then add ground meat and season
with salt, pepper, and sage. Let come to a good boil. Thicken with
meal and flour (two parts flour and one part meal). Cook until it
rolls away from pot, and empty it into pans. When cold, slice one-
half inch thick, and fry a rich brown.

Mrs. Roland Beck, Burke County

LIVER PUDDING

3 1/2 to 4 pounds pork liver
1 or 2 ground onions (to
  taste)
1 cup ground cracklings (or
  5 to 6 slices of ground

bacon or ground side
  meat)
1/2 teaspoon salt (to taste)
1/8 teaspoon pepper (to
  taste)
2 1/2 cups cornmeal

Boil liver in large pot with plenty of water until done. Cook onions
with liver until onions are soft or transparent. (If bacon or meat is
used, it also should be cooked with the liver. Cracklings need not be
boiled.) Brown cornmeal in oven, turning often to avoid burning.
When liver is done, grind it up. Mix all ingredients in liquid left

from boiling liver. Add more water if needed for consistency. Freezes well. Best served hot on top of grits. Makes 5 to 6 pints.

Hazel Koonce, Wake County

Faye Koonce submitted this for her mother-in-law, who has fond memories of her mother making the pudding. When she became a homemaker herself, she would make several pints as part of her regular routine and keep it on hand to serve on grits for a nice, warm breakfast. "I had never eaten liver pudding until I met my husband and visited his mother and father in Rocky Mount, North Carolina. My introduction to this dish was love at first bite. I hope others enjoy this recipe as much as we have. Hopefully our grandchildren will keep the recipe going," says Faye Koonce.

—

LIVER PUDDING OR LIVER MUSH

1 whole fresh hog liver (3 to 4 pounds)
3/4 pound fresh fat from hog's head *or* fresh pork fat
1 teaspoon salt
1 tablespoon ground sage
1/4 teaspoon black pepper
2 cups self-rising cornmeal
1 cup self-rising white flour

Cook on top of stove in a deep black iron pot. Cut hog liver and fat into 2 x 4-inch pieces. Add enough water to cover. Add salt, sage, and black pepper, and stir to mix. Cover. Bring to boil, then reduce heat to low medium. Cook 2 1/2 to 3 hours until tender. Remove from liquid. Set aside. Leave liquid in pot. Sample and add more salt, sage, and black pepper if desired. Put liver and fat through meat grinder, grinding fine; set aside. Sift corn meal and flour together; set aside. Bring liquid to boil, then add ground liver and fat. Stir using a long-handled spoon. As it boils on low heat, sprinkle handfuls of cornmeal-flour mixture, stirring quickly. After all corn meal and flour have been added, cook and stir 10 minutes more. Pour into a 7 x 12-inch glass baking dish. Refrigerate overnight. Will slice well the next day. After slicing, fry as entrée or use cold on sandwiches. May be refrigerated 1 week.

Norene Hill Moll, Henderson County

This has been in my family for many generations. It's great for a farm family.

GERMAN HASH

1 quart tomatoes	Salt and pepper to taste
1 jumbo onion, sliced	1 tablespoon sugar
1 pound hot dogs *or* 3 cans	
Vienna Sausages	

Empty tomatoes into 10-inch frying pan, and crush with fork. Slice onion, and add to tomatoes. Cut hot dogs into 2-inch pieces. Add hot dog pieces to tomatoes and onions. Bring to a boil. Simmer until tomatoes and onions are tender, about 1 hour.

George Daniel, Halifax County

My uncle, Charly Daniel, brought this recipe back from Germany, where he was in the American occupying forces after World War I. I'm sure the Germans used some form of German sausage, but my father always used hot dogs or Viennas when he made it.

SCRAPPLE

20 pounds meat: hog's	2 tablespoons sage
head, jowl, heart, tongue,	2 tablespoons black pepper
sweetbreads, and some	2 tablespoons red pepper
skin	1 teaspoon ginger
Water	1 cup flour
6 tablespoons salt	1 cup buckwheat flour

Cook meat until tender using enough water to cover. Remove meat from pot, cool, and strain. Be sure there are no bones. Grind meat, and put back into liquid. Add seasonings. Thicken with flours. Cook and stir continuously until paddle will stand alone and mixture leaves side of pan. Pour into three 9 x 13-inch pans. Refrigerate to set. Cut in about 1-pound squares. Wrap and freeze. To serve, slice and fry until brown.

Ellen Teague Miller, Guilford County

My dad, Franklin Teague, first ate scrapple in Delaware, and he brought the recipe back to North Carolina with him in the late 1940s. When we kill hogs, we always make scrapple.

SCRAPPLE OR PANHAUS

2 cups ground pork
2 cups ground beef
3 cups beef broth
2 teaspoons salt
1/4 teaspoon pepper

1 1/2 teaspoons sage
1 cup cornmeal
1/8 teaspoon cayenne
  pepper

Combine meats and broth in a large saucepan. Heat to boiling. Add seasonings except cayenne pepper. Sift in cornmeal slowly, stirring constantly. Reduce heat and simmer for 30 minutes, stirring often. Stir in cayenne. Pour into greased 9 x 13-inch pan. Chill until firm. Cut into thin slices, roll in flour, and fry in oil or shortening until

crispy brown. Scrapple freezes well. After chilling, slice into thin strips and wrap family serving size quantities in plastic wrap. Place in freezer bag and freeze. Remove desired quantity as needed. Thaw slightly, not too much, roll in flour, and fry.

Pam Staton, Clay County

When my husband was a child, he enjoyed this dish when his grandmother made it. Today our daughter looks forward to it. We serve it with fried eggs.

SAUSAGE AND CORN

8 ounces hot sausage
4 cups fresh corn

2 tablespoons flour
2 cups milk

Crumble and cook sausage. Add corn and flour, stirring. Add milk, and continue stirring for 10 minutes. Serve over biscuit halves or toast. Serves 4 to 6.

Thelma Shore, Yadkin County

SAUSAGE AND RICE-A-RONI CASSEROLE

1 box chicken Rice-A-Roni,
  prepared
1 pound hot sausage
1 10.75-ounce can cream of
  chicken soup

1 8-ounce container sour
  cream
1 8-ounce package shredded
  cheese

Cook Rice-A-Roni as directed on box. Set aside. Brown sausage, and drain well. Mix sausage, soup, sour cream, and Rice-A-Roni until well blended. Pour into baking dish, and top with cheese. Bake at 350° F. for 30 minutes.

Tina Brown, Cabarrus County

This is a very quick and easy meal, and my family loves it.

—

SAUSAGE-CHEESE LASAGNA

2 pounds hot bulk pork
  sausage
2 10 3/4-ounce cans tomato
  soup
6 cloves garlic, crushed
3 teaspoons dried oregano
3 teaspoons dried basil

1 8-ounce package lasagna
  noodles
3 cups shredded mozzarella
  cheese
3/4 cup grated Parmesan
  cheese
1 16-ounce carton cottage
  cheese

Brown sausage in large skillet, stirring to crumble. Drain off drippings. Stir in soup, garlic, oregano, and basil. Mix well. Cook noodles according to package directions. Drain. Place three noodles in a lightly greased 13 x 9 x 2-inch baking dish. Layer 1/3 each of meat mixture, mozzarella cheese, cottage cheese, and Parmesan cheese over noodles. Repeat layers twice. Cover with aluminum foil. Let stand 2 hours or refrigerate overnight. Bake covered at 350° F. for 25 minutes. Remove foil and bake an additional 10 minutes or until lightly browned. Serves 6 to 8.

Rita Clark, Vance County

One of my family's favorite dishes!

MEXI-MUFFINS

2 pounds mild sausage
  (I prefer Bass Farm)
1 package Velveeta block
  cheese, cubed

1 package Velveeta Mexican
  cheese, cubed
2 packages English muffins,
  split

Brown sausage, and drain. Add cheese, and stir until melted. Spoon onto muffin halves. Freeze. (You must freeze before you can bake). Store in Ziploc bags in freezer. To serve, bake at 350° F. for 20 minutes.

Wanda H. Powell, Nash County

This is a great do-ahead recipe. The muffins can be eaten anytime, or quartered and served as an hors d'oeuvre. Kids like Mexi-Muffins.

—

CHILI-SAUSAGE SQUARES

1 cup biscuit mix
1/2 cup milk
1/2 cup mayonnaise, divided
1 pound bulk pork sausage
1/2 cup chopped onion

1 egg, beaten
2 cups shredded sharp
  cheddar cheese
2 4-ounce cans chopped
  green chilies, drained

Combine biscuit mix, milk, and 2 tablespoons mayonnaise. Stir well. Spread mixture in a greased 13 x 9 x 2-inch baking dish. Set aside. Cook sausage and onion in a skillet until meat is browned, stirring to crumble meat. Drain well, and blot with paper towels. Layer sausage mixture over biscuit mixture. Combine egg, cheese, and chilies, and spread over sausage mixture. Bake at 350° F. for 30 minutes. Let stand 5 minutes before serving.

Jerrie Hasty, Union County

SAUSAGE AND GRITS BREAKFAST CASSEROLE

1 pound bulk pork sausage
3 cups hot cooked grits
2 1/2 cups (10-ounce
  package) shredded
  cheddar cheese

3 tablespoons butter
3 eggs, beaten
1 1/2 cups milk

Cook sausage, drain, and then sprinkle into a greased 9 x 13-inch casserole. Combine hot grits, cheese, and butter. Stir to melt. Combine eggs and milk. Stir into the grits mixture. Mix well. Pour slowly over sausage. Bake 1 hour at 350° F. uncovered. Let rest 10 minutes before serving.

Laura B. Wooten, Wake County

I recommend using at least 2 percent milk. The casserole is watery when it's made with skim milk. It can be made the day before and just assembled when you are ready to bake.

BREAKFAST CASSEROLE

1 pound sausage	6 eggs
3 slices bread	1 cup milk
1 cup grated sharp cheddar cheese	Salt and pepper (optional)

Thoroughly cook, drain, and crumble sausage. Remove crusts from
bread, discard crusts, and cube bread. Place bread cubes in
9 x 12-inch casserole, and top with sausage and cheese. In bowl,
mix eggs, milk, salt, and pepper. Pour over layered ingredients.
Refrigerate overnight. The next day, place in a 325° F. oven, and
bake approximately 45 minutes until set. Serves 8.

Linda N. Aycock, Nash County

This is a traditional Christmas morning breakfast.

SAUSAGE AND EGG BREAKFAST CASSEROLE

6 to 12 slices bread	2 cups grated cheddar
2 pounds hot bulk sausage, browned and drained	cheese
	12 eggs, beaten

Place six slices of bread on bottom of 9 x 13-inch Pyrex casserole
dish. Layer sausage, beaten eggs, and cheese. (If desired, add six
more slices of bread between egg and cheese layers.) Place in
refrigerator overnight. Bake at 325° F. until eggs are done, about 30
to 40 minutes. Serves 12.

Mrs. Doris B. Honeycutt, Columbus County

*This recipe is excellent for a brunch. It can be prepared the night
before and baked the next morning.*

SAUSAGE AND EGG CASSEROLE

1 pound regular or hot sausage	Salt and pepper, to taste
	8 slices loaf bread, cubed
7 eggs	2 cups cheddar cheese, grated
2 cups milk	
1 teaspoon dry mustard	

Brown sausage, and drain well. Set aside. Beat eggs well, and add
milk, mustard, salt, and pepper. Set aside. Cube bread, and put in
bottom of a greased 9 x 13-inch baking dish. Layer sausage on top

of bread. Sprinkle cheese over sausage. Pour egg mixture over all. Cover and place in refrigerator overnight. In the morning, bake at 350° F. for 45 minutes. Let sit for 10 minutes before serving.

Betty Mosley, Union County

This dish is perfect when you have overnight guests or are having a brunch. Just serve it with fruit and muffins, and call me when it's ready!

—

TOMORROW'S BREAKFAST

10 slices bread, cubed	6 eggs
1 pound sausage	3 cups milk
2 cups shredded cheddar	1 teaspoon salt
cheese	1/4 teaspoon pepper

Line an 11 x 13-inch dish with cubed bread. Fry crumbled sausage, and drain. Layer on top of bread cubes. Sprinkle cheese over sausage. Beat eggs, milk, salt, and pepper until frothy or bubbles appear. Pour slowly over cheese and other ingredients. Seal tightly with foil and refrigerate for 12 hours. Bake at 350° F. uncovered for approximately 1 hour or until browned around the edges.

Emily Clapp, Guilford County

This is a great weekend breakfast dish and is also good for brunch.

SAUSAGE-EGG CASSEROLE

1 pound hot sausage,	2 cups milk
browned and drained	6 eggs
4 slices bread, cut in cubes	1 teaspoon dry mustard
1 teaspoon salt	1 cup grated cheddar cheese

Brown sausage, and drain. Spread bread cubes in bottom of a 9 x 13-inch baking dish. Combine salt, milk, eggs, and mustard, and whip. Put sausage on top of bread cubes, then cheese, then pour egg mixture over sausage. Cover and refrigerate overnight. Bake at 350° F. for 35 to 40 minutes. Serves 12.

Dolores Benthall, Hertford County

Start this recipe the night before it is to be served. My family enjoys fruit served with Sausage-Egg Casserole.

CHRISTMAS BREAKFAST CASSEROLE

8 slices white bread
8 ounces shredded cheddar
  cheese
6 eggs
3 cups milk

1/2 teaspoon salt
1/4 teaspoon pepper
1 teaspoon dry mustard
5 to 6 strips uncooked
  bacon

Break bread into small pieces, approximately 1-inch cubes. Spread bread and cheese in bottom of greased 9 x 13-inch casserole dish. In a separate bowl, mix eggs, milk, salt, pepper, and dry mustard. Pour over bread and cheese. Lay strips of bacon lengthwise across dish on top of mixture. Let chill in refrigerator overnight. Bake the next morning at 350° F. for 50 to 55 minutes, or until firm. Serves 8 to 10.

Lisa Freedman, Columbus County

This is a great dish to prepare Christmas Eve and then bake Christmas morning while everyone is opening presents.

SAUSAGE GRAVY

1 pound ground pork
  sausage
1/4 cup all-purpose flour

3 cups milk
1/2 teaspoon salt
1/4 teaspoon pepper

Brown sausage in a large skillet over medium-high heat. Set sausage aside, leaving drippings in the skillet. Reduce heat to medium and combine flour with drippings, stirring constantly until the mixture just turns golden brown. Thoroughly whisk milk into skillet. When mixture is smooth, thickened, and begins to bubble, return sausage to the skillet. Season with salt and pepper. Reduce heat and simmer for about 15 minutes. Serve over homemade biscuits.

Tina Brown, Cabarrus County

Served over homemade biscuits, this Sausage Gravy has become a family tradition on Christmas morning.

HERBED RACK OF LAMB

2 Frenched lamb racks
1 tablespoon olive oil
1 clove garlic, minced
1/2 tablespoon coarsely
  ground black pepper
1/4 teaspoon salt

1/2 tablespoon fresh chervil
  or flat-leaf parsley, minced
1/2 teaspoon fresh rosemary
  or 1/4 teaspoon dried
  rosemary
1/4 teaspoon fresh thyme *or*
  1/8 teaspoon dried thyme

Brush lamb with oil. Combine remaining ingredients, and rub onto lamb. Cover and refrigerate 2 hours. Preheat oven to 475° F. Place lamb racks in shallow roasting pan, meat side down. Roast for 10 minutes, then reduce heat to 375° F. and roast for another 10 minutes. Remove from oven, and let meat stand, covered, for 10 minutes before carving. Serves 2 to 4 and can easily be doubled.

Alice Graham Underhill, Craven County

CRAB QUICHE

3 eggs
1 cup Half & Half
8 ounces Swiss cheese
1 cup crabmeat
1/2 teaspoon cayenne
  pepper

1/2 teaspoon nutmeg
1/2 teaspoon dry mustard
1 9-inch prepared pie shell,
  half baked (follow
  package instructions)

Beat eggs and Half & Half. Add cheese, crabmeat, and spices. Pour into half-baked pie shell (follow package instructions). Bake at 300° F. for about 45 minutes.

Hilda Ray, Columbus County

Crab Quiche is great for a ladies' luncheon.

MILLIE TICE'S CRAB CASSEROLE

8 slices bread, remove crust
  and dice
1 tablespoon margarine
1 pound crabmeat
1/2 cup reduced-calorie
  mayonnaise
1 cup celery, chopped
1 green pepper, chopped

1 medium onion, chopped
4 eggs, slightly beaten
3 cups skim or low-fat milk
1 can cream of mushroom
  soup
1/2 cup shredded cheddar
  cheese

Place half of bread in bottom of a buttered 3-quart casserole dish. Combine crab, mayonnaise, celery, pepper, and onion. Spread over the bread. Place remaining bread on top of crab mixture. Mix eggs and milk together, and pour over bread. Cover and refrigerate for several hours or overnight. Bake at 325° F. for 15 minutes covered. Remove and spoon mushroom soup over top; sprinkle with cheese. Return to oven and bake for 1 hour. Serves 10.

Jessica Tice, Currituck County

This recipe was given to me by my mother-in-law. My husband's family has always enjoyed crabbing each summer, and she was always trying new recipes to use the crab meat. This one became a family favorite. It was always difficult to get enough willing help to pick out the crab meat, but they made it a family event outside on the picnic tables along the waterfront.

FISH STEW

1/2 pound bacon
2 to 3 pounds fish (drum, rock, or flounder), dressed and cut into bite-sized portions
2 to 3 pounds white potatoes, peeled and diced
5 to 6 medium onions, chopped

1 10.75-ounce can tomato soup
Tabasco sauce to taste
Salt and pepper to taste
1/2 to 1 gallon water, as desired
6 to 8 raw eggs

Fry the bacon, and save half of the drippings for seasoning. Put all ingredients except eggs and bacon into a large pot and cover. Bring mixture to a boil. Cook uncovered for approximately 30 minutes, or until done. Crack and add raw eggs one at a time, carefully sliding them into the pot so that the eggs won't run. Cover and cook an additional 20 minutes. Serve with crumbled bacon on top. Serves 6 to 8.

Nancy Lilley, Onslow County

HOLIDAY OYSTERS

1 pint oysters, drained
1/4 cup butter
2 tablespoons dry white
  wine
1 tablespoon lemon juice

1 teaspoon Worcestershire
  sauce
1/2 teaspoon salt
Toast points or rounds of
  Holland Rusk
Lemon wedges

Sauté oysters gently in butter, wine, lemon juice, Worcestershire sauce, and salt for 8 to 10 minutes. Serve on toast or Holland Rusk, which holds up better than the toast and does not get as soggy. Garnish with lemon wedges. Serves 6; doubles easily.

Alice Graham Underhill, Craven County

Holiday Oysters are a great family tradition at Christmas and Thanksgiving. We serve them in the middle of the day, several hours before the big meal. They also make great hors d'oeuvres. (Holland Rusk is found in upscale grocery stores near the salad croutons or in gourmet shops.)

OYSTER CASSEROLE

1 stick butter, melted
2 cups crushed saltine
  crackers
Salt and pepper to taste
1 pint oysters, 1/4 cup liquid
  reserved

2 tablespoons
  Worcestershire sauce
  (more if you like)
3/4 cup Carnation
  evaporated milk

Melt butter, stir with 1 cup crushed cracker crumbs, salt, and pepper. Grease casserole dish. Layer crackers on bottom. Add layer of oysters, another layer of crackers, and another layer of oysters. Set aside. In a separate bowl, mix 1/4 cup reserved oyster liquid with Worcestershire sauce and milk. Pour milk mixture over casserole. Top with cracker crumbs. Bake at 325° F. about 25 minutes.

Faye S. Bunn, Nash County

PETE'S OYSTER DELIGHT

Saltine crackers
1 quart fresh shucked
  oysters with their own
  liquor
1 quart Half & Half *
Butter, salted or unsalted
Sea salt (or regular salt)

Fresh coarsely ground
  black pepper
Cayenne pepper (if you
  want to kick it up a notch)
Other spice/herbs to taste
Fresh parsley for garnish

You may not use the entire quart; too much and the dish is soggy.

Spray a 3 to 4-quart casserole dish with Pam or a similar product. Crush saltines until bite-sized or a tad larger; do not pulverize. Place a layer of saltines in the bottom of the dish. Add enough oysters to cover the saltines, but do not overload. Add several generous pats of butter. Wet these ingredients with Half & Half; do not flood, just liberally dampen. Season this first layer with salt and pepper. (You may experiment with other seasonings, but I recommend using just salt and pepper the first time you make the dish, as the finished casserole will have plenty of flavor of its own.) Repeat this layering process until all oysters are used up. The liquor (oyster juices) should be poured in with the oysters. End with a top layer of saltines and a few pats of butter. Bake in preheated 375° F. oven. Start checking after 30 minutes and do not bake for more than 40 minutes. Serve immediately with fresh parsley garnish.

Pete and Gael Jaeger, Chatham County

My motto is, "Presentation is at least 30 percent of the finished dish." My, it's eye appealing. Bon appetit!

SCALLOPED OYSTERS

Butter a casserole or baking dish. Put a layer of crumbled crackers or biscuits (crackers preferred) on the bottom. Then put in a layer of oysters, sprinkle lightly with salt and pepper, and dot with butter. Repeat layers until dish is nearly full, having a top layer of crumbs. Beat 1 egg, and mix with milk, 1/2 cup if a small dish is used or 1 cup if a large dish is used. Pour over the contents of dish. Bake in a moderate oven until brown.

Mrs. J. S. Payne, Hyde County

This recipe was sent in by Ken Powell in memory of Mrs. Payne.

Sarah Odom of Harnett County brought her Scalloped Oyster recipe back from a vacation in Dare County in the 1950s, and Ethel Pitt of Edgecombe County got her recipe from her mother-in-law. The ingredients are basically the same, but the casseroles are put together slightly differently.

SCALLOPED OYSTERS

1 quart oysters	1 cup milk
Salt and pepper to taste	3/4 to 1 stick butter
1/4 pound salted crackers	

Place a layer of oysters in a 9 1/2 x 13-inch baking dish. Sprinkle with salt and pepper; then add a layer of cracker crumbs. Repeat layers until all oysters and cracker crumbs are used, ending with cracker crumbs on top. Dot generously with butter. Just before baking, pour milk over casserole. Bake at 350° F. until lightly golden in color. Serves 6.

Sarah Odom, Harnett County

Place half of the oysters in a buttered casserole dish. Sprinkle salt and pepper over them. Cut half of the margarine into small pieces, and put over the oysters. Then crumble some crackers, and cover the top of the oysters. Repeat. Pour milk over the top and cook at 400° F. for 30 minutes, or until the cracker crumbs are browned.

Ethel Pitt, Edgecombe County

FARMER'S WIFE SALMON LOAF

1/2 teaspoon garlic powder	2 cups salmon (1 large can)
1 5 1/2-ounce package	1 can cream of celery soup
potato chips, crushed	

Combine all ingredients, and mix well. Turn into baking dish sprayed with olive oil-flavored cooking spray. Bake at 300° F. for 30 minutes.

Wilma B. McCollum, Union County

This is very good served with garlic sauce spread on top. This easy and simple meat dish was used during planting or harvesting season on the farm.

MILLIE'S SHRIMP CREOLE

1 onion, chopped
1 green pepper, chopped
1 to 2 tablespoons
  margarine
1 clove garlic, crushed
1 bay leaf
1 16-ounce can diced
  tomatoes

1 16-ounce can tomato
  sauce
1 to 2 teaspoons chili
  powder
1 tablespoon lemon juice
1 pound shrimp, shelled,
  cleaned, cooked
Cooked rice

Sauté onion and green pepper in margarine in a 12-inch fry pan or electric skillet until tender. Add garlic, bay leaf, tomatoes, tomato sauce, chili powder, and lemon juice. Cook on low heat for 20 to 30 minutes. Before serving, add cooked shrimp. Serve over rice. Serves 6 to 8.

Jessica Tice, Currituck County

This recipe was given to me by my mother-in-law. It was a favorite in my husband's family for years, and now we are continuing the tradition in our family. I have shared this recipe in many local cookbooks.

SHRIMP-RICE CASSEROLE

4 green onions, chopped
1 medium green pepper,
  diced
1 cup chopped celery
3 pounds shrimp, boiled
  and peeled
2 small jars mushrooms

1 1/2 cups white rice,
  cooked
1 cup mayonnaise
1/2 cup heavy cream (or
  Half & Half)
1 teaspoon salt
1 tablespoon
  Worcestershire sauce

Sauté onions, green pepper, and celery. Mix with other ingredients. Put in oblong Pyrex baking dish. Bake at 350° F. for 30 to 45 minutes, or until hot through and through.

Hilda Ray, Columbus County

This is a seafood lover's specialty.

FROG LEGS

1/2 cup butter
1 tablespoon minced garlic
1 medium onion, chopped
6 frog's legs

1/4 cup oil
1/2 cup flour
Salt and pepper to taste

Melt butter in pan. Sauté garlic and onion. Dry the frog's legs to prevent popping (grease spattering) while frying. Dredge oiled frog's legs in flour. In a separate pan, fry legs in 1/4 cup oil until tender. Put fried frog's legs in sauté mixture, and simmer for about 15 minutes. Add salt and pepper to taste.

Betty Mathews, Perquimans County

ROAST GOOSE

Always kill and dress a goose 24 hours before cooking. For several hours before cooking, soak the bird in salt and water. Make a dressing of boiled and mashed Irish potatoes, a lump of butter, and a minced onion, seasoned with salt and pepper. Fill the body of the goose, and place in a roasting pan. Grease the goose with butter, and pour in a teacup of water to the pan. Baste frequently until every part is browned. Serve with onion gravy and apple sauce.

Watauga County Extension and Community Association

QUAIL PIE

Crust:
1 cup self-rising flour
2 cups all-purpose flour
1 cup Crisco shortening
Filling:
10 to 12 quail breasts,
   boiled until cooked, retain
   broth

One medium potato, boiled
   and sliced thin
Salt and pepper
Parsley flakes
2 to 3 pats butter or
   margarine
2 cups quail broth

Mix flours; cut in shortening. Roll out crust for bottom of 9-inch square deep dish or 9 x 12-inch baking dish. Place crust in bottom of dish. Layer the quail breasts, and add a thin layer of sliced potato. Salt and pepper to taste. Sprinkle parsley flakes, and top with several pats of butter or margarine. Add 2 cups of quail broth. Then roll out remaining dough. Cut into strips. Place strips back and forth

to form a lattice on top of pie. Bake at 350° F. for 40 to 45 minutes.
Serves 6 to 8.

Sylvia Smith, Alamance County

My husband goes quail hunting in Texas for two weeks before
Thanksgiving. We use the quail for pies and have a game supper
with squirrel, rabbit, and venison. The hunters enjoy it very much.

—

VENISON STEW

Cut small steaks. Make a dressing with bread crumbs, onion, butter,
pepper, salt, and thyme. Spread dressing on each steak, then roll
each steak up, tie it, and put it in boiling water to stew. Thicken the
gravy with flour.

Watauga County Extension and Community Association

VENISON MEAT LOAF

2 pounds ground venison	Garlic salt and pepper to
1 pound pork sausage	taste
2 eggs	*Sauce:*
1/4 cup bread crumbs	1/4 cup prepared mustard
1/4 cup sweet pickle relish	1/4 cup ketchup
1 small onion, minced	1/4 cup brown sugar

Combine meats, eggs, bread crumbs, pickle relish, onion, garlic salt,
and pepper, and mix thoroughly. Shape into loaf. Bake in preheated
350° F. oven about 1 1/2 hours or until done. While meat loaf is
baking, mix mustard, ketchup, and brown sugar until smooth.
Remove meat loaf 15 minutes before it is done, and spread sauce
over top of loaf. Return to oven and cook for remaining 15 minutes.

Juanita L. Guthrie, Onslow County

CHEESE PUDDING

9 slices bread, crusts
  removed, bread cubed
1/4 pound margarine,
  melted
3/4 pound mild cheddar
  cheese, grated

1/2 teaspoon red pepper
3 eggs, separated
1/2 teaspoon dry mustard
2 cups milk
1/2 teaspoon salt

Remove crust from bread, cube bread, and soak it in melted margarine. Combine cheese, red pepper, slightly beaten egg yolks, dry mustard, milk, and salt. Add to bread-margarine mixture. Stir to combine. Beat egg whites, and fold into mixture. Pour into a buttered large, rectangular baking dish. Let stand covered in refrigerator for 12 hours. Bake for 45 minutes at 350° F. Halfway through cooking time, cover loosely with foil to avoid overbrowning. Serves 12 to 15.

Mrs. Leroy Whitfield, Greene County

Mrs. Henry Thorp of Granville County shared this recipe with our family many years ago, and it's now a family favorite at Thanksgiving and Christmas.

MACARONI AND CHEESE CASSEROLE

1 cup elbow macaroni
2 eggs
2 cups milk

1/2 teaspoon black pepper
1/2 pound cheese, grated
1/2 stick margarine

Cook macaroni in salted water (do not overcook). Lightly beat eggs, and add milk and pepper. Put a layer of macaroni in the bottom of a greased 8 x 8-inch baking dish. Add a layer of grated cheese, then a layer of macaroni, and another layer of cheese. Pour the egg and milk mixture over this. Dot freely with margarine. Bake at 375° F. until slightly browned on top, approximately 1 hour. Serves 8.

Mary Warren, Cleveland County

My children and grandchildren look forward to this. I double the recipe during the holidays, and it always gets eaten.

MACARONI AND CHEESE

2 pounds elbow macaroni
1 medium box Velveeta
  cheese
1/2 cup butter or margarine

1 can undiluted tomato
  soup
1/2 cup milk

Cook macaroni according to package directions. Cut cheese into bite-sized chunks. In a casserole dish, layer a third of the macaroni, a third of the cheese, a third of the butter, and a third of the soup. Repeat twice. Pour milk over the top of the casserole. Cover, and bake at 350° F. for 45 minutes. Serves 8.

Debbie McGilvery, Guilford County

VEGETABLE LASAGNA

9 lasagna noodles, uncooked
Olive oil-flavored vegetable
  cooking spray
1 10-ounce package frozen
  chopped spinach, thawed
  and well drained
2 cups sliced fresh
  mushrooms
1 cup grated carrots
1/2 cup chopped onion
2 tablespoons water

1 15-ounce can tomato
  sauce
1 12-ounce can tomato paste
1 4 1/2-ounce can chopped
  green chilies
1 1/2 teaspoons dried
  oregano
2 cups nonfat cottage cheese
2 cups (8 ounces) shredded
  Monterey Jack cheese
1/4 cup freshly grated
  Parmesan cheese

Cook noodles according to package directions. Drain and set aside. Coat a large nonstick skillet with cooking spray. Place over medium-high heat until hot. Add spinach and next four ingredients. Cook, stirring constantly, until tender. Stir in tomato sauce and next three ingredients. Place five lasagna noodles in a 13 x 9 x 2-inch baking dish coated with cooking spray. Layer with half each of cottage cheese, tomato sauce mixture, Monterey Jack cheese, and Parmesan cheese. Repeat layers with remaining four lasagna noodles, cottage cheese, tomato sauce mixture, Monterey Jack cheese, and Parmesan cheese. Bake uncovered at 375° F. for 30 minutes or until bubbly. Let stand 10 minutes before serving. Serves 8.

Carol Skroch, Ashe County

Breads, Pies, & Pastries

Biscuits
Corn Bread
Yeast Bread
Muffins

Quick Bread
Rolls
Pancakes
French Toast

Dressing & Stuffing
Pies & Cobblers

A Taste of North Carolina's Heritage

Food ... For Thought?

What's the news regarding food for the new millennium?

U.S. agriculture will continue to produce low-cost food and help fee the world. Tomorrow's technologies—genomic science and agricultural biotechnology research carried out in the College of Agriculture and Life Sciences at NC State University—will improv crop yields and nutritional quality, as well as ensure food safety.

The following NC State programs will help improve food:

- Plant and livestock breeders have long recognized the role genetics plays in improving food products, but traditional breeding can take decades. Through genomic science, College o Agriculture and Life Science researchers are learning to identify genes for improved traits in livestock and crops. They also use biotechnology to transfer the beneficial genes to the next generation, without transferring genes for undesirable traits.

- Global Positioning System (GPS) technology helps farmers crea maps showing the varied nutrient needs across a crop field. Such technology, called precision agriculture, can help farmers use nutrients where they are needed most, increase crop yields to fee the world more efficiently, and protect the environment.

- Savvy consumers want to know that the food they eat has the fewest possible chemical residues. Using biotechnology, NC Sta researchers are looking for genetic cues to make crops naturally resistant to certain pests, thereby reducing the need for agricultural chemicals.

CHEESE BISCUITS

2 cups self-rising flour
2 cups grated sharp cheese

1 cup heavy whipping
cream

Preheat oven to 400° F. Combine flour and cheese. Mix in cream, and turn onto a floured board. Knead until no longer sticky. Roll dough 1/4 inch thick. Cut with a glass dipped in flour. Place on a cookie sheet sprayed with cooking spray. Bake 12 to 15 minutes or until golden. Enjoy.

Vicki Heath, Craven County

MAMA LOU'S CHEESE BISCUITS

1/4 cup table fat (lard or
shortening)
2 cups self-rising flour

10 ounces Cracker Barrel
sharp cheese, grated
2/3 cup milk

Cut fat into flour. Mix in cheese and milk. Roll. Cut. Bake 8 to10 minutes at 400° F.

Mac and Blythe Winslow, Wake County

This recipe came from my husband's grandmother.

PARTY BISCUITS

1 stick ParKay margarine,
softened
1 cup sour cream

2 cups self-rising Red Band
flour

Mix ingredients together. Drop batter into little muffin tins. Bake at 375° F. until brown. Some like biscuits light brown; others prefer them a little darker.

Audrey W. Quinn, Craven County

SAUSAGE BISCUITS (PINWHEELS)

2 cups Bisquick
1/2 cup water

1 package (roll) Jimmy
Dean sausage (thawed);
hot, seasoned works well

Mix Bisquick and water. Roll out mixture as thin as preferred. Spread uncooked sausage on rolled-out dough. Keep edges clear. Start from bottom or top and roll the dough. Once rolled, slice 1/4-

inch thick slices (resemble pinwheels). Place circles on greased cookie sheet. Bake at 350° F. until brown, about 20 minutes. Makes 2 dozen.

Lisa Freedman, Columbus County

These also can be made with shredded cheese on top. Some like these with ketchup or mustard. The rolls can also be frozen.

—

THYME FOR BISCUITS
(2001 State Fair winner)

3/4 cup boiling water
4 tablespoons dried
  tomatoes
2 1/4 cups Red Band all-
  purpose flour
1 tablespoon sugar
3 teaspoons baking powder
3/8 teaspoon garlic salt

1/2 teaspoon basil, crushed
1 teaspoon thyme, crushed
1/2 cup butter
1/3 cup shredded Parmesan
  cheese
1/4 cup sour cream
1/2 cup milk

Preheat oven to 425° F. Pour 3/4 cup boiling water over 10 pieces of dried tomatoes. Let sit for 5 minutes to rehydrate. Stir together flour, sugar, baking powder, garlic salt, basil, and thyme. Using a pastry blender, cut in butter until mixture resembles coarse crumbs. Drain dried tomatoes and snip into pieces. Stir cheese and tomatoes into flour mixture. Make a well in the center of the dry mixture. Add sour cream and milk all at once. Stir until just moistened. Turn dough out onto lightly floured board. Flour top of dough and knead two or three times. Lightly roll out 3/4 inch thick. Cut with biscuit cutter. Place on ungreased baking sheet, and bake 12 to 15 minutes, or until lightly brown.

Jackie Wilder, Wake County

YEAST BISCUITS

2 1/2 cups self-rising flour
1/2 teaspoon baking powder
3 tablespoons sugar

1 cup warm buttermilk (not
  hot)
1 package dry yeast
1/4 cup butter, melted

Mix first 3 ingredients. Cut warm buttermilk and yeast into the flour mixture. Knead on a floured board. Roll out to 1/4-inch thickness. Cut out biscuits. Place half on cookie sheet. Melt butter and grease the biscuit tops. Top each biscuit with a second biscuit, making two layers with butter between the layers. Let rise 1 hour in warm spot. (I heat the oven to warm and turn it off for this 1 hour.) Heat oven to 350° F. Bake 15 minutes. Makes 24.

Margaret H. Spencer, Gaston County

BRENDA'S CORN BREAD

Slice of white bread	**3 tablespoons milk**
Hot water	**Dash of salt**
1 1/2 cups plain corn meal	**2 tablespoons shortening**
3/4 cup sugar	

Preheat oven to 450° F. Crumble the slice of bread and add enough hot water to soften. Add corn meal, sugar, milk, and salt. Add enough hot water to make a thin consistency. Melt shortening in an 8 x 10-inch pan. Pour batter into pan. Bake until brown, about 25 minutes.

Brenda Riddick, Perquimans County

Thelma Riddick made this corn bread (passed down from her mother) for more than 35 years; then, as she said, she "lost the rabbit's foot" and she just couldn't make it right. Today, I carry on the tradition.

CORN BREAD

3 cups corn meal	**2 eggs**
1 1/4 teaspoons salt	**3 tablespoons melted fat**
1 1/4 teaspoons baking soda	**3 tablespoons fat to grease**
2 1/4 cups buttermilk	**pan**

Put corn meal, salt, and baking soda in a bowl. Stir well until blended. In a separate bowl, add buttermilk to eggs and stir; add melted fat. Dump egg mixture into corn meal mixture all at once. Stir just enough to mix: mixture will have a rough appearance. Pour about 3 tablespoons of fat in a 15-inch baking pan. Pour in corn meal mixture, and bake at 400° F. for 15 to 20 minutes until browned.

Nancy Schrull, Davidson County

CORNY CORN BREAD

3 eggs slightly beaten
1/2 cup oil
1 cup sour cream

1 16-ounce can cream-style
corn
1 box Jiffy corn bread mix

Mix first four ingredients thoroughly. Stir in Jiffy mix until blended. Pour into 8 x 8 or 9 x 9 or 8 x 10-inch greased casserole dish. Bake at 350° F. for approximately 35 minutes. Recipe may be doubled.

Laura B. Wooten, Wake County

RANDOLPH COUNTY BROCCOLI CORN BREAD

1 10-ounce package frozen
chopped broccoli
1 stick butter or margarine
4 eggs, slightly beaten
1 6-ounce package corn
bread mix

1/4 teaspoon black pepper
1/4 teaspoon garlic salt
1 tablespoon sugar
1 small onion, chopped
6 ounces cottage cheese,
drained

Cook broccoli 2 minutes and drain. Melt butter in a 13 x 9 x 2-inch glass baking dish. Beat eggs slightly. Add corn bread mix, pepper, garlic salt, sugar, and onion. Mix well. Fold in drained cottage cheese and broccoli. Pour over hot, melted butter. Bake in 350° F. oven for 30 minutes or until golden brown. Serves 12.

Lib Thompson, Randolph County

At the county's annual Empty Bowl Luncheon, a big charity fundraiser for the Randolph Extension and Community Association, North Carolina potters provide their pottery soup bowls, and ECA members fill them and serve up their corn bread and best desserts.

OLD-TIMEY SKILLET CORN BREAD

White corn meal
Pinch of salt

Water
1 egg

Put an amount of white corn meal in a bowl with a pinch of salt. Add enough water to make a fairly stiff batter. Mix in an egg. Fry as one large cake in a little fat in a medium-hot cast iron skillet or on a griddle, turning once till crispy golden brown. Cut into wedges and serve hot with plenty of butter (not margarine).

Karl Larson, Wake County

My grandmother used to make this when my mother was a child.

SOUTHERN BAKED CORN BREAD

1 1/2 cups yellow corn meal, plain	1 1/3 cups buttermilk
3/4 teaspoon baking soda	2 eggs, separated
1 teaspoon salt	1/4 cup shortening, melted

Sift corn meal, baking soda, and salt together. Add buttermilk to well-beaten egg yolks. Add to corn meal mixture. Beat well. Add hot melted shortening, and beat again. Fold in stiff beaten egg whites. Pour into a piping hot, greased, heavy 10-inch skillet. Bake 25 to 30 minutes in 450° F. oven. Serves 5.

Betty Jean King, Granville County

Lydia Hart Boyd made this corn bread for her son to take with him when he left to join in the War Between the States. Her husband, William Washington Boyd, passed this story to his grandchildren.

SYLVIA'S CORN BREAD

2 cups yellow corn meal	1 1/2 teaspoons salt
2 cups all-purpose flour	2 1/2 cups milk
1 cup sugar	1 cup vegetable oil
2 tablespoons baking powder	5 large eggs

Preheat oven to 350° F. Grease a 9 x 13-inch baking pan. In a large bowl, sift and stir together corn meal, flour, sugar, baking powder, and salt. Set aside. In a large bowl with an electric mixer, beat the milk, oil, and eggs. Add the corn meal mixture, and stir until combined. Batter will be wet and a little lumpy. Pour into prepared pan, and bake for 40 to 45 minutes. Cool in pan and cut into squares.

Barbara Braswell, Union County

CORN DODGERS

2 cups white corn meal	Pinch of baking soda
Pinch of salt	1 cup buttermilk

Put white corn meal in a bowl. Add a pinch of salt and a pinch of soda and mix together. Add enough buttermilk to make a stiff dough. Pat out the dodgers with your hands, and fry in a little fat in a cast iron skillet over medium heat, turning once. They will be crispy golden brown on the outside and silky soft on the inside. Corn dodgers are best eaten hot and are delicious with collard greens and pinto beans. They can be made with water or milk instead of buttermilk; just omit baking soda.

Karl Larson, Wake County

This is an old recipe that's been around since at least the Civil War era.

—

CORN PONE

Corn meal	1/3 cup molasses
Salt	1 teaspoon baking soda
2 1/2 cups water	1 cup flour
Flour	2 tablespoons shortening
1/4 cup sugar	3/4 cup butter

Make a mush of corn meal, salt, and 2 1/2 cups water. Boil and stir. Move from stove and add a little cold water and corn meal to make another real thick mush. Sprinkle a little flour on top. Sit in a pan of warm water and put in a warm place; let it rise overnight. When you are ready to bake the next day, add sugar, molasses, soda, 1 cup flour, shortening, and butter. Add a little more corn meal if needed. Bake in a heavy bundt pan at 425° F. for about 1 hour or until brown.

Ellen Teague Miller, Wake County

This is a Teague family favorite. It's made mostly in the winter, since the best place to let the dough rise is beside the fire in the fireplace.

HUSH PUPPIES

1 cup corn meal	1/2 cup milk
1 egg	

Blend ingredients in a large bowl. Put oil in a deep fryer until it is about half full. Heat oil on medium high. Drop tablespoons of the mixture into the hot oil, just four or five at a time. Let brown. Continue until mixture is used up. Serves 4.

Erin and Wesley Martin, Wake County

To vary the taste of the hush puppies, experiment with adding sugar and onion to the batter.

OLD-FASHIONED CRACKLIN' BREAD

Sift 1 quart of corn meal; add salt and a teacup of cracklin's,
chopped very fine. Make up with warm water. Bake in pones.

Watauga County Extension and Community Association

OLD-FASHIONED SPOON BREAD

2 eggs, beaten
1/2 cup corn meal
Dash of salt
1 tablespoon sugar

2 cups milk
1/2 stick margarine or
butter

Mix eggs, corn meal, salt, and sugar. Scald milk, then pour over
mixture. Put margarine in 7 x 7 x 3-inch baking dish, and pour in
mixture. Cook at 375° F. until golden brown, usually 30 minutes.
Serves 6.

Madelyn P. Long, Perquimans County

*My neighbor, Mrs. Gatling, lived on the corner and often sent good
food to my family. She passed away many years ago, but I still have
fond memories of her delicious cooking!*

SPOON BREAD

3 cups milk, scalded
1 cup corn meal
3 tablespoons melted butter

1 teaspoon salt
1 teaspoon baking powder
3 eggs, separated

In saucepan, scald milk, and gradually stir in meal. Cook over low
heat until it begins to thicken. Remove from heat, and add butter,
salt, baking powder, and beaten egg yolks. Mix well and let cool.
Fold in stiffly beaten egg whites. Pour into a buttered 2 1/2-quart
dish. Bake at 375° F. for 40 minutes. Serve at once, topped with
butter. Serves 6.

Elizabeth Harper, Edgecombe County

Cracklings

*Crackling bread is corn bread made with cracklings, the crisp
residue left after the fat has been separated from pork skins in
rendering lard.*

SEASONED BUBBLE LOAF
(2001 State Fair winner)

3 to 3 1/2 cups all-purpose
  flour
2 tablespoons sugar
1 teaspoon salt
1 package active dry yeast
1 1/4 cups milk
2 tablespoons oil
1 egg

Topping:
1/3 cup butter, melted
3 tablespoons grated
  Parmesan cheese
1 tablespoon sesame seeds
1 teaspoon seasoned salt
1/4 teaspoon garlic salt
3/4 teaspoon thyme,
  crushed
1/2 teaspoon paprika

In a large bowl, combine 1 1/2 cups flour, sugar, salt, and yeast; blend well. In a small saucepan, heat milk and oil until very warm (120 to 130° F.). Add warm liquid to flour mixture. Blend at low speed until moist; add egg, beat 3 minutes at medium speed. Stir in additional flour by hand until dough pulls away from side of bowl.

Knead bread on a floured surface, adding up to 1/2 cup of flour. Place in a greased bowl; cover; let rise until doubled in size, about 45 to 60 minutes. Punch down to remove all air bubbles. Divide into 36 pieces; shape into balls. Dip each ball into melted butter. Place half of balls in greased 5 x 9-inch loaf pan, forming one layer. Combine topping ingredients; sprinkle half of topping over balls. Make second layer with balls of dough. Pour any remaining butter over balls. Sprinkle with remaining topping.

Cover. Let rise in warm place until light and doubled in size, about 30 to 45 minutes. Heat oven to 375° F. Bake 25 to 30 minutes or until browned and loaf sounds hollow when tapped. Cool 5 minutes; remove from pan. Makes 1 loaf.

Jackie Wilder, Wake County

Kneading Bread

As you knead dough, the gluten in the flour breaks down, and the dough becomes increasingly smooth, elastic, and soft. This allows the bread to rise properly. Yeast makes carbon dioxide gas that makes yeast bread rise. Quick breads, on the other hand, rely on other leavening agents, such as baking powder and baking soda. Never knead a quick bread.

BLUEBERRY MUFFINS

1 1/2 cups flour
1/2 cup sugar
2 teaspoons baking soda
1/2 teaspoon salt
1/4 cup shortening

1 egg
1/2 cup milk
1 cup fresh blueberries,
  drained, *or* 3/4 cup canned
  blueberries, drained

Mix together all ingredients, except blueberries. Stir just until blended. Fold in drained blueberries. Fill greased muffin pan two-thirds full. Bake in 400° F. oven for 20 to 25 minutes.

Juanita L. Guthrie, Onslow County

These muffins make a good dessert. I am a member of the Silverdale Extension ECA.

FRESH BLUEBERRY MUFFINS

1 egg, beaten
2 or 3 tablespoons sugar (I
  use more; I like mine
  sweeter)

1/3 cup shortening or oil
1/2 cup milk
1 3/4 cups self-rising flour
3/4 cup fresh blueberries

Beat egg. Add sugar, oil, and milk. Add flour, mixing only until ingredients are moistened. Gently add berries. Batter will be lumpy. Pour into muffin tins that have been greased, or use paper muffin cup liners. Bake at 400° F. approximately 20 minutes.

For Fresh Apple Muffins: You may omit blueberries and use 1 cup grated apples and 1/2 teaspoon cinnamon. Bake this version a little longer.

Pearl Freedman, Columbus County

I like to use these to welcome a new neighbor to the community. Fresh muffins make them glad they moved in!

HEALTHY BLUEBERRY MUFFINS

1 egg
1/2 cup milk
1/4 cup corn oil or other
  vegetable oil
1/2 cup sugar
1/2 teaspoon salt

1 1/2 cups all-purpose flour
2 teaspoons baking powder
1 teaspoon lemon juice
1 cup fresh blueberries

Beat eggs; stir in milk and oil. In a separate bowl, sift together dry ingredients. Add dry ingredients to egg-milk mixture. Stir only until moistened. Mix lemon juice with blueberries. Add blueberry-lemon juice mixture to batter, and blend gently. Bake in a greased or paper-lined muffin tin at 400° F. for 20 to 25 minutes. Makes 12 muffins.

Martha W. Walker, Orange County

I freeze the extra berries from my blueberry bushes so that I can bake up these easy-to-make, good, and healthy muffins year-round.

—

ORANGE MUFFINS

1 large orange with peel, cut into small pieces, seeds removed
2 tablespoons butter
1 cup sugar
1 1/2 teaspoons baking powder
1 1/2 teaspoons baking soda
1 cup sugar
1 teaspoon salt
1/2 cup orange juice
1 egg
2 cups all-purpose flour
Chopped dates or pecans (optional)

Place orange pieces with peel in food processor and chop well. Place in bowl. Add butter and sugar; mix well. Add remaining ingredients except dates or pecans, and mix together. Fold in chopped dates or pecans. Bake in greased muffin pan at 350° F. until done, about 25 minutes. Makes 12 muffins.

Sarah Lee, Beaufort County

RAISIN BRAN MUFFINS

4 eggs, beaten
1 quart buttermilk
5 teaspoons baking soda
3 cups sugar
5 cups unsifted all-purpose flour
1 cup cooking oil
15-ounce box of raisin bran flakes

Combine all ingredients well, and refrigerate at least overnight. Batter will keep as long as six weeks. Spoon desired amount of batter into greased muffin tins. Bake at 400° F. for 15 to 20 minutes. Makes 6 dozen muffins.

Shirley Pendergrass, Franklin County

SWEET POTATO MUFFINS

1 cup oil	1 cup pecans, chopped
2 cups sugar	1 teaspoon cinnamon
3 cups self-rising flour	1 teaspoon nutmeg
3 eggs	1 teaspoon cloves
2 cups cooked and mashed	1 teaspoon baking soda
sweet potatoes	

Mix all ingredients well. Spray mini muffin tins with vegetable spray. Fill two-thirds full. Bake at 350° F. for 15 to 20 minutes. Cool on wire rack. Makes 96 mini muffins.

Virginia Williams, Wilson County

I have served these at our annual Farm Bureau meeting for many years.

HEALTHY PUMPKIN BRAN MUFFINS

1 package Martha White	2 egg whites
Bran Muffin Mix	1/4 cup skim milk
1/3 cup sugar	2/3 cup canned pumpkin
1/2 teaspoon cinnamon	Cinnamon sugar

Preheat oven to 425° F. Grease 8 large or 10 medium muffin cups. Combine all ingredients except cinnamon sugar in a medium-sized mixing bowl. Stir just until blended. Fill muffin cups two-thirds full. Sprinkle each muffin with cinnamon sugar topping. Bake 12 to 14 minutes or until done. Serves 8 to 10.

Brandon Tice, Currituck County

This recipe is special because I was the North Carolina State Winner of the 1992 Martha White Muffin Mania Recipe Contest when I was a 4-H'er in the Currituck 4-H Program. You won't believe how many muffins my family ate until I could get the recipe right, but it was worth it. We had a great time playing with the Super Nintendo that I won. Participating in 4-H gave me many opportunities to learn about foods, nutrition, and food preparation.

BANANA CHOCOLATE CHIP BREAD

5 ripe bananas	3 eggs
1 18 1/2-ounce yellow cake	1 teaspoon vanilla extract
mix	1 cup chocolate chips

Preheat oven to 350° F. In a large bowl, mash bananas and add all ingredients except chocolate chips. With an electric mixer, mix 2 minutes at medium speed. Fold in chocolate chips. Pour into a buttered 5 x 9-inch loaf pan, and bake 1 hour.

Dayle Oakley, Wake County

This has been a favorite with everyone who tries it. I bake it in smaller loaf pans and give it as gifts or office treats.

—

BANANA NUT BREAD

3 cups all-purpose flour	**3 eggs, beaten**
3/4 teaspoon salt	**1 cup oil**
1 teaspoon baking soda	**2 cups ripe bananas,**
2 cups sugar	**mashed**
1 teaspoon ground	**1 8-ounce can crushed**
cinnamon	**pineapple, drained**
1 cup chopped pecans	**2 teaspoons vanilla**

Combine first 5 ingredients. Stir in pecans. In a separate bowl, combine remaining ingredients. Add to flour mixture, stirring just until dry ingredients are moistened. Spoon batter into two greased and floured 8 1/2 x 4 1/2 x 3-inch loaf pans. Bake at 350° F. for 1 hour and 10 minutes. Remove and cool on racks.

Mildred M. Harper, Edgecombe County

This is the best banana bread recipe I have ever tried!

BEST BANANA BREAD

1 stick butter, room	**1 cup mashed ripe bananas**
temperature	**1 1/4 cups all-purpose flour**
1 cup sugar	**1/2 teaspoon salt**
2 eggs	**3/4 teaspoon baking soda**

Cream butter and sugar. Add eggs one at a time. Beat in until creamy. Stir in bananas. In a separate bowl, sift and measure flour. Add salt and baking soda to the flour. Mix dry ingredients with banana mixture. Pour into greased 8 1/2 x 4 1/2 x 3-inch loaf pan. Bake at 325° F. for approximately 50 minutes. Cool on wire rack 15 minutes before turning out of the pan.

Laura B. Wooten, Wake County

The secret to really good and moist banana bread is really, really ripe, almost black bananas. This recipe doubles nicely. It also freezes well.

POPPY SEED BREAD

3 cups all-purpose flour
2 1/2 cups sugar
3 eggs
1 1/2 cups milk
1 1/8 cups oil
1 teaspoon salt
1 1/2 teaspoons baking powder

1 1/2 teaspoons vanilla flavoring
1 1/2 teaspoons butter flavoring
1 1/2 teaspoons almond flavoring
1 heaping tablespoon poppy seeds

Use a spoon or a whisk to mix all ingredients except poppy seeds together in a bowl. Fold in poppy seeds. Pour into two large or four small loaf pans. Bake at 325° F. for 1 1/4 hours or until done.

Sarah Lee, Stanly County

PUMPKIN BREAD

3 cups sugar
1 cup oil
4 eggs
1 1/2 cups pumpkin
3 cups self-rising flour
1/2 teaspoon nutmeg

1/2 teaspoon cloves
1/2 teaspoon ginger
1/2 teaspoon allspice
1 teaspoon cinnamon
2/3 cup chopped nuts
2/3 cup raisins

Cream sugar and oil. Add eggs one at a time. Add pumpkin. Stir. In a separate bowl, sift dry ingredients together. Sprinkle part of the flour mixture over nuts and raisins. Stir to coat. Stir the rest of the flour mixture into pumpkin mixture. Then stir the raisins and nuts into pumpkin mixture. Spray three 5 x 9-inch loaf pans with vegetable spray. Bake at 350° F. for 1 hour. Use toothpick to check for doneness.

Dorothy Fisher, Nash County

LOW-FAT PUMPKIN BREAD

2 1/2 cups sugar
1/2 cup canola oil
1/2 cup applesauce
4 egg substitutes (see
   package for measurement)
1 1/2 cups pumpkin
3 cups self-rising flour

1/2 teaspoon nutmeg
1/2 teaspoon cloves
1/2 teaspoon ginger
1/2 teaspoon allspice
1 teaspoon cinnamon
2/3 cup chopped nuts
2/3 cup raisins

Cream sugar and oil. Stir in applesauce. Add egg substitutes slowly. Add pumpkin. Stir. In a separate bowl, sift dry ingredients together. Sprinkle part of the flour mixture over nuts and raisins. Stir to coat. Stir the rest of the flour mixture into pumpkin mixture. Then stir in raisins and nuts. Spray three 5 x 9-inch loaf pans with vegetable spray. Bake at 350° F. for 1 hour. Use toothpick to check for doneness.

Dorothy Fisher, Nash County

GRANNY RITA'S PUMPKIN BREAD

2/3 cup shortening (butter
   flavor if available)
2 2/3 cups sugar
4 eggs
1 16-ounce can (2 cups)
   pumpkin
2/3 cup water
3 1/3 cups flour

2 teaspoons baking soda
1 1/2 teaspoons salt
1/2 teaspoon baking powder
1 teaspoon cinnamon
1 teaspoon cloves
2/3 cup chopped nuts
2/3 cup raisins

Heat oven to 350° F. Grease two 9 x 5 x 3-inch loaf pans. In a large bowl, cream shortening and sugar until fluffy. Stir in eggs, pumpkin, and water. Blend in flour, soda, salt, baking powder, cinnamon, and cloves. Stir in nuts and raisins. Pour into pans. Bake about 70 minutes, or until wooden toothpick inserted in center comes out clean. Note: Can be baked in large tube pan as a cake.

Jennifer Mitchell, Harnett County

The Pumpkin Bread and Strawberry Bread (recipe follows on the next page) are recipes from my father's mother, my Granny Rita. She was born outside Buies Creek and later moved to Sanford.

SESAME SEED BREAD

2 cups Bisquick
1/2 cup water
1/4 teaspoon garlic powder

2 tablespoons butter or
margarine
Sesame seeds

Mix 2 cups Bisquick, 1/2 cup water, and 1/4 teaspoon garlic powder
with fork to form a soft dough. Place dough in center of ungreased
cookie sheet and form into a circle. Melt 2 tablespoons butter and
brush top of dough with it. Sprinkle sesame seeds on top. Bake at
425° F. for 15 to 20 minutes, or until golden brown.

Pam Byington, Wake County

STRAWBERRY BREAD

1 1/4 cups salad oil
2 cups sugar
4 eggs
3 cups all-purpose flour
3 teaspoons cinnamon

1 teaspoon baking soda
1 teaspoon salt
2 10-ounce packages frozen
strawberries
1 cup chopped nuts

Heat oven to 350° F. Grease two 9 x 5 x 3-inch loaf pans. In large
bowl, beat oil, sugar, and eggs. In a separate bowl, mix flour,
cinnamon, baking soda, and salt together. Add flour mixture to
sugar mixture, and mix well. Mash strawberries well, and mix in.
Fold in chopped nuts. Pour batter into pans, and bake 30 to 35
minutes or until a wooden toothpick inserted in center comes out
clean.

Jennifer Mitchell, Harnett County

SWEET POTATO BREAD

3 cups all-purpose flour
1 teaspoon baking soda
1 teaspoon salt
3 teaspoons cinnamon
2 cups sugar

2 cups cooked sweet
potatoes
1/2 cup chopped nuts
4 eggs, well beaten
1 1/4 cups oil or melted
shortening

In a large mixing bowl, mix together flour, soda, salt, cinnamon,
sugar, sweet potatoes, and nuts. With spoon, make a deep well in the
center, and add eggs and oil. Stir carefully, just enough to dampen all
the dry ingredients. Pour into 2 loaf pans. Bake at 350° F. for 1 hour.

Delicious served with spiced tea. If desired, mix 3 ounces cream cheese and 3 ounces butter, and serve with bread. Serves 16.

Linda N. Aycock, Nash County

A great way to enjoy North Carolina sweet potatoes any time of day.

—

TIN CAN BREAD

1 tablespoon margarine
2 to 2 1/2 cups raisin, date,
  and nut mixture
1 teaspoon baking soda
1 cup boiling water
2 eggs

1 cup sugar
1 teaspoon lemon extract
2 cups flour
2 teaspoons baking powder
1/2 teaspoon salt

Thoroughly wash and remove paper labels from four 16-ounce tin cans. Dry, grease, and flour lightly. Combine margarine, raisin mixture, and baking soda. Pour boiling water over, and let cool to room temperature. Beat eggs until light. Gradually add sugar and extract. In a separate bowl, stir together dry ingredients, and add to egg mixture. Spoon into tin cans. Bake at 325° F. for 55 minutes. Remove by turning cans upside down so loaves will fall out. Cool on wire rack. Slice and serve with cream cheese or butter.

Shirley Pendergrass, Franklin County

ORANGE COFFEE CAKE

1/4 cup butter
1/2 cup sugar
1 egg
1 1/4 cups all-purpose flour
1 teaspoon baking powder
1/2 teaspoon salt
1/4 teaspoon baking soda
1/2 cup orange juice

Grated peel from 1 1/2
  oranges
Topping:
1/2 cup rolled oats
1/2 cup brown sugar
1/2 teaspoon cinnamon
2 tablespoons butter, melted
1/2 cup chopped nuts

Cream butter and sugar until light and fluffy. Add egg, and beat well. In a separate bowl, sift together dry ingredients. Add to creamed mixture, alternately with orange juice. Stir in orange peel. Turn into greased 8 x 8 x 2-inch baking pan. Combine topping ingredients and sprinkle over batter. Bake in moderate oven, 375° F., for 25 minutes or until done.

Reba Anderson, Pender County

Our family loves all kinds of sweets, and this recipe is one of our favorites. Good with a cold glass of milk and warm conversation.

—

CROUTONS

French, Italian, whole wheat, whole grain bread or day-old white bread
Low-fat margarine or spray margarine

Your favorite herbs, such as garlic powder, parsley, oregano, basil, chili powder, sage, thyme, dill weed

Cut bread into bite-sized pieces. Spread with melted low-fat margarine or use one of the spray margarines. Place on baking sheet, and sprinkle with some of your favorite herbs, such as garlic powder, parsley, oregano, basil, chili powder, sage, thyme, dill weed, or whatever herbs may be interesting and add flavor. Bake in a 250° F. oven until the bread is dry. Rotate the pan or stir the bread cubes around during the cooking time. Store croutons in a covered container in the refrigerator for up to a couple of weeks.

Melinda M. Houser, Lincoln County

REFRIGERATOR ROLLS

1 package yeast
1 teaspoon sugar
1/4 cup lukewarm water
1 cup milk
1 cup butter or margarine

3 eggs
3 tablespoons sugar
1 teaspoon salt
4 cups flour

Combine yeast, 1 teaspoon sugar, and water. Let sit 10 minutes. Gently heat milk, and add butter. In a separate bowl, combine eggs, 3 tablespoons sugar, and salt, and heat well. To this mixture, add milk, sifted flour, and yeast mixture. Mix with electric beater, as you would cake batter. Cover and place in the refrigerator overnight.

Next day shape into rolls or divide, shape, and place in two loaf pans. Let double. Bake at 350° F. for 20 minutes. Makes 24 rolls.

Ellie Herman, Onslow County

Since part of the preparation is done the day before, these rolls are easy to make for company and holidays.

PLANTATION ROLLS

1 yeast cake *or* 1 envelope
   yeast
2 cups lukewarm water
1/3 cup sugar
2 1/2 teaspoons salt

6 cups flour
2 eggs
1 cup melted shortening (*or*
   1/2 cup margarine and 1/2
   cup lard)

Dissolve yeast cake in lukewarm water. Add sugar and salt. Beat in 2 cups flour with mixer. Add unbeaten eggs, beat, and add more flour. Then add cooled shortening, and beat in remainder of the flour. Brush top of dough with melted butter. Cover and let rise a couple of hours until doubled. Up to 1/2 cup flour may be added if dough is too soft, but dough needs to be soft for light rolls. Stir down and refrigerate for several hours or overnight. Shape rolls, and let rise 2 or 3 hours, until doubled. Bake at 425° F. until golden brown.

Jennifer Mitchell, Harnett County

This recipe is from my father's mother, Granny Rita, as I always called her. I can remember, as a little girl, sitting in her kitchen and "helping" her make some of these.

SAN TAN YEAST ROLLS

3 tablespoons sugar
3 tablespoons Crisco
   shortening
1 cup hot water
1 package Fleishman's yeast
1/4 cup lukewarm water

3 to 4 cups Gold Medal
   Flour (or enough to make
   a soft dough)
1 1/2 teaspoons salt
Butter, melted

Dissolve sugar and Crisco in hot water. Dissolve yeast in lukewarm water. When first mixture is cool, add dissolved yeast. Sift in flour and salt to make a soft dough. Let rise 1 hour, push down, and let rise again. Roll dough and cut into strips. Cut strips in small squares, and place squares in greased muffin tins. Spread with melted butter and let rise 1 hour. Bake at 400° F. for about 20 minutes, until almost brown. Butter again and finish browning. Brush again with butter and serve. Serves 8.

Mrs. Franklin Teague, Guilford County

Mrs. Teague won the 1961 National Gold Medal Flour Bake-Off with this recipe.

SOUR CREAM ROLLS

1 cup sour cream	2 packages yeast
1/3 cup sugar	2 eggs
1 teaspoon salt	4 cups sifted all-purpose
1/2 cup margarine, melted	flour
1/2 cup warm water	

Gently heat sour cream. Stir in sugar, salt, and melted margarine.
Cool until lukewarm. Measure warm water into a large bowl.
Sprinkle in yeast and stir. Add sour cream, eggs, and flour. Mix.
Cover tightly, and refrigerate overnight. Turn dough out onto a
lightly floured board. Divide into four parts. Roll each part into a
20-inch circle. Cut each circle into 12 wedge-shaped pieces. Roll
each piece beginning at the wide end. Place on a greased baking
sheet. Cover and let rise in a warm place until doubled in bulk,
about 1 hour. Bake at 375° F. for about 15 minutes, or until brown.
Remove and brush with melted butter, if desired. Makes 4 dozen.

Faye S. Bunn, Nash County

BREAKFAST NUT ROLLS

Margarine	1 cup chopped pecans
1/4 cup brown sugar	1 can biscuits

Grease 9-inch round pan heavily with margarine. Scatter thin layer
of brown sugar on bottom. Scatter chopped nuts over brown sugar
layer. Sprinkle a little water on top. Place canned biscuits over that.
Cook at 375° F. until biscuits are done, about 15 minutes. Turn over
onto plate. Serves 4 (2 rolls each).

Vicki Walton, Wake County

*My mother made these for breakfast a lot, and my brothers and I
enjoyed eating the sugar left in the pan.*

BUTTERMILK PANCAKES

1/2 package active dry yeast	1 tablespoon sugar
2 tablespoons warm water	1/2 teaspoon salt
2 cups sifted all-purpose	2 cups buttermilk
flour	2 tablespoons salad oil
1 tablespoon baking powder	3 eggs
1 tablespoon baking soda	1/2 cup cream

Sprinkle yeast over warm water to soften yeast. Sift flour, baking powder, baking soda, sugar, and salt in a bowl. Pour in buttermilk, and stir until batter is smooth. Mix in the softened yeast and oil. Beat eggs slightly, and stir into batter along with cream; do not beat. Makes one quart. Serve with Fresh Blueberry Sauce, recipe below.

Millie Evans, Brunswick County

When I made these pancakes, my late husband always came to the kitchen to help. He loved pancakes for dinner when he'd had a late lunch of meat and potatoes. I found this recipe in the McCall's *magazine in March 1957, titled "Pancakes & Coffee." I had hunted for years for pancakes to suit him, and he loved them!*

FRESH BLUEBERRY SAUCE

1/2 cup sugar	3 tablespoons margarine
1/4 cup water	1 pint fresh blueberries
1 tablespoon lemon juice	

Mix sugar, water, and lemon juice in medium skillet. Stir over medium heat. Add margarine. Heat to boil. Stir in blueberries. Do not cook.

Millie Evans, Brunswick County

FEATHER PANCAKES

1 egg, slightly beaten	2 tablespoons baking
1 cup milk	powder
2 tablespoons oil	2 tablespoons sugar
1 cup all-purpose flour	1/2 to 1 cup fresh or thawed
1/2 teaspoon salt	frozen blueberries
	(optional)

In mixing bowl, combine egg, milk, and oil. Use wire whisk to stir. Add dry ingredients. Beat with whisk until smooth in consistency. Gently stir in blueberries. Pour onto preheated, lightly greased griddle. Cook until bubbles appear on top. Turn and brown on other side. Makes 8 (5-inch) pancakes. Serve with warm maple syrup.

Kristen Elizabeth Britt, Nash County

GRANNY CLARK'S PANCAKES

1 cup flour	1 1/4 cups buttermilk
1 tablespoon sugar	1 egg
1 teaspoon baking soda	2 tablespoons melted butter
1/4 teaspoon salt	

Mix flour, sugar, baking soda, and salt. Add buttermilk and egg. Stir in melted butter. Cook in electric skillet at 375° F. Makes 6 or 7 (5-inch) pancakes.

Margaret Clark, Wake County

PANCAKES

2 cups self-rising flour	1 egg
1 tablespoon sugar	Enough milk to blend to
3 tablespoons oil	desired thickness

Combine ingredients. Spray skillet with non-stick spray. Pour pancake-sized portions of batter onto hot skillet. Turn pancakes when batter bubbles. Cook on second side until golden brown.

Vicki Walton, Wake County

We had pancakes and bacon or sausage on cold nights for supper.

OVEN FRENCH TOAST

One 8-ounce loaf French bread, cut into 1-inch thick slices	*Topping:*
	1 stick unsalted butter, softened
6 large eggs	1 cup light brown sugar
1 1/2 cups milk	2 tablespoons light corn
1 1/2 cups Half & Half	syrup
1 teaspoon vanilla	1 cup coarsely chopped
1/4 teaspoon nutmeg	pecans

Heavily butter a 9-inch square baking dish. Fill with bread slices so the dish is completely covered with bread and filled to the top. Mix together the eggs, milk, Half & Half, and vanilla. Pour over bread slices. Dust with nutmeg, cover, and refrigerate overnight. The next morning, preheat the oven to 350° F. *Prepare topping:* Combine butter, brown sugar, and corn syrup. Stir in pecans. The mixture is stiff, but spread it as evenly as you can over the bread slices. Bake until puffed and golden, about 40 minutes. Let stand 5 minutes before serving. A wonderful breakfast when served with fruit.

Carolyn Ritz Lemon, Clay County

I have had this recipe for a number of years, and it is a favorite of my father's. I always make it for my parents when they come to visit. You can assemble it the evening before, bake it in the morning, and not spend a lot of time in the kitchen.

—

DECADENT FRENCH TOAST

2 1/2 cups light brown sugar
1 1/2 sticks butter
4 tablespoons light Karo
  syrup
24 slices bread

14 eggs
6 cups milk
3 tablespoons vanilla
  extract

Spray two roaster pans with Pam cooking spray. In a small saucepan, heat brown sugar, butter, and Karo syrup over medium-low heat to form a caramel mix. Divide the caramel mix between the two roaster pans. Take 8 slices of bread and cover the bottoms of both pans. Repeat until you have three layers of bread. In a large bowl, whisk eggs, milk, and vanilla. Using a ladle, evenly distribute the egg mixture over the bread. Let stand in the refrigerator overnight. Cook at 350° F. for 30 minutes or until brown. Serve with bananas and whipped cream, if desired. No syrup is needed.

Sarah Lee, Stanly County

OYSTER DRESSING

2 cups whole milk
1/3 stick margarine
1 pint oysters
10 to 12 4 x 4-inch squares
  of corn bread, crumbled

1/4 teaspoon salt
20 saltine crackers,
  crumbled
3 hard-boiled eggs, chopped

Combine milk, margarine, and oysters in a saucepan. Bring to a boil. Simmer for 3 minutes. In a large bowl, combine crumbled corn bread, salt, crumbled crackers, and chopped eggs. Pour oyster stew over dry ingredients, and mix well. Rub butter in a 9 x 13-inch pan. Put in mixture, and bake at 350° F. for 30 minutes. Serves 15.

Faye Kennedy, Onslow County

*My grandmother used this recipe when she made Oyster Dressing
for holiday meals. It has been in the family since the 1800s.*

OYSTER DRESSING

8 to 10 small biscuits,
  crumbled
1 1/2 cups water
Piece of butter (size of an
  egg)

2 eggs
1 quart oysters, thoroughly
  washed and drained
Salt and pepper to taste

Crumble biscuits fine, and scald with water. Add butter, and let
stand a while. Add eggs, seasoning, and the oysters. Pour in greased
baking dish or pan, and bake at 350° F. until solid, about 30
minutes.

Mrs. J. L. Tunnell, Hyde County

*Mrs. Tunnell, who is deceased, was the grandmother of Dick
Tunnell, who submitted the recipe.*

TURKEY DRESSING

1 large loaf white bread,
  cubed
1 8-ounce package
  Pepperidge Farm corn
  bread stuffing
1 cup celery, chopped
2 medium onions, finely
  chopped
Chopped turkey giblets, if
  desired

1 tablespoon salt
1 tablespoon poultry
  seasoning
1/2 teaspoon black pepper
1 teaspoon sage
3 beaten eggs
1 cup turkey broth
1 cup water
1/2 cup melted butter or
  margarine

Combine all ingredients, mixing well. Bake in a greased 9 x 13-inch
pan at 350° F. for 35 to 40 minutes. Serves approximately 15.

Dolores Benthall, Hertford County

*This recipe is a holiday treat at my house. One of my daughters
says, "It is the best dressing in the world."*

TURKEY AND OYSTER DRESSING

1 pint turkey broth
3 8-ounce cans broth
1 can water
2 sticks margarine
1 16-ounce package herb
stuffing mix

1 1/2 packages corn bread
stuffing mix
1 1/2 pints North Carolina
oysters, chopped

Heat turkey broth, canned broth, water, and margarine until warm and combined. Add mixture to combined stuffings. Add oysters last, and mix thoroughly. Make into patties. Lightly grease a pan to prevent sticking. Bake patties at 375° F. until set and brown. Makes 25 to 30 patties.

Emily Clapp, Guilford County

This dressing has become a tradition at our Thanksgiving and Christmas dinners and was our grandmother's original recipe.

THANKSGIVING CORN BREAD PAN DRESSING

1 pan of corn bread (recipe
follows)
4 cups turkey broth or
chicken broth (we boil a
hen for this)
Salt and pepper to taste
8 to 10 pieces of bread,
toasted, or about 8
leftover biscuits, crumbled

1/2 bunch of celery (5 or 6
stalks), chopped
6 green onions, fresh out of
the garden, chopped
1 small white onion,
chopped
6 to 8 hard-boiled eggs,
chopped
2 tablespoons oil

The day before, make a batch of the Corn Bread (recipe on next page), let it cool, then crumble. Boil a hen to make 4 or 5 cups broth (or use canned chicken or turkey broth). Assemble and chop all of the other ingredients except the oil, and refrigerate. (If you hard-boil eggs that are about a week old, they will peel easier.)

About 3 hours before dinner, in a large bowl, mix the crumbled corn bread, crumbled toast, onions, celery, and eggs. Stir in broth until very soupy (falls off the spoon). Add salt and pepper to taste (it may take a lot). Pour about 2 tablespoons oil into bottom of 15-inch baking dish, pour in dressing, and bake at 450° F. until browned on top. Keep warm until served.

Nancy Schrull, Davidson County

For the past 50 years, this dressing recipe has been the dressing of choice for my family at Thanksgiving and all special turkey meals. The extended family has grown large enough to need four or five pans of corn bread dressing to take us through Thanksgiving dinner and supper that night. We all fight over who gets to do all the chopping. It usually takes a small army, as it is traditional that we use only knives. Some of our fondest childhood memories are of helping Meme, our grandmother, prepare the corn bread and of chopping the vegetables on Wednesday night. We have anywhere from 50 to 80 relatives each year from all over the country.

CORN BREAD FOR DRESSING

3 cups corn meal
1 1/4 teaspoons baking soda
1 1/4 teaspoons salt
2 eggs

2 1/4 cups buttermilk
3 tablespoons melted fat
3 tablespoons fat to grease pan

Put corn meal, salt, and soda in a bowl. Stir well until blended. Add buttermilk to eggs and stir. Add melted fat. Dump egg mixture into corn meal mixture all at once. Stir just enough to mix; mixture will have a rough appearance. Pour about 3 tablespoons of fat in a 15-inch baking pan. Pour in corn meal mixture, and bake at 400° F. for 15 to 20 minutes until browned.

Nancy Schrull, Davidson County

WHITE BREAD DRESSING

1 loaf of white bread (best if slightly stale)
1/2 cup onion, finely chopped
1/2 cup celery, finely chopped

1 to 2 teaspoons poultry seasoning
Salt and pepper to taste
Turkey drippings

Break slices of bread into large pieces into a large mixing bowl. Lightly stir in remaining dry ingredients. Pour in turkey drippings, stirring lightly until very moist, but not swimming in broth. Bake in 9 x 13-inch pan at 375° F. for 45 minutes to 1 hour, until well browned, top and bottom. Serve with turkey, giblet gravy, and lots of cranberry sauce.

Pam Staton, Clay County

My husband's grandmother used to make this easy white bread dressing for Thanksgiving, so corn bread dressing just won't do at our house.

—

ALL-AMERICAN APPLE PIE

1/4 cup packed light brown
  sugar
4 1/4 cups granulated sugar
1 tablespoon all-purpose
  flour
1 teaspoon grated lemon
  peel
1/4 teaspoon ground
  cinnamon
1/4 teaspoon ground
  nutmeg
6 medium Granny Smith
  apples, peeled, cored, and
  thinly sliced (about 2
  pounds)
1 cup dark raisins
1 unbaked, ready-made, *or*
  homemade 9-inch deep-
  dish pie crust

Preheat oven to 425° F. Spray a 9-inch deep-dish pie plate with vegetable cooking spray. In a large bowl, combine sugars, flour, lemon peel, cinnamon, and nutmeg. Mix well. Add apples, stirring until coated. Stir in raisins. Spoon into prepared pan. Place pie crust on top of filling. Trim edges, pressing against edge of pan. Using a sharp knife, cut steam vents in pie crust. Bake until pie crust is golden brown, about 35 to 40 minutes. Place on a wire rack, and cool for 30 minutes. Serves 10.

Juanita L. Guthrie, Onslow County

FAMILY APPLE PIE

3 cups tart apples, pared
  and sliced
1 cup sugar
1/2 cup water
Pie crust:
2 cups self-rising flour
1/2 cup shortening
1/4 cup ice water

Place apples in deep dish or 8 x 8-inch pan. Sprinkle with sugar, and add water. *Prepare pie crust:* Cut shortening into flour with two knives, fork, pastry blender, or fingers until mixture is coarse but uniform. Add water, and mix. Roll pie crust to fit top of pie. Place pie crust on top of filling. Bake at 400° F. until pie crust is golden brown, about 35 to 40 minutes.

Donna Edsel, Wilkes County

My mother-in-law, Pauline Edsel, developed this recipe as a delicious way for all of us to enjoy the apples they, as commercial apple growers, grew in the Brushy Mountain community.

—

GRATED APPLE PIE

1 cup sugar
3/4 stick margarine,
  softened
1 teaspoon cinnamon

1 egg
2 cups grated apples (peel,
  grate, then measure)
1 unbaked pie shell

Cream sugar and margarine. Add cinnamon, egg, and apples. Stir well. Pour into unbaked pie shell. Bake at 350° F. for 45 minutes.

Pearl Freedman, Columbus County

Everyone asks for the recipe when I take my apple pie to special functions.

APPLESAUCE SHIRTTAIL PIE

1 1/2 quarts applesauce
1 cup apple juice
1/4 teaspoon lemon zest
1/4 teaspoon orange zest
1/2 teaspoon cinnamon
1/2 teaspoon nutmeg

1 teaspoon vanilla extract
12 leftover biscuits
Topping (optional):
1 cup brown sugar, firmly
  packed
1/2 teaspoon cinnamon

Combine the applesauce and juice. Add the next 5 ingredients, and mix well. Slice the biscuits in half or thirds, depending on the thickness. Butter the biscuits, and toast crisply. Cover the bottom of a 9 x 9-inch pan with applesauce mixture; add a layer of toasted biscuits, then a layer of applesauce mixture. Continue alternating applesauce and biscuits to fill the pan. Top with applesauce mixture. *Prepare topping:* Mix ingredients together, and sprinkle on top. Bake at 350° F. for 30 to 45 minutes. Serves 6.

Corean S. Ruffin, Person County

My parents and the children were canning applesauce, and we had some extra applesauce and some leftover biscuits, and thus a dessert was born. It is a family favorite.

APPLE BISCUITS

20 canned small biscuits
Applesauce
2 cups sugar

2 sticks margarine
1 cup water

Make a dent in the center of each unbaked biscuit, and place the biscuits in a 9 x 13-inch casserole dish. Fill the dents with applesauce. Boil the sugar, margarine, and water, and pour over biscuits. Bake at 350° F. until biscuits are slightly brown, about 8 to 10 minutes. Serves 20.

Lula Mae Tyndall, Sampson County

Apple biscuits are easy, quick, and good.

GRANDMA'S APPLE STRUDEL PIE

2 cups grated apples
3/4 cup sugar
3 tablespoons brown sugar
1 teaspoon vanilla
1 teaspoon cinnamon
1/8 teaspoon nutmeg
1 egg

1 tablespoon flour
1 stick margarine, melted
Unbaked pie shell
1 large can biscuits
1/2 cup confectioners' sugar
3 tablespoons milk

Mix first 9 ingredients, and pour into unbaked pie shell. Roll out canned biscuits, and cut into strips for lattice top. Brush strips with milk and sprinkle with sugar. Bake at 350° F. for 45 minutes. Cool on wire rack. Mix confectioners' sugar and milk until creamy and drizzle over pie, crisscrossing.

Sharon Hester, Granville County

This is great for the apple lovers.

BROWN BETTY

2 cups stale bread crumbs,
  coarse
6 cups tart apple slices
1/2 cup sugar
1/4 teaspoon cinnamon

1/4 teaspoon salt
3 tablespoons lemon juice
1/4 cup water
2 tablespoons butter

Put a third of the bread crumbs in a buttered 11 x 7-inch casserole dish, and cover with half of the apples. Mix sugar, cinnamon, and salt. Sprinkle half of this mixture over the apples. Add another one-third of bread crumbs, another layer of apples, and sprinkle the other half of the sugar mixture. Top with last third of crumbs. Pour lemon juice and water over these layers. Dot with butter. Cover, and bake at 350° F. for 30 minutes. Uncover, and bake 15 minutes longer. Serve hot or cold, with or without cream. Serves 5.

Pearl King Morton, Granville County

Amelia Elizabeth "Bettie" Satterwhite King made this cake and joked that it was named after her. Her husband, Billy, had his daughters make this cake for him after Bettie died.

—

BLUEBERRY PIE

4 cups fresh blueberries
3/4 to 1 cup sugar
3 tablespoons flour
1/2 teaspoon grated lemon
  peel
Dash salt

1/2 teaspoon cinnamon
  (optional)
1/2 teaspoon nutmeg
  (optional)
1 to 2 teaspoons lemon juice
1 tablespoon butter
Pie pastry

Line 9-inch pie plate with pastry. Combine blueberries, sugar, flour, lemon peel, salt, and spices (if desired). Fill pie shell. Sprinkle with 1 to 2 teaspoons lemon juice. Dot with 1 tablespoon butter. Put crust on top of pie, and seal with a fork. Bake at 400° F. for 35 to 40 minutes. Serve warm with Cool Whip or ice cream. Serves 6.

Mary Warren, Cleveland County

We have several blueberry bushes. We enjoy pies made with fresh berries during the season and use frozen berries later on.

APPLE PIZZA

Crust:
1 box white or yellow cake
  mix
1 1/4 cups quick-cooking
  oats
6 tablespoons margarine
1 egg

Topping:
2 tablespoons margarine
1/4 cup brown sugar,
  packed
1/2 teaspoon cinnamon
1/2 cup chopped nuts
1 can apple pie filling
Cool Whip

Mix cake mix, oats, and 6 tablespoons margarine well. Set aside 1 cup of mixture for topping. Blend egg with the rest of the mixture, and mix well. Press into a 13 x 9-inch pan. Bake at 350° F. for 12 minutes. To the reserved 1 cup of crumbs, add 2 tablespoons margarine, brown sugar, cinnamon, and chopped nuts. Spread 1 can apple pie filling on the baked base. Sprinkle with the cinnamon and crumb mixture. Bake 20 minutes longer, or until light brown. Cool completely. Top with Cool Whip.

Mildred Moxley, Alleghany County

BLUEBERRY PIZZA

1 1/2 pints blueberries	2 dashes of salt
3/4 cup sugar	3/4 cup chopped nuts
2 teaspoons cornstarch	8 ounces cream cheese
1 1/2 sticks margarine,	(room temperature)
melted	2 cups powdered
1 teaspoon sugar	confectioners' sugar
1 1/2 cups all-purpose flour	2 cups Cool Whip

Combine blueberries, 3/4 cup sugar, and cornstarch in small saucepan. Cook 15 minutes over medium heat until thick, stirring constantly. Set aside and let cool. Combine margarine, sugar, flour, salt, and chopped nuts. Mix well. Press into bottom of a pizza pan. Bake at 350° F. for 10 to 20 minutes. Let cool. Mix cream cheese and powdered sugar. Then fold in 2 cups Cool Whip, and spread on cool crust. Finally, spread blueberry mixture on top, and cool in the refrigerator. Serves at least 12.

Mrs. Georgia Pate Love, Robeson County

A wonderful couple, Cliff and Carolyn Hammond, from my hometown of Rowland, grew blueberries and always shared their bounty with friends and neighbors. Mrs. Carolyn shared this recipe with us many years ago, and it is still a family favorite when fresh blueberries are in season. My mother would make a fun trip out of picking blueberries to use in our pizza recipe. Now my husband I continue this tradition.

BROWN SUGAR PIE

3 eggs, beaten
3 cups brown sugar
8 tablespoons butter or
margarine

1 cup milk
3 tablespoons flour
2 9-inch unbaked pie shells

Mix eggs with brown sugar, butter, and milk. Add flour, and mix well. Pour into pie shells. Bake at 350° F. for approximately 1 hour, or until knife inserted in center comes out clean.

Shirley A. Pendergrass, Franklin County

GANNA'S CHEESE CUSTARD PIE

1/2 cup sugar
1 cup cottage cheese
2 eggs
1 teaspoon vanilla
1/2 teaspoon salt

1 cup Half & Half dairy
creamer
1 unbaked pie shell
Trace of nutmeg

Preheat oven to 450° F. Blend the sugar, cottage cheese, and eggs. Add the vanilla, salt, and Half & Half, mixing well. Pour into pastry-lined pie tin. Dust with a trace of nutmeg. Bake for 25 minutes. Remove, place on a rack, and let get cold before cutting. Keep refrigerated.

Carolyn Ritz Lemon, Clay County

Ganna's Cheese Custard Pie originated from my grandmother. My mother baked this pie for us, and it is now a favorite of my family.

CHERRY YUM-YUM

Crust:
3 cups graham cracker
crumbs
2 sticks margarine, melted
6 tablespoons confectioners'
sugar

Filling:
2 packages Dream Whip,
prepared
2 8-ounce packages cream
cheese
2 cups sugar
2 teaspoons vanilla
2 cans cherry pie filling

Mix crust ingredients, and press into a 9 x 13-inch pan. Mix prepared Dream Whip with cream cheese, sugar, and vanilla, and pour into crust. Top with cherry pie filling.

Sandra Calhoun, Surry County

ONE EGG CHESS PIE

1 cup brown sugar, packed
1 heaping tablespoon flour
1 egg
3 tablespoons margarine,
    melted
3 tablespoons milk

1 teaspoon vanilla
1/2 cup chopped pecans or
    coconut or raisins or dates
    or chocolate chips
    (optional)
9-inch pie shell, unbaked

Mix brown sugar and flour in mixing bowl. Add remaining ingredients, and whisk until smooth. Pour into unbaked pie shell. Bake in preheated 375° F. oven for 20 to 25 minutes, or until pie is firm in the middle. Recipe may be doubled for two pies.

Sarah M. Nixon, Lincoln County

We lived in the country, but the hens never seemed to lay enough eggs with my mother's cooking three meals a day for a husband and nine children! She found this pie recipe 70 years ago in the Charlotte News *and was thrilled to death that it used only one egg. I was 9 years old at the time and watched her make many a pie with variations and always with only one egg. I've used it and shared it at our Lincoln County and Mount Holly ECA Pie Days as a lower-calorie pecan pie. Our four children's families and now a fourth generation are using it.*

MAMA'S CHESS PIE

1/4 cup butter
1 cup granulated sugar
2 eggs, separated
1 tablespoon corn meal
1/2 cup sweet cream
1/2 teaspoon lemon extract
    or vanilla extract

1 9-inch pastry shell
    (homemade or frozen)
Meringue (optional):
2 egg whites
2 tablespoons sugar

Cream butter. Add sugar, and mix well. In separate bowl, lightly beat egg yolks until smooth, and add to mixture. Mix corn meal into cream, and add to mixture. Add flavoring, and stir until smooth (do not overbeat). Pour into pastry shell and bake at 300° to 325° F. for 1 hour. Remove. We prefer pie without meringue, but if desired, beat egg whites to stiff peaks. Continue to whip, and add sugar. Top pie with meringue. Return to oven, and brown top. Serves 6 to 8. I always double the recipe; it freezes well.

Sarah Ann Butts Sasser, Carteret County

Mealtime was always a celebration! Mama was an outstanding "home demonstration club member" in Halifax County and baked cakes and pies for "The Curb Market" in the 1930s, '40s, and early '50s. I was a 4-H club member, and our Extension Family Home Business helped to send me to college—and prepared me for a career in Cooperative Extension.

—

CHESS PIE

3 eggs
1 1/2 cups sugar
1/4 stick margarine, cut into
  small pieces
1/2 cup milk

2 tablespoons all-purpose
  flour
Dash salt
Unbaked pie crust

Combine all ingredients. Pour into uncooked pie crust. Bake at 350° F. for 1 hour, or until the middle of the pie is fully cooked. Serves 6 to 8.

Vicki Walton, Wake County

This recipe belonged to my husband's grandmother, and she baked one for him every Thanksgiving and Christmas.

PERFECT EGG-WHITE MERINGUE
(for pies and puddings)

4 eggs, room temperature
1 teaspoon cream of tartar

1/2 cup sugar
1 teaspoon vanilla

Divide eggs. Place only the whites in a metal mixing bowl. Beat with an electric mixer on high. Add cream of tartar while beating. When whites are full of air, continue to whip while you add sugar. Mix on medium, and add vanilla. When mixture will hold a stiff peak, spoon onto the pie, and bake at 350° F. for approximately 15 minutes, watching closely.

Karen Scalf, Duplin County

Meringue Tip

When you spread the meringue over the pie filling, make sure it touches the pie crust all around. This will help keep the meringue from shrinking and slipping.

CHOCOLATE PIE

Ready-made pie crust
1 square unsweetened
  baking chocolate
2/3 cup sugar
4 tablespoons flour
1/4 teaspoon salt
1 1/2 cups milk

2 medium egg yolks
2 teaspoons butter
1/2 teaspoon vanilla
Meringue:
2 egg whites
2 tablespoons sugar

Bake a ready-made pie crust at 450° F. for about 12 minutes. Remove pie crust, and lower oven temperature to 300°. *Prepare filling:* Melt chocolate in a double boiler. In a bowl, mix sugar, flour, and salt together. Stir into melted chocolate. Remove the mixture from heat. Stir in 2 tablespoons of milk, stirring until the mixture is without lumps and well mixed. Separate egg whites and yolks, retaining whites for meringue. Add egg yolks to chocolate and flour-milk mixture. Beat well with spoon. Stir in rest of milk slowly. Add butter. Return to double boiler and cook until mixture thickens, about 15 minutes. Stir frequently to prevent lumps. Remove from heat. Add vanilla. Beat until smooth. Pour into baked pie crust. *Prepare meringue:* Beat egg whites until foamy. Add sugar and beat until meringue is stiff enough to hold its shape. Spread over pie filling. Brown in oven at 300° F. for about 15 to 25 minutes. Serves 8.

Dorothy Ballance, Wayne County

We always have Chocolate Pie for family birthdays and special occasions like Thanksgiving and Christmas. It's our family's favorite dessert.

CHOCOLATE MERINGUE PIE

3 eggs, separated
1 cup sugar
1/2 stick margarine, melted
Pinch salt
3 tablespoons cocoa
1 tablespoon flour
1 teaspoon vanilla

1 12-ounce can Carnation
  evaporated milk
Unbaked 9-inch pie shell
Meringue:
3 egg whites
1/2 teaspoon vanilla
1/4 teaspoon cream of tartar
6 tablespoons sugar

Beat egg yolks with whisk. Add sugar, margarine, salt, cocoa, flour, and vanilla, stirring well after each addition. Gradually add evaporated milk, stirring with whisk. Pour into unbaked 9-inch pie shell. *Prepare meringue:* Beat egg whites, vanilla, and cream of tartar until soft peaks form. Gradually add sugar, beating continuously until stiff peaks form. Spread over pie filling. Bake at 350° F. for 10 to 12 minutes, or until meringue is lightly browned.

Linda H. Harris, Vance County

This delicious pie is a winner with my family.

—

CHOCOLATE MERINGUE PIE

2 cups milk
1 cup sugar
1/4 cup plus 2 tablespoons
  cornstarch
1/4 cup plus 2 tablespoons
  cocoa
1/4 teaspoon salt
3 egg yolks

1 tablespoon butter or
  margarine
1 teaspoon vanilla extract
Meringue:
3 egg whites
1/4 teaspoon cream of tartar
1/3 cup sugar
1 baked 9-inch pie crust

Place milk in a double boiler. Combine dry ingredients, and add to milk, using wire whisk. Cook until thickened, stirring constantly. Stir in egg yolks carefully with wire whisk. Cook 2 or 3 minutes. Remove from heat and add butter and vanilla. Beat a few minutes, and allow to cool. *Prepare meringue:* Beat egg whites and cream of tartar, adding sugar gradually until stiff. Pour chocolate custard into pie shell. Top with meringue. Bake at 350° F. for 8 to 10 minutes, until brown. Serves 6.

Ann Kilian, Warren County

This is my family's favorite dessert.

FOOLPROOF CHOCOLATE PIE
(makes 2 pies)

2 cups sugar
3/4 cup flour
1/2 cup cocoa
6 eggs, separated
3 cups milk, Half & Half, or
  Carnation evaporated
  milk
1/2 stick butter

1 teaspoon vanilla
2 prepared pie shells
Meringue:
Dash of salt
6 egg whites
12 tablespoons sugar
1 teaspoon vanilla

Mix sugar, flour, and cocoa together in a large saucepan. Beat egg yolks with some of the milk, and then add to the sugar-flour mixture. Add the rest of the milk. Cook on low heat stirring constantly, until mixture is thick. Add butter and vanilla. Brush some of the egg whites over the pie shells; bake empty shells for 7 to 9 minutes at 350° F. Add pie mixture. *Prepare meringue:* Sprinkle a dash of salt over egg whites. Allow to stand 5 minutes before beating. Beat egg whites until foamy. Add sugar and vanilla. Continue beating until stiff peaks form. Spread over pie mixture, and bake until lightly browned in a 350° F. oven for 12 to 15 minutes. Watch meringue carefully so that it doesn't burn. (You can also use this recipe to make Coconut Pies. Omit the cocoa, cook the mixture, and add 8 ounces frozen coconut.)

Maxine Jordan, Bladen County

I have used this recipe for 30 years, and it's foolproof. The neighbors always enjoy these pies.

—

HOMECOMING CHOCOLATE PIE

1 cup sugar
5 tablespoons Hershey's
   cocoa
4 tablespoons self-rising
   flour
1/8 teaspoon salt
3 egg yolks
2 cups whole or low-fat milk

1/2 stick butter or
   margarine
1 teaspoon vanilla flavoring
1 baked frozen 9-inch pie
   shell *or* baked graham
   cracker crust
Meringue:
3 egg whites
6 tablespoons sugar

Stir together dry ingredients: sugar, cocoa, flour, and salt in 2-quart saucepan. Beat egg yolks with 2 cups milk in bowl, and add mixture to dry ingredients in saucepan, stirring well. Cut 1/2 stick butter or margarine in six pieces, and add to saucepan. Cook over low to medium heat until mixture is thick and bubbling. Stir continuously while cooking (or cook in double boiler). Stir in vanilla flavoring. Pour into baked pastry pie shell or baked graham cracker crust. Cool 5 minutes and top with meringue. *Prepare meringue:* Use your favorite meringue recipe, or beat 3 egg whites until they hold a stiff peak. Slowly add 6 tablespoons sugar, beating well. Spread on pie, and bake until lightly browned in a 325° F. oven (about 10 minutes, but check periodically since oven temperatures vary.) Refrigerate after cooling to room temperature. Serves 6.

Kay Wallace Bullock, Rowan County

Four generations of our family have made this pie and served it to their families, friends, and at church homecomings. They have all been besieged for the recipe. The pie filling is also delicious served as individual chocolate puddings.

—

MAMA'S CHOCOLATE PIE

2 1/2 squares unsweetened
  baking chocolate, grated
2 1/2 cups milk
4 tablespoons flour
1 cup sugar
1/2 teaspoon salt
3 eggs, separated
2 tablespoons butter

2 teaspoons vanilla
1 baked pie shell
Meringue:
3 egg whites
1/2 teaspoon vanilla
1/4 teaspoon cream of tartar
6 tablespoons sugar

Place grated chocolate and milk in a double boiler. Heat until chocolate is melted and smooth. Combine flour, sugar, and salt, and add to beaten egg yolks. Pour a little bit of milk and chocolate mixture over egg yolk mixture, and then add this back to milk mixture in saucepan. Cook until thick, stirring constantly. Remove from heat; add butter and vanilla. Pour into pie shell. *Prepare meringue:* Beat egg whites with vanilla and cream of tartar until soft peaks form. Gradually add sugar, beating until stiff, glossy peaks form and all sugar is dissolved. Spread over pie filling, sealing to edge of pastry. Bake at 350° F. for 12 to 15 minutes. Cool.

Elizabeth Harper, Edgecombe County

I've never tasted better.

CHOCOLATE CHESS PIE

4 eggs
2 cups sugar
4 tablespoons cocoa
2 teaspoons vanilla

1 cup butter, melted
1 cup evaporated milk
2 unbaked 9-inch pie shells

Beat eggs with sugar. Then add cocoa, vanilla, and melted butter. Mix well. Bring milk to a slight boil (do not overheat). Add gradually to the mixture. Pour into two unbaked, 9-inch pie shells. Bake at 350° F. for 45 minutes.

Patricia Herring, Wayne County

We always had this pie for Sunday lunch at my grandmother's house. You can bake the pie without a crust. Just pour mixture into a medium-sized casserole dish, and bake. My grandmother called this "poor man's pie."

—

COCONUT PIE

2 cups Angel Flake coconut
   or grated coconut
3 eggs
2 cups sugar
3/4 stick margarine

1 13-ounce can evaporated
   milk
1 teaspoon vanilla flavoring
2 pie shells, unbaked

Mix all ingredients, and pour into pie shells. Bake at 350° F. until filling is firm in center of pie.

Elizabeth Parrish, Chowan County

This pie is always good, especially for supper at church.

COCONUT CREAM PIE

1 pie shell, unbaked
3/4 cup sugar
5 tablespoons cornstarch or
   flour
1/4 teaspoon salt
2 cups milk

3 beaten egg yolks
1 1/3 cups coconut, divided
1 tablespoon butter
1 teaspoon vanilla
Meringue

Bake pie shell at 350° F. until lightly brown. In double boiler, combine sugar, cornstarch or flour, and salt. Gradually stir in milk and egg yolks. Cook until thickened. Remove from heat. Add 1 cup of coconut, butter, and vanilla. Pour into baked pie shell. Top with meringue. Sprinkle 1/3 cup coconut over meringue. Bake at 350° F. until meringue is lightly browned, 12 to 15 minutes.

Betty Wood, Craven County

EASY COCONUT PIE

2 eggs
3/4 cup sugar
2 tablespoons all-purpose
flour
Pinch of salt
3/4 cup milk

1 teaspoon vanilla
1 cup coconut (Baker's)
2 tablespoons margarine,
melted
1 9-inch pie crust, unbaked

Beat eggs well. Stir sugar, flour, and salt together, and add to eggs.
Beat well. Add milk, vanilla, coconut, and melted margarine. Stir.
Pour into unbaked 9-inch pie crust, and bake at 350° F. for 45
minutes, or until golden brown and firm.

Kathleen W. Penninger, Davidson County

This pie is easy to make and a favorite of friends at church lunches.

MOCK COCONUT PIE
(makes 5 pies)

6 cups sugar
5 eggs
5 tablespoons flour
2 sticks margarine, melted
6 teaspoons lemon flavoring

6 teaspoons coconut
flavoring
9 1/2 cups yellow squash,
grated into long strings
5 9-inch pie shells
(uncooked)

Blend first six ingredients together. Grate squash in long strings.
Add squash to other ingredients, and mix. Pour into pie shells. Bake
at 375° F. for 45 minutes. Test for doneness by inserting straw in
center. If it comes out clean, the pie is done. Makes 5 pies, each of
which serves 6. Freezes well.

Helen J. Bess, Gaston County

Do you wonder what to do with all that squash from your garden?
Helen Bess uses some of hers in a dessert. The family enjoys the
pies, and they even freeze well.

All-Purpose and Self-Rising Flour

Self-rising flour is a mixture of regular all-purpose flour, baking
powder, and salt. If you don't have self-rising flour on hand, add
1 1/2 teaspoons baking powder and 1/2 teaspoon salt to 1 cup of all-
purpose flour for each cup of flour called for in the recipe.

APPLE-WALNUT COBBLER

4 cups tart apples, peeled,
   thinly sliced (I prefer
   Rome apples)
1 1/2 cups sugar, divided
1/2 teaspoon cinnamon
3/4 cup walnuts, coarsely
   chopped (pecans may be
   used)

1 cup sifted all-purpose
   flour
1/4 teaspoon salt
1 egg, well-beaten
1/2 cup evaporated milk
1/3 cup margarine

Place apples in bottom of a greased 8 1/4 x 1 3/4-inch baking dish.
Mix 1/2 cup sugar, cinnamon, and 1/2 cup walnuts. Sprinkle over
apples. Sift together flour, 1 cup sugar, and salt. In a separate bowl,
combine egg, milk, and margarine. Add flour-sugar mixture, and
mix until smooth. Pour over apples. Sprinkle remaining walnuts on
top. Bake at 325° F. for about 55 minutes. Serve warm with vanilla
ice cream or cinnamon whipped cream.

Pearl Freedman, Columbus County

Yum, yum, good, especially on a cool, crisp fall day.

FANCY FRUIT PIE

(Blue Ribbon winner, 2001 State Fair)

1 cup sugar
2 eggs, beaten
Pinch of salt
1 stick butter, melted
1 tablespoon vinegar

1/2 cup flaked coconut
1/2 cup seedless raisins
1/2 cup chopped pecans
1 9-inch Pillsbury
   Refrigerated Pie Crust

Mix sugar, eggs, salt, butter, and vinegar. Add coconut, raisins, and
pecans. Pour into pie crust. If desired, cut designs from a second
crust to lay on top or make a handle with a basket weave on top.
Bake at 350° F. until filling doesn't shake.

Ronda Hayes, Person County

FRUIT COBBLER

1 stick margarine
1 cup sugar
1 cup self-rising flour

3/4 cup milk
1 can fruit pie filling

Melt margarine in a 3-quart casserole or baking dish. In a separate bowl, mix sugar, flour, and milk. Pour mixture over margarine, but do not stir in margarine. Spoon pie filling over the mixture. Bake at 350° F. for 1 hour, or until golden brown. Serves 9.

Vicki Walton, Wake County

MAGIC COBBLER

1 cup flour
3/4 cup sugar
3 teaspoons baking powder
Dash salt

1/2 cup milk
1/4 stick of butter
Quart of sweet fruit

Mix flour, sugar, baking powder, and salt. Add milk. Melt butter in 8 x 8-inch baking dish. Pour batter on top of butter. Bring fruit to a boil. Spoon fruit on top of batter. Bake at 400° F. for 30 to 40 minutes, or until brown.

Desma Young, Buncombe County

OLD-FASHIONED PEACH COBBLER

4 cups fresh peaches, sliced
1 cup sugar
1/2 cup butter or margarine
1 1/2 cups all-purpose flour

3/4 teaspoon salt
1/2 cup shortening
1/4 cup plus 1 tablespoon
  cold water

Combine first three ingredients in medium pan, bring to a boil, and cook over low heat until peaches are tender and mixture thickens. Pour mixture into lightly buttered 10 x 6 x 2-inch baking dish, and set aside. Combine flour and salt. Cut in shortening until mixture resembles coarse meal. Sprinkle water evenly over flour mixture, and stir with a fork until all ingredients are moistened. Shape pastry into a ball. Roll out pastry, 1/8 inch thick, on lightly floured board. Cut into 1-inch strips, and arrange half the strips in lattice design over peaches. Bake at 350° F. degrees for 35 minutes. Remove from oven, and gently press baked pastry into peach mixture. Repeat lattice design over peaches with remaining pastry strips. Return to oven, and bake another 40 minutes. Serves 6.

Pat Nash, Brunswick County

I am a member of Brunswick County ECA. This recipe originally came from Mrs. Alda Lewis, a homemaker and mother of Mary Russ, retired Extension Agent for Brunswick County. I was born and raised in Mecklenburg County, so I am a native Tar Heel. I collected cobbler recipes for many years and have now thrown all of them away in favor of this one.

—

SURRY COUNTY FRUIT SONKER

Pastry:
3 cups flour
1 teaspoon salt
1 cup shortening
1 whole egg
10 tablespoons cold water
2 tablespoons vinegar
1/4 cup sugar
2 tablespoons butter or
   margarine, cut into small
   pieces
Filling:
8 cups sliced fresh fruit
   (blueberries, blackberries,
strawberries, peaches,
   cherries)
1/3 cup all-purpose flour
2 cups sugar
1 teaspoon ground
   cinnamon
1 cup water
1/2 cup butter or
   margarine, melted
1 teaspoon almond extract
Dip:
3/4 cup sugar
1/4 cup cornstarch
1 quart milk
1/4 teaspoon vanilla

Prepare pastry: Mix flour and salt. Cut in shortening. Add remaining pastry ingredients except 1/4 cup sugar and 2 tablespoons butter or margarine. Mix lightly. Chill. (Can be frozen at this point until ready for use.) On a lightly floured surface, roll pastry to about 1/4-inch thickness. Cut into strips for lining pan and for making lattice topping.

Prepare fruit: Dredge fruit in flour. Add sugar, cinnamon, water, melted butter, and almond extract, and mix well. Set aside.

To assemble sonker: Line bottom of 9 x 13-inch pan with strips of pastry. Bake about 10 minutes at 350° F. Do not brown. Remove from oven; pour prepared fruit mixture over crust strips. Cover with small strips of pastry, lattice style, crisscrossed (or make your own design). Sprinkle lightly with 1/4 cup sugar and add pieces of butter or margarine. Bake at 375° F. for 30 to 40 minutes or until top is brown.

Prepare dip: Mix together sugar and cornstarch; add milk and vanilla. Cook in double boiler until thickened. Pour dip over individual servings of sonker. Recipe serves 12.

Elaine W. Whitaker, Surry County

Ask most Surry Countians how long sonkers have been around and they'll tell you, "For as long as I can remember." Their grandmas could stir one up in a jiffy. Most poured "Dip," a milk-based topping, over individual servings. "Sonker" is another word for a cobbler. Some say the name was derived from the appearance of the irregularly shaped crust, which suggested a grass saddle; some say it had to do with how it was made. We may never really know who or how the name got started, but all seem to agree that sonkers are a tasty tradition in Surry County.

—

ONE-CRUST EGG CUSTARD

3 tablespoons margarine	3 eggs, beaten
1/2 cup granulated sugar	1 tall can evaporated milk
3 tablespoons self-rising flour	1 teaspoon vanilla extract

Melt margarine in pan while oven preheats to 350° F. Mix sugar and flour. Add beaten eggs, milk, and vanilla extract. Beating constantly, add melted margarine. Pour back into baking pan. Bake for 30 to 35 minutes. If desired, turn on broiler, and brown top.

Margaret Helton, Rutherford County

OLD-FASHIONED EGG CUSTARD PIE

2 large eggs	1 1/2 cups whole milk
1/2 cup sugar	1 pie shell
1 teaspoon vanilla	Nutmeg

Beat eggs, sugar, and vanilla. Scald 1 1/2 cups whole milk, and pour into egg mixture. Mix well, and pour into pie shell. Sprinkle with nutmeg. Bake at 400° F. for 20 minutes.

Dorothy E. Fender, Alleghany County

LEMON PIE

2 cups sugar
2 tablespoons corn meal
2 tablespoons flour
1/4 teaspoon salt
1/4 cup lemon juice

4 teaspoons grated lemon
  rind
4 eggs unbeaten
1/2 cup melted butter
1/4 cup milk
1 unbaked pie crust

Mix sugar, corn meal, flour, salt, lemon juice and rind, eggs, butter, and milk. Pour mixture into pie shell. Bake 35 minutes at 325° F. This recipe can also be made using unbaked tart shells.

Pattie M. Brauer, Warren County

LEMON PIE

1 1/2 cups sugar
5 1/2 teaspoons cornstarch
1 1/2 cups hot water
3 eggs, separated
3 tablespoons butter
4 tablespoons fresh lemon
  juice

1 1/3 tablespoons grated
  lemon rind
1 baked pie shell
Meringue:
3 egg whites
1/4 teaspoon cream of tartar
1/2 teaspoon vanilla
6 tablespoons sugar

Mix sugar and cornstarch in saucepan. Add hot water, stir, and cook until mixture thickens and boils. Boil 1 minute. Remove from heat. Beat 1/2 cup hot mixture into 3 slightly beaten egg yolks. Return this mixture to the mixture in the saucepan. Cook 1 minute longer, stirring constantly. Remove from heat, and blend in butter, lemon juice, and lemon rind. Pour into baked pie shell. *Prepare meringue:* Beat egg whites, cream of tartar, and vanilla until frothy and soft peaks form. Gradually add sugar, and beat until sugar dissolves and stiff peaks form. Bake at 350° F. for 12 to 15 minutes.

Laura B. Wooten, Wake County

This recipe doubles nicely.

Beating Egg Whites

Recipes sometimes call for a small amount of acid, such as cream of tartar, lemon juice, or vinegar, to stabilize beaten egg whites and allow them to reach their full volume and stiffness.

LEMON SPONGE PIE

1 unbaked single pie crust
3 eggs, separated
1 cup sugar
2 teaspoons grated lemon
 peel
3 tablespoons flour

1 tablespoon margarine,
 softened
1/8 teaspoon salt
1/3 cup lemon juice
1 cup skim milk

Bake pie shell at 375° F. for 10 minutes. Reduce oven temperature to 325° F. Beat egg whites until stiff peaks form; set aside. In large mixing bowl, beat egg yolks, sugar, lemon peel, flour, margarine, and salt with mixer until well blended. Add lemon juice, beat well, and blend in milk with wire whisk. Fold egg whites into lemon mixture. Place pie shell in oven. Pour filling into it. Bake about 35 minutes, or until top is golden and appears set.

Ann Kilian, Warren County

This is a light version of lemon chess pie!

NUTTY BUDDY PIE

(makes 3 pies)

2 cups confectioners' sugar
8 ounces cream cheese,
 softened
2/3 cup crunchy peanut
 butter
1 cup milk
2 8-ounce containers Cool
 Whip

3 graham cracker pie crusts
 and/or Oreo cookie pie
 crusts
Chocolate syrup
1 cup chopped unsalted
 peanuts

Mix sugar, cream cheese, and peanut butter together. Add milk and Cool Whip. Pour into pie crusts. Swirl with chocolate syrup. Sprinkle pies with chopped nuts. Freeze. Keep frozen.

Cynthia Burton, Surry County

PEANUT BUTTER PIE

2 tablespoons honey
1 8-ounce container Cool
 Whip

1 cup chunky peanut butter
1 prepared Oreo Cookie pie
 shell

Warm honey in microwave, about 30 to 40 seconds. Mix Cool
Whip, peanut butter, and honey until smooth. Pour into cookie pie
shell. Put in freezer for about an hour. Serves 8.

Michele Quinn, Cabarrus County

*This is a quick and easy dessert that's great when you need
something at the last minute.*

—

DELIGHTFUL PEANUT BUTTER PIE

Crust:
**Almost 1 cup powdered
   confectioners' sugar**
**1/2 cup smooth peanut
   butter**
**1 baked pie shell *or* 1
   prepared graham cracker
   crust**
Cream filling:
3 eggs, separated
**1/4 cup cornstarch *or* 1/3
   cup all-purpose flour**

1/2 cup sugar
1/4 teaspoon salt
2 cups milk
**2 tablespoons margarine or
   butter**
1 tablespoon vanilla
Meringue:
3 egg whites (chilled)
4 to 5 tablespoons sugar
**1 teaspoon cream of tartar
   (optional)**

Prepare crust: Mix powdered sugar and peanut butter until
crumbly. Spread crumbly mixture evenly in bottom of baked pie
shell or graham cracker crust, saving 2 tablespoons for top of
meringue.

Prepare cream filling: Separate eggs. Place egg whites and egg
beaters in refrigerator (they need to be cold to make the meringue).
Combine cornstarch, sugar, salt, egg yolks, and milk. Cook until
thick, stirring constantly. Remove from stove. Add margarine and
vanilla. Stir until margarine melts. Pour hot cream filling on top of
crumbly mixture in pie shell.

Prepare meringue: Remove egg whites from refrigerator. Using
chilled beaters, add cream of tartar and 1 tablespoon of sugar at a
time until stiff peaks form. Cover cream filling with meringue,
sprinkle on reserved crumbly mix, and bake at 325° F. until golden
brown, about 25 minutes. This pie is best if allowed to set all day or
overnight in refrigerator.

Edith Roby Edwards, Rutherford County

PECAN PIE
(can also be used to make Coconut or Chess Pie)

2 9-inch unbaked pie shells
About 1 1/2 cups pecans, chopped
3 whole eggs
1 2/3 cups packed brown sugar
1 stick margarine, melted
Dash of salt
1 teaspoon vanilla
1 teaspoon vinegar

Cover the bottoms of unbaked pie shells with chopped pecans. Set aside. Beat eggs. Add brown sugar, melted margarine, salt, vanilla, and vinegar. Mix well. Pour mixture over pecans in pie shells. Place on cookie sheet, and bake 35 minutes at 350° F. To make Chess Pie, omit pecans. To make Coconut Pie, omit pecans and add 1 1/2 cups coconut. Each recipe makes two pies, and each pie serves 6 to 8.

Juanita Fisher Lagg, Rowan County

I never liked pecan pie until a friend of mine gave me this recipe. Not so sweet, has a nice crunchy top, and everyone I have given this pie to wants the recipe. Use coconut instead of pecans and you have Coconut Pie. Leave out the nuts and coconut, and you have a wonderful Chess Pie. Maybe it ought to be called 3-in-1 Pie. My grandfather, James Gibson Brown, was the first farmer in Rowan County to deliver milk, butter, and eggs.

PECAN PIE

1 pound light brown sugar
2 tablespoons flour
2 tablespoons cornmeal
3 eggs, well beaten
3/4 cup milk
1 stick margarine or butter, melted
1 cup pecans, chopped
1 teaspoon vanilla

Mix sugar, flour, and cornmeal together. Add eggs, milk, butter, pecans, and vanilla. Bake at 350° F. for 30 to 40 minutes. Makes enough filling for one deep-dish pie or two regular-dish pies.

Cynthia Burton, Surry County

PECAN PIE

3 eggs, beaten
1 cup sugar
2 tablespoons flour
1/4 cup dark Karo syrup
1 cup chopped pecans
1 teaspoon vanilla

Blend eggs, sugar, and flour. Add syrup, pecans, and vanilla. Pour into a 9-inch pie crust. Bake at 350° F. for 40 to 45 minutes. Makes one pie.

Helene Daugherty, Craven County

PECAN PIE

3 tablespoons flour
1/3 cup margarine
3/4 cup light brown sugar
1/4 teaspoon salt
1 teaspoon vanilla flavoring

1 cup light Karo syrup
3 eggs
2 1/2 cups pecans, coarsely
chopped

Mix all ingredients together. Pour into two unbaked pie shells. Bake at 350° F. for 45 minutes. Makes two small pies.

Audrey W. Quinn, Craven County

PECAN PIE

3 eggs, beaten
1/2 cup sugar
2 tablespoons margarine,
melted
1 teaspoon vanilla

1 cup light Karo syrup
1/8 teaspoon salt
1 1/4 cups pecans, chopped
or broken

Beat eggs with whisk. Add sugar, and beat. Add melted margarine, vanilla, Karo syrup, salt, and pecans, stirring after each addition. Pour into unbaked pie shell. Bake at 325° F. for 50 to 55 minutes, or until set.

Linda H. Harris, Vance County

This makes a smooth pie that is not too terribly sweet.

GRANDMOTHER'S PECAN PIE

1/2 cup sugar
1/4 cup butter, softened
1 cup light corn syrup
1/4 teaspoon salt

1 teaspoon vanilla extract
3 eggs
1 cup pecans, chopped
1 9-inch pie shell

With mixer, cream together sugar and butter. Add syrup, salt, and vanilla. Add eggs, one at a time, beating well after each addition.

Stir in pecans. Pour into pie shell, and bake in a preheated 300° F. oven for 45 minutes. Serves 6.

Brenda Rhodes Batten, Johnston County

This pecan pie was the finishing touch to family get-togethers at my grandmother's house. She knew we liked her pie the best! It was always made with the best pecans, straight off her own trees.

—

CHOCOLATE-PECAN PIE

3 cups sugar
7 tablespoons cocoa
1 stick butter, melted
Pinch of salt
4 eggs, well beaten
1 teaspoon vanilla

1 12-ounce can evaporated
  milk
2 cups coconut
1 cup chopped pecans
3 9-inch pie shells, unbaked

Combine ingredients. Mix well. Pour into pie shells, dividing evenly. Bake at 350° F. for 45 minutes. Serves 18.

Ruth M. Phipps, Ashe County

This family favorite freezes well. We are Century farmers.

PECAN TARTS

Crust:
3 ounces cream cheese
1 stick margarine
1 cup all-purpose flour
Filling:
1 egg

1 tablespoon margarine,
  melted
3/4 cup brown sugar,
  packed
1/2 cup chopped pecans
1 teaspoon vanilla extract
Pinch salt

Prepare crust: Mix cream cheese, 1 stick margarine, and flour together. Cover bowl, and chill. Pinch off small portions of dough, and press into tiny muffin tins to form crusts for tarts. *Prepare filling:* Mix egg, 1 tablespoon melted margarine, brown sugar, pecans, vanilla, and salt. Drop 1 teaspoon of mixture into each crust. Bake in preheated 350° F. oven for 30 minutes. Serves 24.

Susan Harper Britt, Nash County

One of my favorite recipes, this was given to me by my mother.

HOLIDAY PINEAPPLE PIE

1 1/2 cups sugar
2 tablespoons flour
1 teaspoon vanilla
2 eggs

1 8 1/4-ounce can crushed
pineapple, drained
2 tablespoons margarine,
melted
1 unbaked pie shell

Mix all ingredients well, and pour into unbaked shell. Bake at 350°
F. for about 45 minutes, or until pie is firm and lightly brown.

Sharon Hester, Granville County

*This was passed down to me from my mother-in-law, and we always
have it at Thanksgiving and Christmas.*

GRANDMA'S PINEAPPLE PIE

(makes 3 pies)

1 20-ounce can crushed
pineapple
2 cups sugar
4 egg yolks

4 heaping tablespoons flour
2 cups boiling water
3 baked pie shells

Combine first five ingredients, and cook until thick. Remove from
stove, and let cool for 5 minutes. Pour into 3 baked pie shells.
Prepare meringue using your favorite recipe, and cover pies with it.
Bake until brown, about 12 to 15 minutes at 350° F.

Mrs. Barbara Thompson, Ashe County

*My Grandma made these; she passed the recipe to my mother, and
now I make them.*

NO-COOK PINEAPPLE PIE

(makes 2 pies)

1 20-ounce can crushed
pineapple, well drained
1 9-ounce container Cool
Whip topping
1 14-ounce can Eagle Brand
condensed milk

1/4 cup lemon juice (or less)
1 cup crushed pecans
2 9-inch graham cracker
crusts

Drain pineapple well or your pies will be soggy. Mix all ingredients
together, and pour into crusts. Place in refrigerator overnight.

Johnsie C. Cunningham, Granville County

My reputation is based on what is fast, easy, and GOOD...but does not require cooking. This dessert is not just a pretty dish, but is also a family favorite.

PUMPKIN PIE

3/4 cup brown sugar,
  packed
1/2 teaspoon salt
1 tablespoon flour
3/4 teaspoon cinnamon
1/2 teaspoon ginger
1/4 teaspoon ground cloves

1/2 teaspoon nutmeg
2 eggs
1 16-ounce can pumpkin
1 can evaporated milk
1/2 cup water
1 pie crust

Mix all ingredients. Pour into pie crust. Bake at 350° F. until set, about 1 hour. Serves 6 to 8.

Helen Walton, Wake County

TAWNY PUMPKIN PIE

1 1/2 cups cooked or canned
  pumpkin
3/4 cup sugar
1/2 teaspoon salt
1 teaspoon flour
1/4 teaspoon ground ginger

1 teaspoon cinnamon
2 eggs, slightly beaten
1 cup evaporated milk
2 tablespoons water
1/2 teaspoon vanilla
1 unbaked 9-inch pie shell

Combine pumpkin, sugar, salt, flour, and spices in a mixing bowl. Add eggs; mix well. Add evaporated milk, water, and vanilla. Mix. Pour into unbaked pie shell. Bake at 425° F. for 45 to 50 minutes, or until knife inserted near center comes out clean.

Dorothy C. Fisher, Nash County

RHUBARB PIE

1 1/4 cups sugar
1/3 cup flour
Dash of salt

4 cups rhubarb, cut into 1-
  inch pieces
Pastry for double crust pie
2 tablespoons butter

Stir together sugar, flour, and salt. Add sugar mixture to rhubarb pieces, and toss to coat. Let mixture stand for 15 minutes. Put pastry into a 9-inch pie plate, and fill with rhubarb mixture. Dot with butter. Cover with top crust. Seal, and flute edges. Cover edge of crust with foil. Bake at 375° F. for 25 minutes. Remove foil, and bake 25 minutes longer. Serve warm. Serves 8.

Margaret H. Spencer, Gaston County

Growing up, my parents had a large garden. We all enjoyed my mother's rhubarb pie, and she made the pie often because we had a lot of rhubarb. This recipe could be 100 years old or older as her mother passed it on to her.

—

CRUNCHY TOPPED FRENCH RHUBARB PIE

1 unbaked pie shell
Filling:
1 cup sugar
2 tablespoons flour
1 egg
1 teaspoon vanilla
2 cups fresh rhubarb, cut
  into small pieces

Topping:
1 cup quick cooking
  oatmeal
1/3 cup brown sugar
1/3 cup softened butter
1/2 teaspoon cinnamon

Mix 1 cup sugar and 2 tablespoons flour together. Then add rest of the filling ingredients, and mix well. Pour into unbaked pie shell. Mix topping ingredients together, and sprinkle over filling. Bake in preheated 400° F. oven for 10 minutes. Then lower temperature to 350° F., and bake an additional 30 minutes. Makes 1 pie.

Sandy Smith, Wake County

STRAWBERRY PIE DELUXE

1 quart fresh strawberries
  (or 16-ounce package of
  frozen whole strawberries)
1/2 cup sugar
1 envelope unflavored
  gelatin

1 tablespoon lemon juice
1 baked 9-inch pie shell,
  cooled
1 large banana

Using potato masher, crush 3 cups of strawberries. Halve or slice remaining berries. Set aside. Strain crushed berries. Add water to juice to equal 1 cup of liquid. Reserve crushed berries. In medium saucepan, stir sugar and gelatin. Add 1 cup strawberry liquid. Cook and stir over medium heat until gelatin and sugar are dissolved. Stir in remaining crushed berries and lemon juice. Pour into bowl and chill until partially set (consistency of unbeaten egg whites). Pour half of the mixture into the cooled pie shell. Thinly slice banana, and arrange slices in a single layer over the berry mixture. Top with the remaining berry mixture. Arrange reserved berry halves or slices on top. Chill several hours, or until firm. Makes 1 pie.

Janet Singleton, Wake County

STRAWBERRY CREAM CHEESE PIE

1 envelope whipped topping
  mix
1 8-ounce package cream
  cheese
1/2 cup sugar
1 baked 10-inch graham
  cracker crust, cooled

1 3-ounce package
  strawberry flavor gelatin
1 cup boiling water
1 pint strawberries, halved
  and sweetened

Prepare topping mix as directed on package. Whip cream cheese until soft; beat in sugar, then blend in whipped mixture. Pour into crust, mounding high at edges. Dissolve gelatin in boiling water. Drain berries, adding cold water to juice to make 1/2 cup. Add to gelatin. Chill until slightly thickened; fold in strawberries. Then pour over top of pie, leaving a narrow rim of cream filling around edge. Chill until gelatin is set, at least 3 hours.

Mrs. Foil W. McLaughlin, Wake County

STRAWBERRY PIE

1 cup sugar
2 tablespoons cornstarch
2 tablespoons strawberry
  Jell-O mix
1 cup water

1/2 quart fresh
  strawberries, sliced
1 baked pie shell
Small container Cool Whip

Combine dry ingredients and water. Bring to a boil until thickened. Let cool. Place sliced berries in a baked pie shell. Pour cooled filling over berries. Top with Cool Whip.

Karen Scalf, Duplin County

STRAWBERRY PIE

1 Bisquick pie shell, baked
  and cooled (see below)
Sliced strawberries
1 cup sugar
4 tablespoons cornstarch
1 cup hot water

2 tablespoons strawberry
  Jell-O
Cool Whip
Pie Shell:
1 cup Bisquick mix
1/4 cup margarine, softened
3 tablespoons boiling water

Place sliced strawberries on top of pie crust. Mix sugar, cornstarch, hot water, and Jell-O. Pour on top of sliced strawberries. Let set in refrigerator. Top with Cool Whip. *Prepare pie shell:* Mix all ingredients in a small bowl. Stir quickly until very soft dough forms. Make pie crust. Bake 8 to 10 minutes in a 400° F. oven. Cool before adding filling.

Evelyn Sneed, Granville County

SWEET POTATO PIE
(makes 2 pies)

4 medium sweet potatoes,
  cooked and mashed
1/4 cup of allspice
1/4 cup of nutmeg

1/4 cup of sugar
2 eggs
2 pie shells, uncooked

Boil or bake sweet potatoes until done; peel and mash. In a large bowl, blend the allspice, nutmeg, sugar, eggs, and mashed sweet potatoes until you have a smooth batter. Brown pie shells at 350° F. for 10 minutes, or according to package instructions. Be careful not to let the crust burn. Spoon batter into the pie shells, and bake at 350° F. for 15 minutes.

James and Lossie Edwards, Wayne County

MRS. BURNS' SWEET POTATO PIES
(makes 5 pies)

4 1/2 pounds sweet potatoes
3 cups sugar
1 cup Pet evaporated milk
2 sticks margarine

1 tablespoon vanilla
1 tablespoon lemon
  flavoring
6 eggs, separated

Peel sweet potatoes, cook, and then mash them. Add all ingredients except egg whites, and mix. Fold in beaten egg whites last. Pour
200

into five prepared pie shells. Bake at 325° F. for 30 minutes, or until
crust is light brown. Pies freeze well.

Marilyn Zone, Lee County

*Eleanor Burns' family runs Bud's BBQ in Cumnock. She is a
wonderful, generous, well-loved member of the Cumnock Extension
Club.*

—

SWEET POTATO PIE
(makes 2 pies)

**2 1/2 cups cooked, mashed
  sweet potatoes
1 1/4 cups milk
1 cup sugar
1 stick margarine, melted**

**1 3-ounce box instant
  vanilla pudding
2 eggs
1 cup chopped nuts**

Mix everything together. Put into two 9-inch pie crusts. Bake pies at
350° F. for 30 to 40 minutes, or until set.

Bill Braswell, Rowan County

This Sweet Potato Pie is for those of us who have high sugar.

SWEET POTATO PIE

**1 1/4 cups sweet potatoes,
  cooked and mashed
1/2 cup brown sugar, firmly
  packed
1/2 teaspoon salt
1/4 teaspoon cinnamon**

**2 eggs, well beaten
3/4 cup milk, evaporated is
  best
1 tablespoon melted butter
1 8-inch pastry shell
Pecan halves (optional)**

Prepare pastry for an 8-inch pie, and let chill while making filling.
Combine cooked, mashed sweet potatoes, brown sugar, salt, and
cinnamon in a bowl. In a separate bowl, mix together eggs, milk,
and butter, and stir into sweet potato mixture. Mix thoroughly, and
pour into chilled pastry shell. If desired, arrange a circle of pecan
halves around edge. Bake at 400° F. for 45 minutes, or until knife
comes out dry when inserted in the center. Serves 8.

Margaret Helton, Rutherford County

*This is a pie we enjoy year 'round whenever we have a hankering
for sweet potato pie. It is so delicious with ice cream or Cool Whip
or by itself.*

SWEET POTATO PIE

Pie crust:
1 cup all-purpose flour
1/2 teaspoon salt
7 tablespoons lard
4 tablespoons ice water
Filling:
1 1/2 cups mashed sweet
  potatoes

1 cup brown sugar
1/2 cup butter, melted
2 eggs, beaten
2 teaspoons apple pie spice
1 teaspoon vanilla
3/4 cup milk
1 cup self-rising flour

Prepare pie crust: Mix flour and salt. Cut lard into flour-salt mixture with pastry blender until mixture is the size of peas. Add ice water 1 tablespoon at a time. Mix with hands, and form into a ball. Roll out on a generously floured surface. Place in 9-inch pan and trim. Prick with fork. *Prepare filling:* Combine and beat first seven filling ingredients. Add flour. Beat until well blended. Pour into unbaked pie crust. Bake pie in preheated 350° F. oven for 40 minutes. Serves 8.

Janice Carter, Onslow County

For large gatherings, my mother stacked three or four pies on a cake plate and sliced it like cake.

Cakes, Cookies, & Desserts

Candies
Fudge
Peanut Brittle
Pralines
Cakes, Icings, &
   Frostings

Pound Cake
Fruit Cake
Cookies
Drop Cookies
Rolled & Shaped
   Cookies

Bar Cookies
Pudding
Ice Cream
Other Desserts

A Taste of North Carolina's Heritage

How well do we eat, and what should we eat?

The Food Guide Pyramid for a healthy diet is built like this: At the top are fats, oil, and sweets, all foods that we should eat most sparingly. At the next, larger level are milk, yogurt, cheese, meat, poultry, fish, dry beans, eggs, and nuts, a food group that should be consumed in some form three times daily. At the third, even larger level are vegetables and fruits, which should be eaten five to nine times daily. At the pyramid's base are the foods we should eat the most—bread, cereal, rice, and pasta—six to 11 servings daily. Research and Extension professionals in the College of Agriculture and Life Sciences at NC State University are involved in a number of efforts to promote healthy eating.

Food Guide Pyramid

OLD-FASHIONED CINNAMON CANDY

3 3/4 cups sugar
1 1/2 cups light corn syrup
1 cup water
1 teaspoon cinnamon oil
  (food grade)

Red food coloring
Pam Original Cooking
  Spray
1 cup confectioners'
  powdered sugar

Mix sugar, corn syrup, and water in a 2-quart saucepan. Hook a candy thermometer on the side of the pan. Make sure it is not touching the bottom of the pan. Stir over medium heat until sugar dissolves. Let mixture boil *without stirring* until temperature reaches 310° F. Remove from heat. After boiling has ceased, stir in cinnamon oil with a wooden spoon. Be careful: the fumes will be strong. Add red food coloring until desired color of red is reached.

Pour onto a 10 x 15-inch cookie sheet that has been sprayed with Pam. Let candy cool. Break up into bite-sized pieces using a hammer and an ice pick. Mix with the powdered sugar. Add more powdered sugar if desired. Store in an airtight container. Makes more than 2 pounds of candy.

Shawn Poe, Chatham County

MINTS

1 quart sugar
3/4 pound butter
1 cup boiling water

Mint flavoring (optional)
Food coloring (optional)

Mix sugar, butter, and water in large saucepan. Boil without stirring until candy will crack or break when put in cold water. Pour on marble slab, and leave until almost cool. Add a few drops of mint and coloring, if desired, before pulling.

Mrs. Roland Beck, Burke County

How Do You Pull Candy?

Pour candy onto a buttered marble slab or platter. Let cool enough to handle easily. Butter hands lightly. Pull and fold, pull and fold. When it stops being shiny, stop pulling and cut it immediately. Cut into pieces with well buttered scissors. If you pull it too long, it turns to sugar and gets crumbly. Wrap candies in foil, store in a closed tin.

NUTTY BUTTERSCOTCH CANDY

1/2 cup butterscotch
  topping
1/2 cup peanut butter
1/2 cup powdered milk

1/2 cup confectioners' sugar
1/4 teaspoon salt
1/4 cup chopped peanuts

Combine all ingredients except nuts. Using your hands, roll butterscotch mixture into 3/4-inch balls. Roll in chopped peanuts. Chill.

Dorothy Fender, Alleghany County

WONDERFUL FUDGE

4 1/2 cups sugar
1 12-ounce can evaporated
  milk
1 stick butter
1/2 pound marshmallows
12 ounces chocolate bits

2-ounce square baking
  (unsweetened) chocolate
3 3-ounce bars German
  chocolate
2 teaspoons vanilla
1 cup nuts, chopped

Place sugar, milk, and butter in a heavy saucepan. Stir together, bring to a boil, cover, and let boil for 5 minutes. Beat in marshmallows. Add chocolate, one kind at a time, beating well after each addition. Add vanilla and nuts. Pour into buttered pans. Makes 5 pounds; freezes well.

Ruth M. Phipps, Ashe County

This fudge has been a favorite of my family for years, and it never fails.

Saving Calories?

On may labels, the word "light" refers to a reduced-calorie version of a food. So if you use light corn syrup, you may think that you are saving calories. Actually, "light" in this case refers to the color of the corn syrup, not calorie content. Some older recipes call for "white" or "clear" corn syrup. This is the same as light corn syrup.

PEANUT BRITTLE

1 cup sugar	2 cups raw shelled peanuts
1/2 cup light Karo syrup	1 teaspoon baking soda
1/4 cup cold water	

Measure sugar, syrup, and water into a heavy saucepan. Cook over medium heat, stirring frequently, and bring to a boil. Add peanuts and continue stirring mixture until temperature reaches 293° F. on a candy thermometer (peanuts will stop "popping"). Remove from heat, and stir in soda. Pour onto greased cookie sheet or jelly roll pan. Allow to cool, then break into pieces. Store in airtight container. This recipe can be doubled easily. Do not attempt to make Peanut Brittle on damp or humid days as the candy will remain sticky.

Harriet Coleman Edwards, Wake County
Sarah Odom, Harnett County
Anne Porter, Wake County

Harriet Edwards says, "My grandmother used to make this candy and set it out on the screened-in back porch to cool. Sometimes my sister and I were allowed to help break it up when it was ready. Grandmother Hester never needed a candy thermometer to know when the brittle was ready."

Sarah Odom's recipe was passed to her by her mother. "It is a family favorite, especially around Christmastime." Sarah uses 1 1/2 teaspoons baking soda and adds 1 teaspoon of salt.

Anne Porter says, "This was my grandmother's, Maude Chappell's, recipe. She lived in Perquimans County and used good old North Carolina peanuts!" Anne uses 2 teaspoons baking soda and adds a dash of salt.

POP TAYLOR'S PEANUT BRITTLE

2 cups granulated sugar	3 cups raw, shelled,
1 cup light Karo syrup	unblanched peanuts
1/2 cup hot water	1 tablespoon baking soda
1/4 teaspoon salt	

You will need a candy thermometer, large wooden spoon, and two shallow buttered metal trays. Mix sugar, syrup, hot water, and salt together. Bring to a rolling boil. Add peanuts, stirring constantly. Cook slowly to 293° F. Remove from heat. Add baking soda. Beat rapidly. Pour onto buttered trays. Spread to 1/4 to 3/8-inch thick. Allow to cool. Remove from tray and break pieces into desired size.

Jeri Gray, Wake County

PEANUT BUTTER FUDGE

2 cups sugar
1 large can Pet evaporated
    milk
1 cup crunchy peanut
    butter

2 cups miniature
    marshmallows, *or* 16 large
    marshmallows

Cook sugar and milk to soft boil stage. Remove from heat, and pour over the peanut butter and marshmallows. Beat fast to mix well. Pour into 8 x 8-inch pan. Let set. Cut into 1-inch squares.

Dixie Porter, Wake County

This recipe has been made a million times, and folks around the country love it. It's even been mailed to the United Kingdom.

PECAN PRALINES

2 cups sugar
1 teaspoon baking soda
1 cup buttermilk

1 pinch salt
2 tablespoons butter
2 1/2 cups pecans

Mix together sugar, baking soda, buttermilk, salt, and butter in a heavy 8-quart saucepan; mixture foams up. Cook briskly, stirring frequently for 5 minutes or until candy thermometer registers 210° F. Add pecans. Stir continuously for 5 minutes until syrup forms a soft ball in cold water. Remove from heat. Cool slightly for 1 minute. Beat till thick and creamy. Drop by teaspoonful on wax paper.

Virginia Pearl Davis Baker, Harnett County

This is a very old family recipe that originally came from Tidewater Virginia. It is unbelievably good and so simple to make.

PRALINES

1 cup brown sugar	1 cup white sugar
1/2 cup evaporated milk	2 tablespoons butter
1 cup pecans	

Mix ingredients. Cook to 228° F. on a candy thermometer, then raise temperature to 238° F. (Make sure candy thermometer isn't touching the bottom of the pan.) Remove from heat, and beat 1 minute. Pour quickly onto waxed paper. Makes about 24 pralines.

Carolyn Tyndall, Duplin County

PRALINES

1 1/2 packs graham crackers	1/2 cup firmly packed brown sugar
1 1/2 sticks butter or margarine, melted	1 cup chopped pecans, black walnuts, or almond slices

Preheat oven to 350° F. Break crackers apart at lines, and place on a foil-lined cookie sheet. Blend together butter and sugar; bring to a boil for 3 minutes. Pour liquid over each cracker and sprinkle nut meats on top. Bake for 10 minutes. When cool, pull off foil and store pralines in airtight container. You may place an apple slice in the container of cookies to keep them moist.

Edith Edwards, Rutherford County

I used this recipe for the Natural Resources meeting's Auxiliary Hospitality Room at the Grove Park Inn, Asheville.

POTATO CANDY

1 1/2 potatoes, peeled and cooked	Peanut butter (smooth or chunky, your preference)
Powdered sugar (amount needed to make workable dough)	

Boil potatoes until done, and drain. Mash potatoes real well. Work powdered sugar in until you're able to roll the dough out (like you would a pie crust). Roll it out and spread peanut butter thinly on top. Then roll it up like a jelly roll. Slice and enjoy.

Judy W. Cogdell, Harnett County

Daddy always made Potato Candy for Christmas, and I have continued the tradition.

—

SEA FOAM

3 1/2 cups sugar
1 cup Karo syrup
2 egg whites

Vanilla or peppermint
flavoring

Moisten sugar with a little hot water. Add syrup, and boil until it threads. Pour 4 tablespoons of the boiling syrup over beaten egg whites. Let balance of syrup cook until it hardens in cold water. Then pour over the eggs, and beat constantly until it begins to get stiff. Add flavoring and drop on tin to cool.

Mrs. Roland Beck, Burke County

1-2-3-4 CAKE

1 cup butter or shortening
2 cups sugar
4 eggs, separated
3 cups sifted cake flour

1/4 teaspoon salt
3 teaspoons baking powder
1 cup milk
1 teaspoon vanilla

Preheat oven to 350º F. Cream shortening and sugar until fluffy. Add egg yolks one at a time, beating thoroughly after each is added. Sift dry ingredients together three times, and add alternately with milk and vanilla to creamed mixture, beating until smooth after each addition. Fold in stiffly beaten egg whites. Pour into 3 pans lined with wax paper, and bake for 25 minutes. Makes three 9-inch layers.

Sandy Smith, Wake County

My husband's aunt, Evelyn Sneed, used to make this delicious cake, but I didn't have a recipe for it until I found a copy in an old cookbook called Favorite Recipes of North Carolina, *which was published by the North Carolina Department of Agriculture. The cake gets its name from the main ingredients: 1 cup of butter, 2 cups of sugar, 3 cups of flour, 4 eggs.*

Try a 1-2-3-4 Cake with one of the following old-fashioned fillings. Use the frosting of your choice to finish off the cake.

COCONUT CAKE FILLING
(may be used with 1-2-3-4 Cake)

1 1/2 cups sugar	2 large coconuts, grated,
3 tablespoons cornstarch	reserve milk
1 1/2 cups milk	1/4 tablespoon lemon
3 tablespoons butter	extract
3 egg whites, beaten until	
stiff	

Combine sugar and cornstarch in a saucepan. Add milk, and cook until thickened, stirring frequently. Add butter, and stir to melt. Set aside to cool. Fold in stiff egg whites, shredded coconut, and lemon extract. Add enough coconut to make filling stiff enough to hold together. Makes enough filling to frost three layers and sides. Use reserved coconut milk to moisten layers; I use 1/2 cup per layer.

Laura B. Wooten, Wake County

This was my grandmother's recipe. I use a basic 1-2-3-4 Cake for the layers.

GRANDMOTHER'S PINEAPPLE CAKE FILLING
(may be used with 1-2-3-4 Cake)

3/4 cup sugar	1 20-ounce can crushed
3 tablespoons cornstarch	pineapple, drained,
1 cup milk	reserve juice
1 egg	1 teaspoon butter
	1/4 tablespoon lemon
	extract

Mix sugar and cornstarch in saucepan. Add milk. Cook until slightly thickened. Let cool. Beat egg thoroughly; add to milk mixture. Cook until thickened; add pineapple, and cook a few minutes more. Add butter and lemon flavoring. Cool before icing cake. Use reserved juice to moisten cake layers; I use 1/2 cup juice on each layer.

Laura B. Wooten, Wake County

MENDA'S PINEAPPLE CAKE FILLING
(may be used with 1-2-3-4 Cake)

1 16-ounce can (2 cups)
  crushed pineapple
2 tablespoons water to rinse
  out can
1 cup sugar

2 teaspoons flour or
  cornstarch
Water to make a paste
1 tablespoon butter

Empty can of crushed pineapple into saucepan. Use 2 tablespoons of water to rinse out can, and add water to pineapple. Add sugar and cook about 5 minutes. In a bowl, use just enough water to make a paste of the flour. Add to pineapple mixture. Boil a few minutes to thicken. Remove from heat, and stir in butter. Cool slightly. Spoon between layers.

Lydia M. Booth, Nash County

This recipe from the late 1930s is good with basic vanilla, lemon, or orange cake. We grew our own wheat, raised chickens for our own eggs, and made our own butter. Pineapple was inexpensive and was a good change from the Knock Up a Cake, which was a plain cake we cooked in layers or a tube pan.

ANGEL BAVARIAN

4 egg yolks
1 cup sugar
2 tablespoons flour
Pinch of salt
1 pint milk, scalded
1 envelope Knox gelatin
1/2 cup cold water

4 egg whites
1/2 pint whipping cream, *or*
  8 ounces whipped topping
1 purchased angel food
  cake, tube-pan size
Pineapple or strawberries,
  if desired

Beat egg yolks in top of double boiler. Add sugar, flour, and pinch of salt. Pour scalded milk into mixture. Cook in double boiler at simmering point until mixture coats a spoon. In a separate bowl, dissolve gelatin in cold water. Add to hot custard. Allow to cool. In a large mixing bowl, beat egg whites. Fold into cooled custard. Fold in cream (or whipped topping). Break angel food cake into pieces into a 9 x 13-inch glass or plastic serving container. Pour in custard-cream mixture. Chill. May be topped with drained pineapple or strawberries or enjoyed plain. Serves 8 to 10.

Patsy H. McNeill, Stanly County

This is my children's favorite dessert. Sometimes, they ask for it instead of a birthday cake.

—

APPLE SNACK CAKE

3/4 cup vegetable oil
2 eggs
2 cups sugar
2 1/2 cups all-purpose flour
1 teaspoon baking soda
1 teaspoon baking powder
1 teaspoon salt
1 teaspoon ground cinnamon
3 cups peeled, finely chopped apples
1 cup chopped pecans
1 6-ounce package butterscotch morsels

Preheat oven to 350° F. Combine oil, eggs, and sugar in a large mixing bowl. Beat at medium speed with electric mixer until well mixed. In a separate bowl, combine flour, soda, baking power, salt, and cinnamon, and stir. Add dry ingredients alternately with apples to egg mixture, mixing well. Stir in pecans and half of butterscotch morsels. Spread batter into a greased 13 x 9 x 2-inch baking pan. Sprinkle batter with remaining morsels. Bake at 350° F. for 55 to 60 minutes or until done.

Bertie Vaughn, Iredell County

This has been a favorite in my family from way back. My aunt (now deceased) used this recipe when I was a little girl, and now I am most fortunate to use it. I always try to use North Carolina apples.

Oven Temperature

Although all of the recipes use degrees, old recipes sometimes use words to describe oven temperature. Here's the modern translation.

Slow oven is 250 to 300° F.
Slow moderate oven is 325° F.
Moderate is 350°
Qquick moderate is 375°
Moderately hot is 400°
Hot is 425 to 450°
Very hot is 475 to 500° F.

AUTUMN APPLE CAKE

2 cups granulated sugar
1 1/3 cups vegetable oil
2 eggs, well beaten
1 tablespoon vanilla
1 large banana, mashed
3 cups all-purpose flour,
   sifted

1 teaspoon baking soda
1/2 teaspoon baking powder
1/2 teaspoon salt
3 cups apples, chopped
1/2 cup pecans, chopped
   (optional)

Preheat oven to 350° F. Mix sugar and vegetable oil. Add eggs, vanilla, and banana. Add flour, soda, baking powder, and salt, and mix. Batter will be stiff. Pour into greased and floured bundt pan. Bake approximately 60 minutes. Cool. Frost with Cream Cheese Frosting (recipe follows).

Hilda McGee, Davidson County

CREAM CHEESE FROSTING

1 stick margarine
8 ounces cream cheese,
   softened

1 1/2 cups confectioners'
   sugar
1 teaspoon vanilla
Chopped pecans

Cream margarine and cream cheese. Mix in sugar, vanilla, and pecans. Spread over cake.

Hilda McGee, Davidson County

In the past, this was a must for corn shuckings and similar get-togethers. Now, it's just delicious eating.

North Carolina Apples

North Carolina apple growers received $18 million in cash receipts from sales in 2000, according to the North Carolina Department of Agriculture. Red Delicious, Golden Delicious, Rome, and Gala make up the bulk of our state's apple production.

DRIED APPLE CAKE

2 1/2 cups dried apples,
  cooked
3 teaspoons baking soda
1 cup shortening
2 cups brown sugar
2 eggs, beaten
4 cups sifted all-purpose
  flour

1 cup chopped pecans or
  walnuts
1 pound raisins
1/2 pound dates, chopped
1 cup fig, strawberry, or
  pear preserves
1 teaspoon vanilla flavoring

Preheat oven to 350° F. Sprinkle baking soda on hot apples. Cream
shortening and sugar together. Add beaten eggs to creamed mixture.
Then gradually add flour. Stir in nuts, raisins, and dates. Lastly, stir
in preserves and vanilla flavoring. Mix well. Pour into greased and
floured tube pan. Bake for 80 to 90 minutes. Cake is done when
toothpick inserted in center comes out clean. Cool cake for 10
minutes on wire rack before removing from pan. Freezes well.

Helen F. Rhyne, Gaston County

*My mother-in-law (now 97 years old) always made this for the
Christmas holidays. We like it better than fruit cake. We use our
own dried apples.*

FRESH APPLE CAKE

2 cups sugar
1 cup oil
1 teaspoon vanilla
3 eggs

2 1/2 cups self-rising flour
3 cups raw apples, chopped
1 cup pecans
Cinnamon to taste

Preheat oven to 300° F. Put all ingredients in bowl, and stir with a
spoon (do not use mixer). Then mix by hand until well blended.
Pour into a tube pan. Bake for 1 hour.

Sue Arnette, Duplin County

Fresh Fruit Garnishes

*Garnish desserts with fresh fruits like whole raspberries, blue-
berries, blackberries, strawberries, sliced kiwi fruit and orange
sections, which do not brown, and can be placed on the cake or
pudding just before serving.*

UNION COUNTY FRESH APPLE CAKE

1 cup cooking oil
2 cups sugar
2 eggs, well-beaten
2 teaspoons vanilla

3 cups self-rising flour
3 cups fresh chopped apples
1 cup chopped nuts
1 box chopped dates

Preheat oven to 325° F. Combine oil and sugar. Add well-beaten eggs and vanilla. Add flour. Stir in apples, nuts, and dates. Pour into 9 x 13-inch pan. Bake for 1 hour and 15 minutes. Top with Fresh Apple Cake Glaze (recipe below).

Dale Evans, Union County

FRESH APPLE CAKE GLAZE

2 cups brown sugar
5 tablespoons cream or milk
1/2 cup butter

1 teaspoon vanilla
1/2 teaspoon baking powder

Mix sugar, cream, butter, and vanilla together in a saucepan. Heat until melted. Stir in baking powder. Spread on top of cake.

Dale Evans, Union County

MOUNTAIN APPLE CAKE

3 eggs
1 1/2 cups oil
2 cups sugar
3 cups flour
1/2 teaspoon salt
1 teaspoon baking soda
2 teaspoons cinnamon
2 teaspoons vanilla extract
3 cups apples, chopped

1 1/2 cups pecans and black
    walnuts, chopped and
    mixed
Topping:
1 cup brown sugar
1/2 cup milk
1/2 cup butter
1 teaspoon vanilla

Preheat oven to 350° F. Mix eggs, oil, and sugar; blend well. In a separate bowl, sift flour, salt, soda, and cinnamon together. Add to egg mixture. Add vanilla, apples, and nuts. Mix well. Pour into greased 8-inch tube or bundt pan. Bake 1 hour. I check cake at 50 minutes with toothpick.

Prepare topping: Combine all ingredients, and cook 2 1/2 minutes.

Pour hot topping over cake while it is still in the pan. Let cool.
When cake is completely cool, remove from pan.

Juanita McKnight, Wayne County

*My family loves apples, and we have many apple trees in our yard.
This is just one other way of using a product that we grow and love
so much.*

—

APRICOT NECTAR CAKE

1 package lemon cake mix	1 cup apricot nectar
4 eggs	*Glaze:*
1/2 cup sugar	2 cups powdered sugar
1/2 cup oil or butter	1/4 cup apricot nectar

Preheat oven to 300° F. Mix cake ingredients, and pour into a tube
pan. Bake at 300° F. for 1 hour. Cool in pan 10 minutes. Invert onto
plate. Mix glaze ingredients, and pour over warm cake.

Jennifer W. Ballance, Wayne County

BANANA SNACK CAKE

1 cup margarine, softened	2 cups flour
1 cup sugar	1 cup quick rolled oats
2 eggs	1 1/2 teaspoons baking soda
1/2 cup buttermilk	1/2 teaspoon salt
1 cup (2 medium) bananas, mashed	1 6-ounce package semisweet chocolate chips
1 teaspoon vanilla	1/2 cup chopped nuts

Preheat oven to 350° F. In a large bowl, combine margarine, sugar,
and eggs, and mix well. Stir in buttermilk, bananas, and vanilla;
blend thoroughly. Lightly spoon flour into a measuring cup and
level off. Stir in flour, oats, soda, and salt; mix well. Stir in chips.
Spread batter in 9 x 13-inch greased pan. Sprinkle nuts evenly over
the top. Bake 30 to 35 minutes.

Janet Singleton, Wake County

*This is an easy scratch cake that doesn't need any frosting. I would
say it serves 12, but actually most people have seconds, or even
thirds.*

BETTER THAN KISSES CAKE

1 yellow cake mix
3 eggs
1/2 cup water
1/2 cup oil
1 large instant pudding mix,
  chocolate or vanilla

1 cup sour cream
4 ounces German chocolate
  squares, grated
1 cup chocolate chips

Preheat oven to 350° F. Mix first 6 ingredients well. Fold in chocolate and chocolate chips. Put in greased tube pan, and bake for 45 minutes, or until top is firm.

Sandra Vann, Northampton County

BETTER THAN SEX CAKE

Duncan Hines butter cake
  mix
1 teaspoon butter flavoring
1 20-ounce can crushed
  pineapple
1 cup sugar

1 3-ounce package instant
  vanilla pudding
2 cups coconut
2 cups milk
1 16-ounce container Cool
  Whip

Mix cake according to directions on box, adding butter flavoring. Bake in a 10 x 15-inch baking dish (or 8 x 8-inch or 7 x 11-inch dish). Remove from oven, and make holes in cake with a fork. Boil the pineapple and sugar for 5 minutes, then pour over cake. Cool. Make pudding according to package directions, and add 1 cup coconut. Pour over cake. Put on layer of Cool Whip, and sprinkle 1 cup coconut over cake.

Mrs. Jack (Martha) Shore, Yadkin County

This is an easy recipe!

BLACK BOTTOM CAKE

1/2 cup cocoa	2 teaspoons white vinegar
3 cups flour	*Topping:*
2 cups sugar	8 ounces cream cheese
2/3 cup oil	2/3 cup sugar
1 teaspoon vanilla	2 eggs
2 teaspoons baking soda	1/4 teaspoon salt
1 teaspoon salt	1/2 cup chopped nuts
2 cups water	1/2 cup chocolate chips

Preheat oven to 350° F. Mix cake ingredients together. Pour into ungreased bundt pan. *Prepare topping:* Mix cream cheese, eggs, sugar, and salt together. Pour over cake batter. Sprinkle nuts and chocolate chips over top of cake. Bake for 45 to 60 minutes.

Evelyn Sneed, Granville County

BLUEBERRY TEA CAKE

1/3 cup shortening	1 cup sugar
2 cups all-purpose flour	3/4 cup milk
2 teaspoons baking powder	1 egg
1/4 teaspoon salt	1 cup blueberries

Preheat oven to 350° F. Stir the shortening to soften. In a separate bowl, sift together flour, baking powder, salt, and sugar. Add to shortening, and mix well. Add milk. Beat vigorously at least 2 minutes. Add egg. Beat 1 minute. Stir in blueberries carefully. Pour into greased 9 x 9 x 2-inch cake pan. Bake about 50 minutes.

Theresa McIntyre, Pender County

This recipe has always been special to me. My grandmother always made it when her grandchildren came to visit.

Decorating Your Cake

Garnish your cake with fresh fruit, chopped nuts, coconut, crushed candy, or chocolate shavings. You can use food coloring to tint coconut. Use the palm of your hand to press sliced almonds, chopped nuts, or crushed candy onto frosted cake sides.

BUTTER PECAN CAKE

Betty Crocker butter pecan
cake mix
4 eggs
1 cup water
3/4 cup oil

Betty Crocker coconut
pecan icing
1/4 cup powdered sugar
1/4 cup chopped nuts

Preheat oven to 350° F. Beat cake mix, eggs, water, and oil with mixer until well beaten. Fold pecan icing into batter. Spray bundt pan well. Put powdered sugar and nuts in bottom of pan, and pour batter in pan. Bake for 50 to 60 minutes.

Elizabeth Parrish, Chowan County

Good any time and easy to make.

BUTTER PECAN CHEESECAKE

1 1/2 cups graham cracker
crumbs
1/3 cup sugar
1/3 cup butter or
margarine, melted
1 1/2 cups finely chopped
toasted pecans, divided
3 8-ounce packages cream
cheese, softened

1 1/2 cups sugar
3 eggs
2 8-ounce cartons sour
cream
1 teaspoon vanilla extract
1/2 teaspoon butter
flavoring

Combine graham cracker crumbs, 1/3 cup sugar, butter, and 1/2 cup pecans. Set aside 1/3 cup of this mixture. Firmly press rest into bottom of a 9-inch springform pan. Beat cream cheese with an electric mixer until light and fluffy. Add 1 1/2 cups sugar, mixing well. Add eggs, one at a time, mixing well after each addition. Add sour cream and flavorings, and mix well. Stir in 1 cup pecans. Spoon mixture into pan. Sprinkle with reserved graham cracker crumb-pecan mixture. Bake at 475° F. for 10 minutes, then reduce temperature to 300° F. and bake an additional 50 minutes. Let cool at room temperature.

Jerrie Hasty, Union County

CARAMEL CAKE

1 box of Duncan Hines
  butter recipe golden

Icing:
1 stick butter (no
  substitutions)

1 16-ounce box light brown
  sugar
1 5-ounce can evaporated
  milk
1 teaspoon vanilla

Follow directions on cake box, and make three layers. *Prepare icing:* Mix first three ingredients until sugar is melted. Start cooking slowly, then increase until boiling. Cook 4 or 5 minutes until it forms a soft ball in cold water. Remove from heat, and add vanilla. Beat until creamy. I set saucepan in cold water to cool it quicker. As it starts to cool down, start putting some on the bottom cake layer. Check to see if it has cooled down so it will not run too much when you get to the top layer. Chopped nuts may be added.

Eva Ketelsleger, Duplin County

Everyone has a Carrot Cake of their dreams. Here are five North Carolina versions, and the first two don't even involve grating carrots!

CARROT CAKE

2 cups sugar
3 eggs
1/2 cup oil
2 jars junior carrot baby
  food
1 6 1/2-ounce can crushed
  pineapple, do not drain

2 1/2 cups self-rising flour
1 teaspoon salt
1 teaspoon cinnamon
1 teaspoon baking soda
1 teaspoon vanilla

Preheat oven to 350° F. Cream together sugar, eggs, and oil. Add carrots and pineapple. Mix well. Add flour and remaining ingredients. Pour into three greased and floured pans. Bake for 30 minutes. Let cool; then frost with Cream Cheese Frosting (recipe follows).

Dot Ballance, Wayne County

CREAM CHEESE FROSTING FOR CARROT CAKE

1 stick margarine
8 ounces cream cheese
1 pound confectioners'
  sugar

1 teaspoon vanilla
1 cup nuts

Cream together softened margarine and cream cheese. Add powdered sugar, vanilla, and nuts. Spread on cooled cake.

Dot Ballance, Wayne County

CARROT CAKE

2 cups sugar
2 1/2 cups self-rising flour
1 teaspoon salt
1 teaspoon baking soda
2 teaspoons cinnamon

3 eggs
1/2 cup oil
2 jars of stage 3 baby food
  carrots
1 teaspoon vanilla

Preheat oven to 350° F. Grease three 9-inch round baking pans. Mix sugar, flour, salt, soda, and cinnamon. Then add eggs, oil, baby food carrots, and vanilla. Blend together. Pour into pans. Bake for 35 minutes. Top with icing (recipe follows).

Jenny Odom Ballance, Wayne County

ICING FOR CARROT CAKE

1 1/2 sticks butter, softened
12 ounces cream cheese,
  softened
1 1/2 teaspoons vanilla

1 1/2 16-ounce boxes
  confectioners' sugar
1 cup nuts

Mix together softened butter and cream cheese. Add vanilla and confectioners' sugar. Hand-blend together, then add nuts. Ice layers.

Jenny Odom Ballance, Wayne County

Plain Flour

Some old recipes call for plain flour. Others don't specify a type of flour. In both cases, you should use all-purpose flour.

CARROT CAKE

2 cups self-rising flour
1 teaspoon cinnamon
1 teaspoon baking soda
1/4 teaspoon salt
2 cups sugar

4 eggs
1 1/4 cups vegetable oil
2 cups grated carrots,
    packed

Preheat oven to 350° F. Sift together flour, cinnamon, baking soda, and salt. Mix together sugar, eggs, and vegetable oil. Combine all ingredients, including the carrots. Pour into three greased and floured 9-inch cake pans. Bake for approximately 40 minutes, or until center is firm. Top with icing (recipe below).

Marie Joyner, Nash County

CARROT CAKE ICING

1/2 stick margarine
1 16-ounce box
    confectioners' (powdered)
    sugar
1 teaspoon vanilla

1 8-ounce package cream
    cheese
1 cup chopped pecans
1 teaspoon milk (more if
    needed to get to spreading
    consistency)

Mix all ingredients together. Spread over cooled cake layers. Serves 18 to 20.

Marie Joyner, Nash County

Good for any occasion.

CARROT CAKE

1 1/4 cups oil
2 cups sugar
4 eggs
2 cups all-purpose flour
2 teaspoons baking soda

2 teaspoons cinnamon
1 teaspoon salt
2 teaspoons vanilla
3 cups grated carrots
1 cup chopped pecans

Preheat oven to 350° F. Mix oil and sugar. Add eggs. Mix with mixer. Add all dry ingredients and vanilla, and beat well. Fold in carrots and nuts. Grease and put waxed paper in three pans, and pour in batter. Bake for 25 to 30 minutes. Top with frosting (recipe below).

Elizabeth Parrish, Chowan County

CARROT CAKE FROSTING

1 8-ounce package cream
  cheese, softened
1 teaspoon vanilla

1 package confectioners'
  powdered sugar

Mix cream cheese and vanilla. Beat in sugar a little at a time. If the frosting is too thick, add a little milk. Spread on top and sides of cake.

Elizabeth Parrish, Chowan County

My husband and boys love this Carrot Cake. We always have it for Christmas and sometimes for their birthdays.

FRESH CARROT CAKE

3 1/2 cups sugar
1/2 cup oil
1/4 cup cold water
4 eggs, separated
3 cups self-rising flour

1 teaspoon baking powder
2 teaspoons cinnamon
1 cup chopped pecans
2 cups grated carrots

Preheat oven to 325° F. Mix sugar and oil. Add water, and mix thoroughly. Add egg yolks, and mix thoroughly. Add flour, baking powder, and cinnamon, and mix thoroughly. Add nuts and well-beaten egg whites, and mix thoroughly. Add grated carrots. Bake for 1 hour if you are making a two-layer cake or using a tube pan. Bake for 35 to 40 minutes if using a single layer pan.

Freida Culler, Watauga County

This cake is a favorite at Christmas.

—

CHERRY NUT CAKE

1 16-ounce can pie cherries
1 teaspoon baking soda
1 cup sifted flour
1 cup sugar
1 egg
4 tablespoons butter
Pinch salt

1 cup chopped pecans
Cherry Sauce:
Juice from cherries
1 cup sugar
1 tablespoon cornstarch
1/2 cup water

Preheat oven to 350° F. Drain juice from cherries into saucepan, and set aside. In a bowl, mix baking soda with cherries, and stir until soda is well mixed. Set aside. Mix flour, 1 cup sugar, egg, butter, and salt in bowl. Add cherries and pecans to mix. Pour into greased 8 x 8-inch pan, and bake for 40 minutes. *Cherry Sauce:* Mix juice from cherries, 1 cup sugar, cornstarch, and water in saucepan; boil until clear. Pour over cake before serving.

Evelyn Stevens, Wake County

I make this every February for George Washington's birthday.

30-MINUTE CHOCOLATE CAKE

2 cups all-purpose flour
2 cups sugar
1/4 teaspoon salt
1 teaspoon cinnamon
2 sticks margarine
3 tablespoons cocoa, sifted
1 cup hot water

2 eggs
1 teaspoon vanilla
1 teaspoon baking soda
1/2 cup buttermilk, *or* use
  1/2 cup milk with 1
  tablespoon vinegar

Preheat oven to 350° F. In a large bowl, mix together flour, sugar, salt, and cinnamon. In a saucepan, bring margarine, cocoa, and water to a rolling boil. Remove from heat, and stir into flour-sugar mixture. Beat with mixer until smooth. Add eggs and vanilla. Dissolve baking soda in buttermilk. Add to mixture, and beat. Batter will be thin. Pour into 9 x 13-inch pan, and bake for 30 minutes.

Pour Quick Chocolate Frosting (recipe follows) over hot cake.
Serves 24.

Deane Avett, Cherokee County

QUICK CHOCOLATE FROSTING

1 cup sugar
1 stick margarine
4 tablespoons cocoa (1/4
   cup), sifted

1/2 cup evaporated milk
1 teaspoon vanilla
1 1/2 to 2 cups sifted
   confectioners' sugar

Mix sugar, margarine, cocoa, and milk together in saucepan. Bring
to a rolling boil, and boil for 1 minute. Remove from heat, and stir
in vanilla and confectioners' sugar. Beat with mixer until smooth,
and pour over hot cake.

Deane Avett, Cherokee County

*My husband and I were in Anchorage, Alaska, in the mid-'60s. A
neighbor of ours served this 30-Minute Chocolate Cake, and I just
had to have the recipe. I have made this cake many times for our
four grown-up children's birthdays and even now when they visit.*

CHOCOLATE ÉCLAIR CAKE

1 package fudge stripe
   cookies, crushed
2 small packages instant
   vanilla pudding
3 cups milk
1 large container Cool
   Whip

Topping:
1 cup sugar
1/4 cup evaporated milk
1/4 cup cocoa
1 stick margarine
1 teaspoon vanilla

Line a 9 x 13-inch dish with half the crushed cookies. Mix together
pudding and milk until it begins to thicken. Fold in Cool Whip.
Spoon half onto the layer of cookies. Repeat with another layer of
cookies and pudding mixture. *Prepare topping:* Boil sugar, milk,
and cocoa for 1 minute. Remove from heat. Add margarine and then
vanilla. Pour over pudding mixture. Chill for several hours before
serving.

Sandra Layton, Durham County

There are never any leftovers with this dessert.

CHOCOLATE ÉCLAIR CAKE

2 packages vanilla instant
  pudding
3 cups milk
1 8-ounce container non-
  dairy topping
1 box graham crackers

Icing:
1/3 cup cocoa
1/4 cup evaporated milk
1 cup sugar
1 stick of margarine
1 teaspoon vanilla
Chopped pecans (optional)

Combine pudding and milk. Beat until thick, then fold in topping.
Layer bottom of a 9 x 13-inch serving dish with whole graham
crackers. Put layer of pudding mixture, then another layer of
crackers and mixture, ending with a layer of crackers on top.
Prepare icing: Bring cocoa, milk, and sugar to boil, stirring
constantly. Let cool 1 minute, and add margarine and vanilla. Mix
thoroughly, and pour over cake. Top with chopped pecans if
desired. Refrigerate overnight.

Glenda Beavers, Duplin County

CHOCOLATE WACKY CAKE

3 cups all-purpose flour
2 cups sugar
4 tablespoons cocoa
2 teaspoons baking soda
1 teaspoon salt

2 or 3 teaspoons vanilla
  flavoring
2 teaspoons vinegar
10 tablespoons margarine,
  melted
2 cups water

Preheat oven to 350° F. Blend together dry ingredients. In a separate
bowl, mix wet ingredients. Combine the wet and dry ingredients.
Pour into greased 9 x 13 x 2-inch baking pan. Bake for 40 minutes,
or until a fine crack forms in center. Serves 16 to 20.

Juanita Wood Haas, Catawba County

*I got this recipe from my mother-in-law. I've made it for my two
sons, and now I make it for my granddaughter, Amelia Haas, who is
allergic to milk. It's a moist dark chocolate cake that needs no
icing.*

COCONUT CAKE

1 cup butter or margarine
1 1/2 cups sugar
1 whole egg and 4 egg yolks
(save egg whites for
frosting)
2 cups all-purpose flour
1 heaping teaspoon baking
powder
1 cup milk

1 teaspoon lemon extract
Filling:
1 coconut, grated, *or* 1 12-
ounce package frozen
coconut (keep enough to
sprinkle over top of cake)
Milk of coconut, strained,
or use about 1 cup milk
1 1/2 cups sugar

Preheat oven to 350° F. Cream butter and sugar, and add whole egg
and yolks one at a time, In a separate bowl, mix flour and baking
powder, then add to butter-sugar-egg mixture. Add milk. Add lemon
extract. Pour into three 9-inch cake pans. Bake at 25 to 30 minutes,
or until cake is done. *Prepare filling:* Mix coconut, coconut milk,
and sugar in a saucepan. Bring the mixture to a boil. Spread filling
between cake layers. For a moist cake, prick layers with spoon
while spreading filling so juice will go through cake. Top with
frosting (recipe below).

Maxine Jordan, Bladen County

FROSTING FOR COCONUT CAKE

4 egg whites
12 heaping tablespoons
sugar

Shredded coconut

Put egg whites and sugar into double boiler over boiling water. Let
water be on high heat. Start beating with electric beater. Beat until it
forms a slick shiny peak. Spread over cake at once. Then sprinkle
coconut on cake while it is still moist so it will stick to cake.

Maxine Jordan, Bladen County
*I have used this recipe for 45 years. I have tried many coconut cake
recipes, but this is worth every minute I put into making it. It seems
long, but it really isn't.*

COCONUT CAKE

2 1/2 cups Red Band self-
  rising flour
2 1/2 cups sugar
1 cup milk
1/2 cup Crisco shortening

2 whole eggs
4 egg yolks (save egg whites
  for frosting)
2 teaspoons vanilla

Preheat oven to 350° F. Mix flour, sugar, milk, and shortening, and beat for 2 minutes. Add eggs and vanilla, and beat another 2 minutes. Pour into three 9-inch greased cake pans. Bake approximately 30 minutes, or until a toothpick comes out clean after inserting in the middle of each layer. Top with Coconut Frosting (recipe follows).

Carnell Autry, Sampson County

COCONUT FROSTING

1 1/2 cups sugar
1/2 cup light corn syrup
5 tablespoons water

4 egg whites
1/2 teaspoon cream of tartar
14 ounces coconut

Boil sugar, syrup, and water until it will spin a thread. While mixture is boiling, beat egg whites and cream of tartar until stiff. Add syrup mixture while still beating. Beat until it reaches consistency to spread. Put coconut and icing between layers and on top and sides.

Carnell Autry, Sampson County

A family favorite for any occasion.

Baking Cakes

Unless the recipe specifies otherwise, preheat the oven. Your cake may crack and have an uneven surface if you start baking from a cold oven. If the oven temperature is too high, your cake may have tunnels and cracks: A coarse texture can be the result of an oven temperature that was too low or not combining fat and sugar well enough.

EASY COCONUT CAKE

1 package Duncan Hines
golden or yellow pudding
cake mix

4 ounces frozen coconut

Make cake as usual, but add approximately 4 ounces of frozen coconut to it before baking. Bake in a greased 9 x 13-inch dish according to package directions. Top with frosting (recipe follows).

FROSTING FOR EASY COCONUT CAKE

2 cups milk
1 1/2 cups sugar
2 ounces coconut

1 8-ounce container
whipped topping

Boil milk and sugar for 1 minute. Cool. Prick holes in cooled cake with a fork. Pour milk mixture onto cake. Mix 2 ounces of coconut into an 8-ounce container of whipped topping. Spread on cake. Sprinkle on additional coconut for garnish. Refrigerate. This cake gets better and better.

Sandra Layton, Durham County

We always have this at Christmas.

SNOWBALL CUPCAKES

1/2 stick butter
1 cup sugar
1/2 cup diluted evaporated
milk

1 2/3 cups self-rising flour
1 teaspoon vanilla flavoring
2 egg whites
Coconut

Preheat oven to 375° F. Cream together the butter and sugar. Add milk, flour, and vanilla. Beat egg whites until fluffy, and fold them into the butter-sugar-flour mixture. Pour into a muffin pan with paper liners. Bake about 30 minutes. Make your favorite white icing, frost cooled cupcakes, and top with coconut.

Ethel Pitt, Edgecombe County

This is my husband's favorite recipe. It was handed down to us from his mother.

DIRT CAKE

1/2 stick butter
1 8-ounce package
  Philadelphia Brand cream
  cheese, softened
1 cup powdered sugar
1 5-ounce package instant
  chocolate pudding

3 1/2 cups milk
2 8-ounce containers of
  Cool Whip
1 20-ounce package Oreo
  cookies, crushed
1 package Gummy Worms

Mix butter, cream cheese, and powdered sugar. In a separate bowl, mix pudding mix and milk until it begins to thicken. Fold in Cool Whip. Combine two mixtures. Fill bottom of bowl with half of the crushed cookies. Add half of the pudding mixture. Add a third of crushed cookies. Add remaining pudding mixture. Top with remaining cookie crumbs. Place Gummy Worms in top layer as if they were coming up out of the dirt. Refrigerate.

Tara Crayton, Cabarrus County

Children love this quick and easy dessert.

EARTHQUAKE CAKE

1 cup chopped pecans
1 cup coconut
1 box German chocolate
  cake mix
Ingredients listed on cake
  mix to make cake

Topping:
1 stick margarine, melted
1 8-ounce package cream
  cheese
1 16-ounce box
  confectioners' sugar

Preheat oven to 350° F. Spray 9 x 13-inch pan with cooking spray. Spread pecans and coconut in bottom of pan. Prepare cake mix as directed on box (I use milk instead of water). Pour mixture over top of nuts and coconut. Melt margarine and cream cheese; add box of powdered sugar. Drizzle over top of cake mixture. Bake for 40 minutes or until done.

Della Stephens, Forsyth County

EGGLESS CAKE WITH COFFEE ICING

1/2 cup butter
1 1/3 cups sugar
1 cup milk
1 cup raisins
2 1/2 cups flour

1/3 level teaspoon salt
3 level teaspoons baking
   powder
1/2 level teaspoon mixed
   spices

Preheat oven to 325° F. Beat butter and sugar until light and creamy. Add milk, then raisins. In a separate bowl, sift flour, salt, baking powder, and spices together. Add this to the other ingredients. Turn into a tube pan, and bake for 75 minutes. Top with Coffee Icing (recipe follows).

Helen Mae Hilliard King, Vance/Warren counties

COFFEE ICING

1/2 cup strong, clear coffee
2 cups granulated sugar

2 teaspoons vanilla extract

Cook the coffee and sugar together until a little dropped in cold water forms a soft ball. Cool. Add vanilla. Beat until stiff enough to spread.

Helen Mae Hilliard King, Vance/Warren counties

Lucy Polk Paschall Hilliard and her husband, Hugh Palmer Hilliard, raised chickens and sold the eggs. When the hens stopped laying, this is the cake Lucy would make.

FIG PRESERVE CAKE

2 cups all-purpose flour
1 teaspoon baking soda
1 teaspoon cloves
1 teaspoon cinnamon
1 teaspoon nutmeg
1 teaspoon salt
1 1/2 cups sugar
1 cup vegetable oil
3 eggs, beaten
1 cup buttermilk

1 cup fig preserves (not
   drained)
1 cup chopped nuts
1 teaspoon vanilla
Sauce:
1 cup sugar
1 tablespoon corn syrup
1 teaspoon vanilla
1/2 cup margarine
1/2 cup buttermilk

Preheat oven to 350° F. Sift together dry ingredients. Add oil, and mix well. Add eggs and buttermilk gradually. Fold in preserves and nuts. Add vanilla. Pour into greased and floured 9 x 13-inch pan. Bake for 45 to 50 minutes. *Prepare sauce:* Mix ingredients together, bring to a boil, and boil for 3 minutes. Pour hot sauce over hot cake.

Wilma B. McCollum, Union County

GERMAN CHOCOLATE DELIGHT

1 box German chocolate cake mix, prepared
1 can Eagle Brand condensed milk
1 4- to 6-ounce jar caramel ice cream topping

1 14- to 16-ounce container Cool Whip
6 Heath Bars crushed (or Butterfingers)

Mix and bake cake as directed on package in 9 x 13-inch dish. After cake is done, punch holes in cake with a wooden spoon handle. Drizzle sweetened condensed milk over top of cake. Cover with caramel. Cool completely. Spoon Cool Whip over the top. Sprinkle with crushed candy bars, then refrigerate.

Nancy Johnston, Buncombe County

GINGERBREAD

2 eggs
1/2 cup brown sugar
1/2 cup sour cream
1/2 cup molasses
1 teaspoon ground ginger
1 1/2 cups flour
1 teaspoon baking soda

1/4 teaspoon salt
1/2 cup margarine, melted
1/2 cup chopped dates (optional)
1/4 cup raisins (optional)
1/4 cup chopped nuts (optional)

Preheat oven to 350° F. Beat eggs and sugar. Add sour cream, molasses, and ginger. Stir until smooth. Sift in flour, baking soda, and salt, and beat again. Add chopped dates, raisins, and nuts, if desired. Stir in margarine. Pour into buttered 8-inch or 9-inch square baking pan. Bake 25 minutes or until done.

Wilma B. McCollum, Union County

Gingerbread may be topped with cinnamon-flavored applesauce. Wilma McCollum is a member of the Union County Farm Bureau Women's Committee and a past chairperson of the N.C. Farm Bureau State Women's Committee.

GINGERBREAD

1 2/3 cups cake flour
1/4 teaspoon salt
1/2 teaspoon baking soda
1/2 teaspoon cinnamon
3/4 teaspoon ginger
1/2 teaspoon allspice

1/3 cup butter
1/2 cup sugar
1 egg
1/2 cup light molasses or
   sorghum
1/2 cup buttermilk

Preheat oven to 350° F. Sift flour, measure, and resift 3 times with salt, soda, and spices. In a separate bowl, cream butter until smooth. Add sugar and egg; beat until light and fluffy. Add molasses, and beat for 2 minutes. Add flour mixture and buttermilk, beginning and ending with flour and beating well after each addition. Pour into a greased 11 x 7 x 1 1/2-inch pan. Bake for 25 to 30 minutes. Let cool 5 minutes, and turn out on rack. Serve with cream or applesauce.

Pearl King Morton, Granville County

Porthenia "Sis" Boyd King had four children to feed alone after her husband, Jimmy Wyatt King, died. She used available foods to make recipes work. This is one of those recipes.

HERSHEY SYRUP CAKE

1 stick margarine
1 cup sugar
4 eggs
1 cup self-rising flour

1 16-ounce can (2 cups)
   Hershey's chocolate syrup
1 teaspoon vanilla

Preheat oven to 350° F. Cream together margarine and sugar. Add eggs one at a time, beating after each addition. Add flour, chocolate syrup, and vanilla, and beat well. Spread evenly into three 8-inch cake pans. Bake for 20 to 25 minutes. When cake has cooled, frost with Chocolate Frosting (recipe follows on next page).

Iris S. Conner, Rockingham County

CHOCOLATE FROSTING

1 stick margarine	1 cup marshmallows
1 cup sugar	1 cup chocolate morsels
1 cup evaporated milk	1/2 teaspoon vanilla

Boil margarine, sugar, and evaporated milk together for 2 to 3 minutes. Add marshmallows and chocolate morsels, and stir until melted. Cool, and add vanilla. Spread on cooled cake layers.

Iris S. Conner, Rockingham County

This recipe is quite old as it was made when Hershey syrup cost only 25 cents a can. My 87-year-old sister baked this cake for her family's birthdays. Her granddaughters named this cake "the Dynamite Cake." The granddaughters are now grown and married with children, and they make "the Dynamite Cake" for their families' birthdays.

HONEY BUN CAKE

1 box yellow cake mix	1 cup brown sugar
3/4 cup oil	3 teaspoon cinnamon
4 eggs	*Topping:*
1 cup milk	1 cup confectioners' sugar
1 cup chopped nuts	3 tablespoons milk
(optional)	1 teaspoon vanilla

Preheat oven to 300° F. Mix cake mix, oil, eggs, and milk until well blended. Pour into a greased 13 x 9-inch baking pan or dish. Mix together the nuts, brown sugar, and cinnamon. Sprinkle over batter, and swirl into batter with a spoon. Bake for 50 minutes. *Prepare topping*: Blend ingredients well, and spread on cake as soon as it is removed from oven. Delicious served warm. Serves 12 to 15.

Rita Clark, Vance County

Confectioners' Sugar

Confectioners' sugar is also known as powdered sugar or 10x sugar. This finely ground sugar dissolves quickly and is often used in frostings and icings. If you see white sugar listed as an ingredient, use white granulated sugar, not confectioners' sugar.

HOT MILK CAKE WITH FIG FILLING

2 cups sugar
2 cups flour
1 1/2 teaspoons baking
  powder
4 eggs, beaten
1 teaspoon vanilla extract
1 cup hot milk

1/4 cup butter
Filling:
1 pound fresh figs, cut up
1 cup water
4 level tablespoons sugar
Juice of 1 lemon

Preheat oven to 350° F. Mix sugar, flour, and baking powder. Add beaten eggs and vanilla. Add hot milk and butter. Pour into 11 x 7-inch baking pan and bake for 30 to 35 minutes. *Prepare filling:* In a saucepan, cook figs, water, and sugar until they form a thick pulp. Add lemon juice and beat well. When cool, spread on cake; if you've made a layer cake, use between layers.

Betty Jean King, Franklin/Warren counties

Susan Sledge Harris Stallings Kness brought this recipe to her husband, Solomon Stallings, and their children from her family in Franklin County. After she married and moved to Warren County, she had a fig bush planted on their farm so that she could make this cake.

ITALIAN CREAM CAKE

5 eggs
1 stick butter or margarine
1/2 cup vegetable
  shortening
2 cups sugar
1 teaspoon baking soda
1 cup buttermilk
2 cups all-purpose flour
1 teaspoon vanilla

Filling:
1 stick margarine (room
  temperature)
1 8-ounce package cream
  cheese
1 pound box confectioners'
  sugar
1 cup Angel Flake coconut
1 cup pecan meal, *or* finely
  chopped pecans

Preheat oven to 375° F. Separate the 5 eggs. Beat the egg whites in a bowl, and set aside. Cream together butter, shortening, and sugar. Add egg yolks one at a time, beating well after each addition. Mix soda and buttermilk in a 2-cup measure as the mixture will bubble up. Add flour and milk alternately, blending well. Lastly, add the vanilla flavoring and fold in the beaten egg whites. Pour into two greased and floured 8- or 9-inch round cake pans. Bake for 30 minutes. *Prepare filling:* Combine ingredients, and beat with an electric mixer until light and fluffy. Use as a filling and frosting on cooled cake.

Juanita Wood Haas, Catawba County

This was a favorite recipe of my mother, Hildreth Norman Wood.

—

KENTUCKY BUTTER CAKE

1 cup butter or margarine
2 cups sugar
4 eggs
3 cups all-purpose flour
1 teaspoon salt
1 teaspoon baking powder
1/2 teaspoon baking soda
1 teaspoon vanilla flavoring
1 teaspoon almond
   flavoring

1 teaspoon butter flavoring
1 teaspoon lemon flavoring
1 cup buttermilk
Butter sauce:
1 cup sugar
1/4 cup hot water
1/2 cup butter or margarine
2 tablespoons rum flavoring
   or sherry

Preheat oven to 325° F. Cream butter and sugar until fluffy. Add eggs one at a time, and beat well. Add remaining ingredients, and blend well. Continue beating for 2 minutes at medium speed. Pour into a 10-inch tube pan that has been greased on bottom only. Bake for 60 to 65 minutes. Take from oven, prick top of cake with a fork, and pour warm butter sauce over warm cake. *Prepare butter sauce:* Combine all ingredients except flavoring in a saucepan, and heat until butter is melted and sugar is dissolved. Do not boil. Remove from heat. Stir in flavoring. Drizzle over hot cake. Cool cake completely before removing from pan.

Scottie Saltz, Clay County

This recipe has been a family favorite since my great-grandmother's time. My mother, who was well known for her wonderful cooking, made this cake often. She also won awards for this delicious cake.

GRANDMA PHELPS' MAYONNAISE CAKE

1 cup raisins
1 teaspoon baking soda
1 1/2 cups hot water
2/3 cup mayonnaise
1 cup sugar

1 1/2 cups self-rising flour
2 eggs
1 cup pecans, broken in
   pieces

Place raisins and soda in water. Let stand 1 hour. Preheat oven to 350° F. Cream mayonnaise and sugar; add to raisin mixture. Add flour and eggs. Add pecans. Mix well. Place in three 8- to 9-inch round cake pans that have been sprayed with vegetable spray and floured. Bake 20 to 30 minutes until done. Ice with Minute Frosting (recipe follows).

Jessica Tice, Currituck County

MINUTE FROSTING

1 1/2 cups sugar	**1 1/2 teaspoons light Karo**
2 egg whites	**corn syrup**
5 tablespoons water	**1 teaspoon vanilla flavoring**

Combine all ingredients, except vanilla flavoring. Blend thoroughly, and place over boiling water. Beat with an electric hand mixer until frosting stands in a peak, approximately 7 minutes. Remove from heat, and add flavoring. Beat until frosting forms swirls and ridges. Cake serves 12 to 16.

Jessica Tice, Currituck County

My grandmother made Mayonnaise Cake for Thanksgiving and Christmas. We always looked forward to those special holiday times as Grandmom would make us our favorite cake. She passed this recipe down to my mother, who also only made it for the holidays, and my mother passed it down to me and my two sisters. Now this is our special cake during the holidays, and we remember Grandmom and the fun times at Grandmom's house. Christmas isn't Christmas without her cake and the fond memories.

MILK CHOCOLATE BAR CAKE

1 18.25-ounce package	**1/2 cup granulated sugar**
Swiss chocolate cake mix	**10 1.5-ounce milk chocolate**
Frosting:	**candy bars with almonds,**
1 8-ounce package cream	**divided**
cheese, softened	**1 12-ounce container frozen**
1 cup powdered	**whipped topping, thawed**
confectioners' sugar	

Preheat oven to 325° F. Prepare cake batter according to package directions. Pour into three greased and floured 8-inch round cake pans. Bake for 20 to 25 minutes, or until a wooden pick inserted in center comes out clean. Cool in pans on wire racks 10 minutes. Remove from pans, and cool completely on wire racks.

Prepare frosting: Beat cream cheese and sugars at medium speed with an electric mixer until mixture is creamy. Chop 8 candy bars finely. Fold cream cheese mixture and chopped candy into whipped topping. Spread icing between layers and on top and sides of cake. Chop remaining 2 candy bars. Sprinkle half of chopped candy bars over cake. Press remaining chopped candy along bottom edge of cake.

Mary Jane Sessions, Columbus County

OLD-FASHIONED MOLASSES STACK CAKE

1 cup packed brown sugar	1 teaspoon ginger
1 cup shortening	Dash of salt
1 cup molasses	5 1/2 cups all-purpose flour
1 cup buttermilk	About 6 1/2 cups apple
2 eggs, beaten	butter, cooked dried
1 teaspoon baking soda	apples, *or* applesauce

Preheat oven to 350° F. Combine sugar, shortening, and molasses. Beat until smooth. Add buttermilk, eggs, soda, ginger, and salt. Mix well. Add flour 1 cup at a time, beating until blended (do not overbeat). Divide dough into 10 portions. Place each one on a greased cookie sheet. Pat into 10-inch circles. Bake for 5 to 7 minutes. Cool layers on rack.

Stack the layers, spreading applesauce, apple butter, or cooked dried apples between them and on top. Let sit in refrigerator a few days to moisten. Makes one large cake.

Joyce Dixon, Alleghany County

MOM'S LAZY DAISY CAKE

1/2 cup milk	1 cup flour
1 tablespoon butter	1 teaspoon baking powder
2 eggs	1/2 teaspoon salt
1 cup sugar	1 teaspoon vanilla

Preheat oven to 350° F. In a saucepan, combine milk and butter, and heat. Do not boil. Beat eggs until light. Add sugar and beat vigorously. Sift together flour, baking powder, and salt. Stir into egg mixture, and add vanilla. Add milk mixture, stirring carefully. Pour into a 9-inch square baking pan. Bake for 30 to 35 minutes. Top with frosting (recipe follows).

Shirley Pendergrass, Franklin County

MOM'S LAZY DAISY FROSTING

2/3 cup brown sugar
1/3 cup butter, melted
2 tablespoons heavy cream

1/2 cup coconut
1/2 cup chopped nuts

Heat sugar, butter, and cream in saucepan, stirring until creamy. Pour over warm cake. Sprinkle with coconut and nuts. Place cake under boiler for 5 minutes to caramelize frosting. Serves 8 to 10.

Shirley Pendergrass, Franklin County

NUT RAISIN CAKE

1 14- to 16-ounce box
  raisins
3 cups self-rising flour
2 sticks butter

5 eggs
2 cups sugar
1 quart nuts

Preheat oven to 325° F. To plump up raisins, put them in a saucepan, and just cover with water. Bring to a boil, then drain. Mix well with flour, butter, eggs, and sugar. Fold in nuts. Pour into 10-inch tube pan. Bake for 1 1/2 hours.

Thelma Blake, Columbus County

My Aunt Lucy made this for holiday meals.

OLD NORTH STATE CAKE

1 pound butter
1 pound (3 cups) sugar
1 pound (6) eggs
1 pound sweet potatoes,
  peeled, raw, coarsely
  grated
3/4 cup chopped pecans

1 pound (4 cups)
  unbleached all-purpose
  flour
1 tablespoon baking powder
1 tablespoon cinnamon
1 cup milk

Preheat oven to 350° F. Using an electric mixer, cream together butter and sugar. Add eggs one at a time, beating after each addition. Remove from electric mixer, and proceed with hand mixing. Stir in grated sweet potatoes and chopped pecans. In a separate bowl, combine flour, baking powder, and cinnamon. Add dry ingredients and milk to the sweet potato mixture, alternating dry with wet and beginning and ending with dry. Pour batter into a floured bundt pan. Bake for 1 hour, or until a toothpick inserted into the cake comes out clean.

Sharon Freeman, Wake County

This cake is an original—a cross between a pound cake and a carrot cake. Applesauce can replace part of the butter to reduce the fat content. Since it's a very moist cake, it doesn't need frosting.

ORANGE SLICE CAKE

4 eggs
2 sticks margarine
2 cups sugar
3 3/4 cups all-purpose flour
1 teaspoon salt
1 teaspoon baking soda
1/2 cup buttermilk
1 teaspoon vanilla
1 8-ounce box cut-up dates

2 cups chopped pecans
1 pound orange slices, cut in small pieces
1 can flaked coconut
Icing:
1 cup orange juice
Grated rind of 1 orange
2 cups powdered confectioners' sugar

Preheat oven to 300° F. Combine eggs, margarine, and sugar in large bowl. Sift flour, salt and soda. Add vanilla, dates, and nuts, which have been rolled in flour. Orange slices should be cut in small pieces and also rolled in flour together with coconut before adding to batter. Bake in tube pan for 2 hours.

Prepare icing: Just before cake is removed from oven, mix orange juice, grated orange rind, and powdered sugar. When you take the cake out of the oven, pour the orange mixture over the hot cake. Let it stand overnight before removing cake from tube pan.

Mildred M. Harper, Edgecombe County

This is a family favorite at Christmas.

EASY OATMEAL CAKE

1 1/2 cups boiling water
1 cup quick cooking oats
1/2 cup margarine
1 cup brown sugar, firmly
  packed
1 cup sugar
2 eggs
1 1/2 cups self-rising flour
1 teaspoon cinnamon
1 teaspoon nutmeg

Topping:
1/4 cup brown sugar, firmly
  packed
1/2 cup sugar
1 cup flaked coconut
1 cup nuts, chopped
6 tablespoons margarine
1/4 cup evaporated skim
  milk
1/4 teaspoon vanilla extract

Preheat oven to 350° F. Pour boiling water over oats; mix well. Cream margarine, brown sugar, and sugar together thoroughly. Beat in eggs. Stir in soaked oatmeal. In a separate bowl, sift together flour and remaining dry ingredients. Stir into oatmeal mixture. Turn into a greased 13 x 9 x 2-inch pan. Bake for 30 to 35 minutes. Cool in pan.

Prepare topping: Combine the first 6 ingredients in saucepan. Heat until bubbly; stir in vanilla. Spread topping over cooled cake. Broil until golden brown, about 5 minutes. Serves 10 to 12.

Jessica Tice, Currituck County

This was one of my favorite cakes when I was growing up in Chowan County. Mom always made this cake for our special treat. Topped off with a tall glass of milk, it makes you yearn for the good old days of swinging in the backyard and eating Mom's oatmeal cake. I now make this cake for my family, and they always come back for more.

OLD-FASHIONED PRESERVE CAKE

1 stick margarine
1 cup sugar
4 eggs
3 cups all-purpose flour
1/2 teaspoon cloves
1/2 teaspoon allspice
1 teaspoon cinnamon

1 teaspoon baking soda
1/2 cup sour milk
1/2 pound raisins
2 1/2 cups preserves
  (blackberry, cherry, fig,
  peach, pear, or any
  combination)

Preheat oven to 325° F. Cream butter and sugar. Add eggs one at a time. In a separate bowl, mix dry ingredients. Mix soda with sour milk. Add these two mixtures alternately to creamed mixture. Fold in raisins and preserves. Pour into greased and floured 10-inch tube pan or two 9-inch layer pans. Bake 1 hour or longer for tube pan or 35 to 40 minutes for layer pans. Turn out, and ice with favorite icing. Caramel icing is good.

Margaret H. Spencer, Gaston County

This is a recipe I have been making for 50 years—one of the first cakes I ever made. I always had good luck with this. I couldn't cook when I got married. Now, many friends tell me I am an excellent cook.

PIG PICKING CAKE

1 can mandarin orange
   slices
1/2 cup oil
4 eggs
1 box Duncan Hines yellow
   cake mix

Icing:
1 large can crushed
   pineapple, drained,
   reserve juice
1 package vanilla instant
   pudding
1 9-ounce container Cool
   Whip
Coconut
Pecans

Drain orange slices, and mash oranges in mixing bowl. Add oil and eggs. Beat well, and add cake mix. Bake according to cake mix instructions. While cake is baking, drain crushed pineapple, retaining juice. When cake comes out of the oven, pour the juice over the hot cake.

Prepare frosting: Mix pineapple and pudding mix. Add Cool Whip. Frost cooled cake, adding coconut and pecans as desired between cake layers.

Karen Scalf, Duplin County

Floral Decorations

If you want to decorate a cake with fresh flowers, use only edible, pesticide-free flowers whether or not you plan to eat the flowers. Some edible flowers include roses, violets, and nasturtium.

PINCH ME CAKE

1 envelope dry yeast
1/2 cup lukewarm water
1 teaspoon sugar
1 cup milk
1/4 cup sugar
1/4 cup shortening
1 teaspoon salt

4 cups flour, divided
2 unbeaten eggs
3/4 cup butter
1 1/2 cups sugar
5 teaspoons cinnamon
1/2 cup finely chopped nuts

Preheat oven to 375° F. Dissolve yeast in lukewarm water with 1 teaspoon sugar. Bring milk to boiling point. Remove from heat, and add 1/4 cup sugar and the shortening, salt, and 1 1/2 cups flour. Mix well. Add eggs and remaining flour. Mix well. Let rise until doubled. Knead down and let batter rise again. Flour table and fold dough in several times. Make balls the size of walnuts. Melt butter. In a separate bowl, combine 1 1/2 cups sugar, cinnamon, and nuts.

Dip dough balls in melted butter, then in sugar-cinnamon-nut mixture. Put foil in 12-inch tube pan. Place dough balls around in pan. Allow to rise. Bake for 35 minutes.

Virginia Hodges, Ashe County

My children liked this cake, which is good with hot chocolate or coffee.

—

JIM GRAHAM'S PINEAPPLE CAKE

Your favorite layer cake
Cooked white frosting or
  whipped cream
Pineapple filling:
1/2 cup sugar
1 tablespoon cornstarch
Dash of salt

2/3 cup pineapple juice
2 egg yolks, slightly beaten
1 tablespoon butter or
  margarine
1 cup crushed pineapple,
  drained, reserve 2/3 cup
  juice

Prepare your favorite layer cake in two 9-inch layers. Cool. *Prepare filling:* Combine sugar, cornstarch, and salt in saucepan. In a separate bowl, add pineapple juice to slightly beaten egg yolks, and blend. Then add gradually to cornstarch mixture, mixing thoroughly. Place over medium heat and bring to a boil, stirring constantly. Remove from heat. Add butter and drained pineapple. Cool before spreading on cake to prevent sogginess. Spread pineapple filling all on one layer. Place second layer over the filling. Frost the cake with cooked white frosting or whipped cream.

Commissioner Jim Graham

PINEAPPLE CAKE

2 cups sugar
1 cup butter or margarine
5 eggs
3 cups flour
2 teaspoons baking powder

1 cup milk
1 cup chopped raisins
2 tablespoons cocoa
1/2 teaspoon cinnamon
1/2 teaspoon cloves

Preheat oven to 350° F. Grease and flour three 9-inch layer pans. Cream sugar and butter. Add eggs, beating after each addition. In a separate bowl, sift flour and baking powder together. Add flour mixture and milk alternately to batter. Pour two-thirds of the batter in two of the greased and floured layer pans. Add the following to the remaining batter: raisins, cocoa, cinnamon, and cloves. Pour this batter in the remaining cake pan. Bake for 25 to 30 minutes. Frost with Pineapple Cake Icing (recipe follows), placing the chocolate layer in the middle. Serves 16 to 18.

Anne S. Boyd, Rockingham County

PINEAPPLE CAKE ICING

1 1/2 cups sugar
2 tablespoons cornstarch

1 20-ounce can pineapple
Juice of 3 small lemons

Mix sugar and cornstarch in saucepan. Add can of pineapple and lemon juice. Cook until syrup is clear. Spread on cooled layers.

Anne S. Boyd, Rockingham County

This recipe was one my mother used for special occasions.

PISTACHIO CAKE

1 box yellow or white cake
  mix
1 package pistachio instant
  pudding

1 stick of margarine
3 eggs
1/2 cup of pecans
1 cup 7-Up

Preheat oven to 350° F. Add ingredients as listed, and mix well.
Bake in 9 x 13-inch pan for 45 minutes. Cool and frost with
Pistachio Frosting (recipe follows).

Lottie Lou Dickens, Nash County

PISTACHIO FROSTING

1 package pistachio instant
  pudding
1 cup milk

1 large 13 1/2-ounce Cool
  Whip

Mix all frosting ingredients together, and spread on cool cake.

Lottie Lou Dickens, Nash County

*This cake is very good for all occasions. It has been handed down
through our family.*

ST. PATRICK'S DAY PISTACHIO CAKE

1 box yellow cake mix
4 eggs
1 cup sour cream
1/2 cup oil

1 3- to 4-ounce package
  pistachio pudding
1 cup chopped walnuts
3 tablespoons sugar
4 teaspoons cinnamon

Preheat oven to 350° F. Mix cake mix, eggs, sour cream, oil, and
pudding in large mixing bowl. In separate small bowl, mix walnuts,
sugar, and cinnamon. Pour approximately half the cake batter into
10-inch tube pan. Sprinkle half the nut mixture onto batter. Pour
remaining batter into pan. Sprinkle remaining nuts on top. Bake for
1 hour.

Joan A. Marion, Bladen County

*This is my mother's recipe. I made it for a bake sale for my
nephew's Cub Scout Den. Now we make it every St. Patrick's Day.*

PRUNE CAKE

1 1/2 cups sugar
1 cup vegetable oil
3 eggs
2 cups flour
1 teaspoon baking soda
1 teaspoon cinnamon
1 teaspoon nutmeg

1 teaspoon allspice
1/2 teaspoon salt
1 cup buttermilk
1 teaspoon vanilla
1 cup nuts
1 cup prunes, cooked,
  seeded, chopped

Preheat oven to 300° F. Blend sugar and oil. Add eggs. In a separate bowl, mix flour, baking soda, cinnamon, nutmeg, allspice, and salt. Add dry ingredients alternately with buttermilk. Add vanilla, nuts, and prunes. Pour into buttered pan. Bake for 45 minutes. Just before removing cake from oven, prepare Buttermilk Icing (recipe follows). Pour over hot cake.

Mrs. Roland Beck, Burke County

BUTTERMILK ICING

1 cup sugar
1/2 cup buttermilk
1/2 teaspoon baking soda

1 tablespoon white corn
  syrup
1/4 cup butter
1/2 teaspoon vanilla

Mix all ingredients in a saucepan, and boil until mixture forms a soft ball. Do not beat after mixture forms a ball. Pour over hot cake.

Mrs. Roland Beck, Burke County

PRUNE CAKE WITH BLACK WALNUTS

2 cups self-rising flour
2 cups sugar
1 teaspoon cinnamon
1 teaspoon nutmeg
1 teaspoon allspice
1 cup black walnuts

1 cup Mazola oil
3 large eggs
3 2 1/2-ounce jars Gerber
  First Foods for Baby
  prunes

Preheat oven to 350° F. In one bowl, mix flour, sugar, cinnamon, nutmeg, allspice, and walnuts. In second bowl, mix oil, eggs, and prunes. Add second mixture to the first, and mix by hand. Bake in floured tube pan for 1 hour.

Margaret Helton, Rutherford County

PUMPKIN CRISP

1 16-ounce can pumpkin
1 large can evaporated milk
1 cup sugar
3 eggs
1 teaspoon cinnamon
1 box yellow cake mix
1 cup pecans

2 sticks margarine, melted
Frosting:
8 ounces cream cheese
1/2 cup powdered
    confectioners' sugar
3/4 cup Cool Whip

Preheat oven to 350° F. Layer 9 x 13-inch pan with wax paper. Mix pumpkin, milk, sugar, eggs, and cinnamon. Pour into pan over wax paper. Sprinkle dry cake mix over mixture. Sprinkle nuts into cake mix. Drizzle melted butter evenly over top. Bake for 50 to 60 minutes. Invert cake onto another pan, cool, and frost. *Prepare frosting:* Mix cream cheese with powdered sugar. Mix in Cool Whip. Spread over top of Pumpkin Cake. Refrigerate dessert for several hours before serving. Serves 10 to 15.

Margaret H. Spencer, Gaston County

A friend gave me this recipe 45 years ago. I have made it for my family ever since, and they have enjoyed it very much.

PUNCH BOWL CAKE

1 box yellow cake mix
1 large box vanilla instant
    pudding
1 large can crushed
    pineapple
1 can cherry pie filling

1 12-ounce package frozen
    coconut
1 large container Cool
    Whip
Fresh cherries for garnish,
    if desired

Bake cake as directed on box, making three layers. Mix pudding, pineapple, and pie filling together, and divide into thirds. Place first layer of cake in a large glass bowl. Spoon a third of the pudding-pie filling mixture on top of layer. Sprinkle with a third of the coconut. Spread a third of the Cool Whip over the layer. Repeat process with subsequent cake layers. Garnish with cherries, if desired. Cover top of bowl with plastic wrap, and refrigerate. Serves 15.

Linda N. Aycock, Nash County

This large cake will keep for several days.

RUM CAKE

1 package Duncan Hines
  butter cake mix
1 small package instant
  vanilla pudding
4 eggs

1/2 cup vegetable oil
1/2 cup light rum
1/2 cup water
1/2 cup pecans, finely
  chopped

Preheat oven to 350° F. Mix cake mix, pudding mix, eggs, oil, rum, and water together, and beat for 2 minutes. Grease and flour a bundt pan. Sprinkle pecans in bottom of pan, and pour in cake batter. Bake for 50 to 60 minutes. Turn cake out of bundt pan while still hot, and pierce top of cake with toothpicks so glaze will soak into cake. Brush Rum Cake Glaze (recipe follows) over cake.

Ann Lowder, Stanly County

RUM CAKE GLAZE

1/4 cup water
1/4 cup rum

1 cup sugar
1 stick margarine

Boil ingredients for 2 to 3 minutes. Put on cake with a pastry brush.

Ann Lowder, Stanly County

This cake is easy to make and always enjoyed by everyone.

Back in the early 1900s, the Chadbourn area of Columbus County was a major strawberry shipping area. In fact, growers there shipped out as much as 180 railroad boxcar loads of strawberries in a single day in 1907. Here's a delicious modern strawberry cake recipe from Chadbourn.

BLUE RIBBON STRAWBERRY CAKE

1 box strawberry cake mix
1 3-ounce box strawberry Jell-O
1 3-ounce box vanilla instant pudding
1 cup Wesson oil
1 1/2 cups milk
4 eggs
1 cup crushed strawberries
Fruit filling:
1 8-ounce container sour cream

1 8 1/4-ounce can crushed pineapple, not drained
2 cups sugar
2 6-ounce packages frozen coconut, thawed
Luscious Strawberry Frosting
1 8-ounce container Cool Whip
1 cup crushed strawberries
1 cup reserved fruit filling

Preheat oven to 350° F. Combine first three ingredients in large mixing bowl. Add oil, milk, and eggs. Beat until thoroughly mixed. Stir in crushed strawberries. Spoon batter into three greased and floured 9-inch round cake pans. Bake for 25 minutes. Let cake cool completely before icing.

Prepare fruit filling: While cake is cooling, mix sour cream, crushed pineapple, sugar, and coconut thoroughly. (*Note:* Reserve 1 cup fruit filling for Luscious Strawberry Frosting.) Spread fruit filling between layers and on top of cake. Mixture will be runny but will gradually be absorbed by the cake.

Prepare frosting: Combine Cool Whip, crushed strawberries, and reserved fruit filling. Mix thoroughly. Spread on top and sides of cake. Place in refrigerator for 24 hours. Serves 16.

Barbara B. Larrimore, Columbus County

As a lifetime resident of Chadbourn, known for delicious strawberries and its N.C. Strawberry Festival in May, I had to concoct a luscious strawberry recipe. This is it! My family and friends rave about this cake, and it's a must for homecomings, reunions, and socials.

STRAWBERRY CAKE

1 box white cake mix	1 3-ounce box Strawberry
2 tablespoons flour	Jell-O
1 cup Wesson oil	4 eggs
1/2 cup water	1/2 cup fresh or frozen
	strawberries

Preheat oven to 350° F. Sift flour and cake mix together. Add oil, water, Jell-O, eggs, and strawberries, and mix well. Pour into a 9 x 12-inch pan. Bake for 30 to 35 minutes. Frost with Strawberry Frosting (recipe follows).

Dale Evans, Union County

STRAWBERRY FROSTING

1 stick butter or margarine	1/2 cup strawberries
1 16-ounce box sifted	
powdered confectioners'	
sugar	

Cream butter. Add box of powdered sugar. Add just enough strawberries so that frosting spreads easily.

Dale Evans, Union County

STRAWBERRY BANANA DELIGHT

2 pints fresh strawberries	1 16-ounce container Cool
1/2 cup water	Whip whipped topping
2 tablespoons sugar	1 tablespoon pure maple
1 package Supermoist	flavoring
French vanilla cake mix	2 medium bananas

Rinse strawberries, cut into thin slices, and place in large bowl with 1/2 cup water. Sprinkle with sugar, and stir. Cover, and place bowl in refrigerator for 5 hours. Stir well when removed. Preheat oven to 350° F. Prepare cake mix according to directions on box, dividing batter equally among three 9-inch greased and floured cake pans. Bake for 25 minutes, or until toothpick inserted in center comes out clean. Cool completely.

To assemble cake: Stir maple flavoring into whipped topping. Place first cake layer on serving plate. Slowly spoon a layer of strawberries and juice onto cake. Slice one banana, and layer slices on top of strawberry layer. Spread thin layer of whipped topping over fruit. Repeat with second cake layer. Place third cake layer on top and spread a layer of strawberries only. Frost sides and top with remaining whipped topping. Garnish with fresh strawberries if desired. Cover cake and refrigerate overnight. Serves 12.

Cynthia M. Jones, Franklin County

This quick and easy recipe is a new tradition at our house. It won first place in the cake category at the 2001 Franklin County Strawberry Festival.

VANILLA WAFER CAKE

2 cups sugar
2 sticks margarine
6 eggs
1/2 cup milk

1 12-ounce box vanilla
  wafers, crushed
1 cup coconut
1 cup pecans

Preheat oven to 325° F. Cream sugar and butter until fluffy. Add eggs one at a time, beating after each addition. Add milk and crushed wafers. Fold in coconut and pecans. Pour into greased and floured tube or bundt pan. Bake for 1 hour, or until done.

Carolyn Tyndall, Duplin County

Home Grown

Statewide, North Carolina strawberry producers earned a total of $17 million from the sale of the 2000 crop of strawberries in 2000, says the N.C. Department of Agriculture. Almost all of these delicious strawberries are eaten right here in the state.

WEDDING CAKE

1 cup butter
3 cups sugar
1 1/2 teaspoons vanilla
    extract
5 cups flour

1 1/2 teaspoons baking
    powder
1 cup milk
12 egg whites, well-beaten

Preheat oven to 350° F. Beat butter to a cream, then gradually beat
in sugar. Add vanilla. In a separate bowl, sift flour and baking
powder together five times. Then add to butter-sugar mixture. Add
milk, and beat until light. Then lightly fold in the well-beaten egg
whites. Pour into three graduated cake pans. Bake until straw
inserted in middle comes out clean. Each layer will have a different
baking time because baking time depends upon the size of the pan.
An 8-inch cake pan should be baked for 30 to 35 minutes, so plan
baking times accordingly.

Helen J. Bess, Gaston County

*This wedding cake recipe, a Jenkins Family recipe, was brought
from England by my maternal great-great-grandmother, and more
than six generations of the girls in the family have used this recipe
for their wedding cakes.*

WORLD WAR CAKE

1 cup brown sugar
1 1/2 cups water
1 cup seeded raisins
2 ounces citron, cut fine
1/3 cup shortening
1 teaspoon ground
    cinnamon

1/4 teaspoon cloves
1/4 teaspoon nutmeg
1/2 teaspoon salt
2 cups flour
5 teaspoons baking powder
1/2 teaspoon vanilla extract

Preheat oven to 325° F. Boil sugar, water, raisins, citron, shortening,
cinnamon, cloves, nutmeg, and salt for 3 minutes. Let cool. In a
large bowl, sift together flour and baking powder. Beat sifted
ingredients into sugar-fruit mixture, adding vanilla, and mix well.
Bake in a well-greased 11 x 7-inch loaf pan for 45 minutes.

Pearl King Morton, Granville County

*Mary Amy King and her husband, Robert Marshall King, both liked
this cake. It's a quick, unfrosted cake.*

7-MINUTE ICING

1 teaspoon vanilla
1/2 cup sugar
2 egg whites

1/4 teaspoon cream of tartar
1/3 cup water

Mix all ingredients. Place in double boiler. Cook, beating constantly with an electric mixer until icing forms peaks and loses gloss, 7 minutes or longer. Remove from heat; beat 1 1/2 minutes, or until icing is easy to spread.

Evelyn Stevens, Wake County

I have used this recipe since I was in 4-H in the 1940s.

7-MINUTE ICING

2 egg whites
1 1/2 cups sugar
1 tablespoon white corn
  syrup
1/3 cup cold water

1/8 teaspoon salt
1/2 teaspoon vanilla
1/2 to 1 cup miniature
  marshmallows

Combine all ingredients except vanilla and marshmallows. Place in double boiler. Cook, beating constantly with an electric mixer, for 7 minutes. Remove from heat, and add vanilla and marshmallows. Beat vigorously. (Make sure marshmallows are melted.)

Hattie Sessions, Columbus County

This icing is great for the outside of a fresh coconut cake.

OLD-FASHIONED FUDGE FROSTING

1 stick butter (1/2 cup)
3 cups sugar
1/3 cup cocoa
Dash of salt

1 large can evaporated milk
1 tablespoon vanilla
  flavoring

Melt butter in a large cast-iron pan over medium heat. Stir in half of sugar. Add cocoa, and mix well. Add the rest of the sugar and salt. Add milk and stir, making sure to get all the sugar from the sides and bottom of the pan. Bring to a full, rolling boil while stirring. Cook for 5 to 6 minutes; frosting will start to thicken. Take pan off heat, and add vanilla. Let cool a few minutes. When frosting starts to thicken more and looks glossy, pour over cake layers. Makes enough for three 8-inch layers.

Pamela Farmer, Clay County

This was my great-grandmother's recipe. Everyone called her Mother because she was an excellent cook and always had goodies in the cupboard. My grandmother always made this for me when I spent the night. It was delicious!

BIRTHDAY POUND CAKE

1 cup Crisco shortening
1 1/2 sticks butter (not margarine)
3 cups sugar
5 eggs
1 teaspoon vanilla
1 teaspoon lemon extract
3 1/2 cups all-purpose flour
1 cup milk

Preheat oven to 350° F. Mix shortening, butter, and sugar. Add eggs, one at a time. Add vanilla and lemon flavorings. Add small amounts of flour, then small amounts of milk until all is used. Spray tube pan with cooking spray, and pour batter into pan. Bake at 350° F. for 1 1/2 hours. Cool for 10 minutes and turn cake out on a plate.

Dixie Chappell Porter, Wake County

I live in Wake County now, but I was raised in Perquimans. Our family has made this cake for many generations, and it has since been passed on to others all over the United States and England!

BLACK WALNUT POUND CAKE

1/2 pound butter
1/2 cup Crisco shortening
3 cups sugar
5 eggs
1 teaspoon black walnut flavoring
1 teaspoon vanilla flavoring
3 cups Gold Medal all-purpose flour
1 teaspoon baking powder
1 cup Half & Half dairy creamer
1 cup black walnuts, chopped
Icing:
1/2 stick butter, melted
3 or 4 tablespoons milk
1 box powdered sugar
1 teaspoon black walnut flavoring
1 teaspoon vanilla flavoring
1 cup black walnut halves (do not chop)

Preheat oven to 325° F. Cream butter and shortening. Add sugar, and beat until light. Add eggs, one at a time, and beat after each. Add flavorings, and mix well. In a separate bowl, mix baking powder with flour. Add flour mixture and Half & Half to creamed mixture, starting and ending with flour. Fold in walnuts. Grease tube pan, line with wax paper, and sprinkle lightly with flour. Pour mixture into pan. Bake at 325° F. approximately 1 hour and 20 minutes. *Do not open oven door during first hour.*

Prepare icing: Add milk and melted butter to sugar. Blend to right consistency for spreading. Add black walnut and vanilla flavorings. Spread on top and sides of cake. Cover top of cake with black walnut halves.

Betty H. Evans, Wayne County

This makes a beautiful and wonderful cake. I have given this recipe to many family members and friends. It is tops at our church auction.

KAY'S BLACK WALNUT POUND CAKE

Follow the Black Walnut Pound Cake recipe (above) but substitute 1 teaspoon of rum flavoring for black walnut flavoring, and do not frost the cake.

Kay Carswell, Rutherford County

CARAMEL NUT POUND CAKE

2 sticks butter, room
  temperature
1/2 cup Crisco shortening
1 16-ounce box light brown
  sugar
1 cup white sugar
5 eggs
3 cups sifted all-purpose
  flour
1/2 teaspoon salt
1/2 teaspoon baking powder

1 cup milk
1 teaspoon vanilla extract
1 cup chopped pecans (I
  always toast them)
Icing:
2 cups light brown sugar
1 cup sugar
1 cup Half & Half dairy
  creamer
1 stick butter

Preheat oven to 325° F. Cream butter and Crisco shortening. Add brown sugar, and cream ingredients. Add white sugar, and cream until fluffy. Add eggs one at a time. Mix dry ingredients together. Set aside 2 tablespoons of flour mixture to toss with nuts. Add flour mixture alternately with milk, beginning and ending with flour. Add vanilla. Stir in nuts. Bake at 325° F. for approximately 1 hour and 30 minutes. Cool cake in pan for 15 minutes before turning out. Ice while warm. *Prepare icing:* In a saucepan, combine first three ingredients. Boil, stirring frequently, until mixture reaches soft ball stage, 325° F. Pour hot mixture over stick of butter in mixer bowl. Stir to melt. Beat until ready to spread.

Laura B. Wooten, Wake County

COLONIAL POUND CAKE

1 cup Crisco shortening	**1/4 teaspoon salt**
2 cups sugar	**2 cups cake flour**
5 unbeaten eggs	**1/2 cup evaporated milk**
1 teaspoon vanilla flavoring	

Beat shortening until creamy. Beat in sugar. Beat in eggs, one at a time. Add vanilla, salt, and flour alternately with milk. Pour into floured tube pan. Turn on oven to 300° F. when you put the pan in the oven. Do not preheat the oven. Cook for 1 1/2 hours.

Margaret Helton, Rutherford County

CRISCO POUND CAKE

3 cups sugar	*Icing:*
1 pound (2 cups)Crisco shortening	**1 16-ounce box powdered sugar**
10 eggs	**1/3 cup Crisco shortening**
3 cups cake flour	**Dash of salt**
1/4 cup evaporated milk	**Rind of 1 lemon**
2 teaspoons lemon extract	**Enough lemon juice to mix**
1 teaspoon vanilla	**above ingredients to**
1/2 teaspoon salt	**spreading consistency**

Cream sugar and shortening. Add eggs, one at a time, beating after each egg. Add flour and milk, alternating. Add vanilla and salt. Bake in a 10-inch tube pan at 300° F. for 2 hours. *Prepare icing:* Mix all ingredients, and spread on cake.

Paula Williams, Duplin County

MILLION DOLLAR POUND CAKE

1 pound butter, softened	3/4 cup milk
3 cups sugar	1 teaspoon almond extract
6 eggs	1 teaspoon vanilla extract
4 cups all-purpose flour	

Preheat oven to 300° F. Cream butter in a large mixing bowl. Gradually add sugar, beating well with an electric mixer at medium speed. Add eggs one at a time, beating after each addition. Add flour alternately with milk, beginning and ending with flour. Stir in flavorings. Pour batter into greased and floured 10-inch tube pan. Bake at 300° F. for 1 hour and 40 minutes or until you insert a wooden toothpick and it comes out clean. Cool cake in the pan for 10 to 15 minutes, then remove it.

Jerrie Hasty, Union County

MY MOTHER'S POUND CAKE

3 1/2 cups all-purpose flour	3 cups sugar
1/2 teaspoon baking powder	6 eggs
1/2 teaspoon salt	1 teaspoon vanilla flavoring
1 cup Crisco shortening	1 teaspoon lemon flavoring
1 stick butter	1 cup milk

Preheat oven to 325° F. Sift flour before measuring. Sift again with baking powder and salt added to measured flour. Cream shortening and butter with sugar. Add eggs one at a time, and beat after each addition. Add flavorings, and beat until creamy. Add flour alternately with milk, and beat thoroughly after each addition. Grease and flour a big tube pan. Bake at 325° F. for 1 hour and 25 minutes. Serves 18.

Bettie H. Hodges, Davidson County

When I was a little girl, my mother did not have a mixer. She would put me on a stool, and I creamed the Crisco, butter, and sugar with my hands. Of course, she had to do it some more. There were nine in our family, and this cake was a favorite.

MYRTLE ASHLEY'S POUND CAKE

1/2 cup butter-flavored
  Crisco shortening
2 sticks butter
3 cups sugar
5 eggs (6 if small)

3 cups cake flour
1 cup Pet evaporated milk
Favoring of choice
Pam cooking spray

Cream shortening and butter. Mix in sugar; then beat well. Add eggs and mix, then beat well. Beginning with flour and ending with flour: add flour and Pet milk a little at a time, and mix well until all flour and milk are used. Add preferred flavoring. Bake in a tube or bundt pan sprayed with Pam. Put cake in a cold oven and set temperature at 275° F. Bake about 2 1/2 hours or until done, using the toothpick test. Cool cake about 30 minutes before taking out of pan. Serves 16.

Susan E. Pope, Wake County

My great-grandmother, Myrtle Ashley (affectionately called "Mammy" by everyone who knew her), made this cake for four generations of Ashleys in Fairmont. She shared this recipe with children, grandchildren, great-grandchildren, nieces, great-nieces, in-laws, neighbors, and friends. Never did a holiday or special occasion pass without one of her pound cakes making the scene. I continue this tradition today and have yet to taste a pound cake that can hold a candle to "Mammy's." While I have updated this recipe over the years, it still tastes like my great-grandmother's pound cake. The key is to constantly mix the batter and to beat in lots of air. It is also vital not to preheat the oven. Most of the people in my family call this a cold-oven cake. Even to this day, making this cake conjures up memories of big family get-togethers, lots of good smells from the kitchen, and arguing over who will get to lick the bowl and beaters! The batter is almost as good as the cake.

WHIPPED CREAM POUND CAKE

2 sticks butter (not
  margarine), softened
3 cups sugar

6 eggs
3 cups all-purpose flour
1/2 pint whipping cream

Soften butter. Add sugar, and mix until smooth. Add eggs to sugar one at a time, and mix. Alternate adding small amounts of flour and whipping cream to butter-sugar-egg mixture, starting and ending with flour. Bake at 325° F. for 1 hour.

Mrs. Vollie Dalton, Rutherford County

ONE-HALF POUND CAKE

1 cup butter	2 cups cake flour
1 2/3 cups sugar	1 teaspoon flavoring, vanilla
5 eggs	or lemon

Cream butter and sugar together. Add eggs one at a time, beating after each addition. Beat well, and add cake flour. Thoroughly mix, and add preferred flavoring. Pour into lightly greased and floured tube pan. Put in a cold oven, and bake at 300° F. for 1 hour. Serves 20 to 24 slices.

Harriett Coleman Edwards, Wake County

This was my grandmother's pound cake recipe. I remember my uncles coming in from the fields and eating warm slices of this cake while standing on the back screened porch on summer afternoons. It is a fail-proof pound cake that is wonderful warm from the oven or covered with fresh strawberries and homemade ice cream.

POUND CAKE WITH FRUIT AND ICING

2 sticks butter, softened	2 kiwi, peeled and thinly
3 cups sugar	sliced
1/2 cup Crisco shortening	*Icing:*
1 cup milk	1 cup + 2 tablespoons
5 eggs	powdered sugar, sifted
3 cups plus 6 tablespoons	3/4 cup Crisco shortening
Softasilk flour	Water as needed for
Glazed fruit:	thickness
1/4 cup water	1 box Jell-O instant vanilla
3/4 cup sugar	pudding, prepared
1 pint strawberries, thinly	1 8-ounce jar strawberry
sliced	preserves

Combine butter, sugar, and shortening, and mix well. Add milk, and mix. Add eggs one at a time. Add flour gradually, mixing well. Grease and flour bundt cake pan. Pour in batter, and place cake in a cold oven. Set temperature at 325° F., and bake for about 70 minutes. Allow cake to cool before assembling.

Glaze fruit: Mix water and sugar, and cook over low heat until mixture becomes liquid. Let cool for 30 minutes. Then dip strawberries and kiwi in glaze, or brush the glaze onto the fruit. *Prepare icing:* Mix powdered sugar, shortening, and water together.

Assemble cake: Slice cooled cake into three layers. Remove the top two layers. Spread prepared pudding onto bottom layer. Place the next layer on top. Spread icing and strawberry preserves on the second layer. Place the final layer on top. Ice the top layer, and arrange fruit on top of the icing. Pipe icing around the base of the cake, and arrange fruit around it.

Paul Taylor, Alamance County

RED VELVET POUND CAKE

3 cups sugar
5 eggs
1/2 cup Crisco shortening
1 cup margarine
1 ounce red food coloring
3 cups all-purpose flour

1/2 cup cocoa
1/2 teaspoon baking powder
1/2 teaspoon salt
1 cup milk
1 teaspoon vanilla

Cream sugar, eggs, shortening, margarine, and food coloring well. In a separate bowl, sift flour, cocoa, baking powder, and salt. Mix milk and flour mixture alternately into creamed mixture. Add vanilla. Mix well, and bake in a 10-inch tube pan at 300° F. for 1 1/2 hours.

Anna Lee Poe, Ashe County

My family enjoys this cake.

VELVET POUND CAKE

3 cups sugar
1 1/2 cups shortening
7 eggs
2 teaspoons vanilla

3 1/2 cups all-purpose flour
1/4 teaspoon salt
1 cup milk

Cream sugar and shortening well. Add eggs one at a time, beating well after adding each one. Add vanilla, then beat well. Mix salt and flour, and add to creamed mixture, alternately with milk. Bake in greased and floured 10-inch tube pan at 325° F. for 1 1/2 hours.

Gladys Patton, Clay County

I have used this recipe for many years, and it is still a popular request when I visit my sisters.

GRANDMA SLATE'S FRUIT CAKE

1 cup soft butter
1 cup light brown sugar
2 cups all-purpose flour
1 teaspoon ground
cinnamon
1 teaspoon allspice
1 teaspoon cloves
1 teaspoon nutmeg
6 large eggs
1 teaspoon baking soda
1/2 cup buttermilk
1/2 cup molasses

1/4 cup all-purpose flour
1 pound raisins
1 pound golden raisins
1 pound citron and fruit
mix
1 cup maraschino cherries
2 1/2 cups black walnuts
2 1/2 cups pecans
Wine (1/2 cup per week
twice a week until cake is
served)

Use an electric mixer to cream butter and brown sugar until fluffy. In a separate bowl, sift flour, cinnamon, allspice, cloves, and nutmeg together. Add eggs alternately with flour and spice mixture to butter and brown sugar mixture. Mix well. Dissolve baking soda in buttermilk. Add molasses and baking soda-buttermilk to batter. In a separate large bowl, flour the fruits and nuts. Add batter and mix well.

Line the sides and bottom of a tube pan with four layers of waxed paper. Spoon batter in tube pan. Place pan with 1 inch of water on bottom rack of the oven. Bake fruit cake at 225° F. for 3 hours. Cool cake in pan. Remove cooled cake and wrap in two layers of cheesecloth. Store in large cookie tin with tight lid. Spoon 1/2 cup of warm wine over cake two times a week. The cake is best when it is made three months before you plan to use it. This recipe will make a 9-pound fruit cake.

Nancy C. Sapp, Forsyth County

This recipe came with my husband's grandmother's wood cook stove in the early 1900s. When our children were small, we made three at a time.

OLD-FASHIONED DARK FRUIT CAKE

2 cups butter
2 1/4 cups sugar
1 dozen eggs
2 apples, grated coarsely
2 teaspoons vanilla
2 pounds currants
2 pounds raisins
3/4 pound diced citron
3/4 pound glazed pineapple
  wedges

1 pound glazed cherries,
  halved
1 pound chopped pecans
4 cups all-purpose flour
1 teaspoon baking powder
2 teaspoons allspice
2 teaspoons ground
  cinnamon
1 teaspoon nutmeg
1 teaspoon ground cloves

Cream butter. Slowly add half the sugar, beating well after each addition. Separate egg yolks and whites. Add 3 egg yolks to the butter-sugar mixture. Continue to add yolks until all are beaten in. Mix in grated apples and vanilla.

Prepare currants and raisins. Rinse well with cold water, drain, and spread in shallow baking pans. Cover with foil and place in 275° F. oven for 20 to 30 minutes to "plump." After currants and raisins cool, place in a large stock pot with remaining fruits and nuts. In a separate bowl, sift together flour, baking powder, and spices. Then sift over prepared fruits and nuts.

Take out two large mixer bowls. In each bowl, beat half the egg whites to big foam stage; begin adding half of the retained sugar slowly as you continue beating whites. Beat until egg whites form good peaks. Add butter-sugar mixture and egg white-sugar mixtures to fruit-nut mixture in the large stock pot. Use your hands to mix well.

Grease loaf pans and tube pans well with margarine or butter, then cut paper to fit sides and bottoms. Fit the paper into the pans; then grease the paper well after fitting. (Oil does not work well.) Fill prepared pans three-fourths full. Cover with foil. Place some water and a rack in the bottom of a stockpot. Carefully place pans inside stockpot. Bring water to a boil, cover the stockpot tightly, and steam breads for 2 hours. Make sure stockpot doesn't boil dry. Bake 1 to 2 hours, depending on pan size, at 250° F. until firm and a toothpick inserted in the center comes out clean.

Place pans of fruit cake back in large stockpot with fresh apples to maintain moisture. Two or three times a week for 2 weeks, drizzle

2 to 4 tablespoons of rum or brandy over the top of each cake.
Don't add too much rum or brandy or the cakes will be soggy.

Isabelle M. Fletcher-Perry, Lenoir County

*My mother made this cake every year, and I have continued the
tradition for more than 60 years. The recipe came from my
mother's mother, Martha May, who was born in Pitt County near
Farmville.*

—

PLANTATION FRUIT CAKE

2 cups seedless raisins
1 16-ounce can cling
  peaches, drained and
  chopped
1 cup shortening
1 cup firmly packed brown
  sugar
1/2 cup cream sherry or
  orange juice
1 16-ounce jar mixed
  candied fruit

2 cups chopped walnuts
4 eggs, beaten
2 1/2 cups sifted all-purpose
  flour
1 teaspoon baking powder
1 1/2 teaspoons salt
1 teaspoon ground
  cinnamon
1/2 teaspoon ground cloves
1/4 cup light corn syrup

Grease a 9-inch bundt pan. Dust with flour; tap out excess.
Combine raisins, peaches, shortening, brown sugar, and sherry (or
orange juice) in a medium saucepan. Heat just to boiling. Remove
from heat and allow to cool. Add candied fruit and nuts to cooled
mixture. Stir in beaten eggs. In a separate bowl, sift flour, baking
powder, salt, cinnamon, and cloves together. Stir into fruit mixture;
mix well. Pour mixture into prepared pan. Bake in slow oven
(300° F.) for 2 hours, or until center springs back when lightly
touched with fingertip. Cool in pan on wire rack for 15 minutes,
then turn out of pan and allow to cool completely. In a small
saucepan, heat corn syrup until bubbly. Brush syrup over cake and
decorate with walnut halves and candied red and green pineapple, if
desired.

Jennifer Mitchell, Harnett County

WHITE CHRISTMAS FRUIT CAKE

1 pound flour
1/2 teaspoon salt
4 teaspoons baking powder
2 pounds candied
  pineapple, chopped
2 pounds candied cherries,
  chopped
1 1/2 pounds citron,
  chopped

1 pound pecans, chopped
1 pound butter, room
  temperature
1 pound sugar
10 large eggs, room
  temperature
1 teaspoon vanilla extract

Sift together flour, salt, and baking powder in a large bowl. Stir in chopped fruit and pecans, mixing well. In a separate bowl, cream butter and sugar. Mix well. Add eggs two at a time, beating on low speed of mixer after each addition. Add vanilla. Pour batter over fruit, nut, and flour mixture and stir well. Pour into a well-greased and floured tube cake pan and bake at 325° F. for 1 1/2 hours.

Jane Stuart, Wake County

This recipe came from a cousin, the late Grace McIntyre Butler of Rowland. I sometimes bake this recipe in smaller loaf pans. The cake freezes well.

BOILED COOKIES

2 cups sugar
4 tablespoons cocoa
1/2 cup milk
1 stick butter or margarine
2 1/2 cups old-fashioned
  oatmeal, uncooked

1/4 cup pecans
2 teaspoons vanilla extract
1 tablespoon peanut butter
  (optional)

Mix sugar and cocoa together. Add milk and butter or margarine. Cook on medium heat until it reaches a full boil, then continue to cook for 1 1/2 minutes. Remove from heat. Stir in uncooked oatmeal, nuts, and vanilla extract. Drop by teaspoon onto wax paper.

Mary Louise Baker Ennis, Harnett County

FRUIT CAKE COOKIES

1/2 cup butter
1 cup brown sugar
1 egg
2 1/2 cups all-purpose flour
1/2 teaspoon baking powder
1/2 teaspoon salt
1/2 teaspoon baking soda

1/2 cup buttermilk
1/2 teaspoon cinnamon
1/2 teaspoon nutmeg
1 cup chopped pecans
1 cup chopped dates
1 cup chopped green and
red candied cherries

Cream butter and sugar. Add egg, and mix well. In a separate bowl, sift together flour, baking powder, salt, and soda. Stir flour mixture and buttermilk into butter-sugar-egg mixture. Add other ingredients, and mix well. Drop by teaspoonfuls on greased cookie sheet. Bake at 325° F. for about 15 minutes.

Faye S. Bunn, Nash County

JANET'S OATMEAL COOKIES

1 1/4 cups (2 1/2 sticks)
  softened margarine
3/4 cup firmly packed
  brown sugar
1/2 cup sugar
1 egg
1 teaspoon vanilla

1 1/2 cups flour
1 teaspoon baking soda
1/2 teaspoon salt
1 teaspoon cinnamon
1/4 teaspoon nutmeg
3 cups uncooked oatmeal

Beat margarine and sugars until creamy. Beat in egg and vanilla. In a separate bowl, combine flour, baking soda, salt, and spices, and mix well. Combine mixtures, and mix well. Stir in oats. Drop onto ungreased cookie sheet. Bake 8 to 9 minutes in a 375° F. oven for a chewy cookie and 10 to 11 minutes for a crisp cookie. Let cool 1 minute on the cookie sheet, and then remove to a wire rack. Makes about 4 1/2 dozen.

Janet Singleton, Wake County

CHOCOLATE CHIP-OATMEAL COOKIES

Omit the nutmeg from Janet's Oatmeal Cookies (above), and add 1/2 cup semisweet chocolate morsels and 1 cup of chopped pecans.

Reba Adams, Craven County

OATMEAL-RAISIN COOKIES

3 eggs, well beaten	2 1/2 cups all-purpose flour
1 cup raisins	1 teaspoon salt
1 teaspoon vanilla	2 teaspoons baking soda
1 cup butter	1 teaspoon cinnamon
1 cup light brown sugar	2 cups quick oatmeal
1 cup white sugar	3/4 cup pecans

Combine eggs, raisins, and vanilla. Let stand 1 hour. In separate
bowl, cream butter and sugars. Add flour, salt, soda, and cinnamon
to butter and sugar mixture. Mix well. Blend in egg-raisin mixture.
Add oatmeal and nuts. Batter will be stiff. Drop on ungreased
cookie sheet, and bake for 10 minutes at 350° F. They are delicious!

Mildred Harper, Edgecombe County

OATMEAL COOKIES

1 cup butter	1/2 teaspoon baking soda
1 cup sugar	1/4 teaspoon salt
2 eggs, beaten	1/4 cup milk
2 cups flour	2 cups oatmeal
1 teaspoon baking powder	1 cup raisins
1 teaspoon cinnamon	1 cup nuts

Heat oven to 375° F. Cream butter and sugar together. Beat in eggs.
In a separate bowl, mix flour, baking powder, cinnamon, baking
soda, and salt together. Add flour mixture and milk to butter-sugar
mixture. Add oatmeal, raisins, and nuts. Drop by spoonful onto
ungreased cookie sheet. Bake 15 to 18 minutes.

Helene Daugherty, Craven County

CAROLINA COOKIES

3 cups flour	1 egg
3 teaspoons baking powder	1/3 cup milk
3/4 cup shortening	1 teaspoon vanilla flavoring
1 cup sugar	

Sift flour and baking powder together. Cream together shortening,
sugar, egg, milk, and flavoring. Add flour mixture gradually. Mix
well. Knead dough lightly, and roll out on well-floured board to 1/4
inch thick. Cut and place on well-greased baking sheet. Bake in

350° F. preheated oven for 10 to 12 minutes or until golden. This recipe can be varied by adding nuts, raisins, etc. If nuts and raisins are added, drop cookies by the spoonful onto the cookie sheet.

Lois Curtis, Clay County

These cookies are among my fondest childhood memories. When my mother would bake them, my brothers and I would enjoy them warm from the oven.

VANILLA DROPS

1 cup shortening	2 cups flour
1 cup sugar	2 teaspoons baking powder
1 teaspoon vanilla	1/2 teaspoon salt
1 egg	1/2 cup milk

Cream shortening until soft. Add sugar, creaming until fluffy. Beat in vanilla and egg. In a separate bowl, combine flour, baking powder, and salt. Add flour mixture alternately with milk to shortening-sugar mixture. Drop small spoonfuls onto ungreased cookie sheet. The cookies will spread as they bake. Bake 8 to 10 minutes in a 375° F. oven until cookies are lightly browned around the edges; centers remain pale. Be careful not to burn the bottoms. Makes 3 dozen small cookies.

Janet Singleton, Wake County

My older sister, Joan, used to make these.

MOLASSES COOKIES

3/4 cup Crisco shortening	2 cups sifted flour
1 cup sugar	1 teaspoon cinnamon
1/4 cup molasses	1/2 teaspoon salt
1 egg	Granulated sugar
2 teaspoons baking soda	

In medium saucepan, carefully melt shortening; let cool. Add sugar, molasses, and egg, and beat well. Sift dry ingredients together. Mix well with molasses mixture. Chill dough 2 to 3 hours. Roll into 1-inch balls, then roll in granulated sugar. Bake at 375° F. for 8 to 10 minutes. Makes approximately 36 cookies.

Anna Braswell, Rowan County

These cookies are quick, easy, and delicious.

268

OATMEAL REFRIGERATOR COOKIES

1 cup butter
1 cup brown sugar
1 cup granulated sugar
2 eggs
1 1/2 cups sifted flour
1 teaspoon baking soda
1 teaspoon salt
1/2 cup shredded coconut
1/2 cup chopped pecans or walnuts
3 cups quick rolled oats, uncooked

Cream butter and sugars. Add beaten eggs. In a separate bowl, sift flour with soda and salt, and add to egg mixture. Stir in coconut, nuts, and rolled oats. Shape into four rolls, wrap in waxed paper, and chill overnight. Cut into 1/8-inch slices, and place 2 inches apart on ungreased cookie sheet. Bake at 375° F. for 12 to 15 minutes.

Ellen Teague Miller, Wake County

My grandmother, Bess Sockwell, used to make these cookies and send them to me at college.

QUICK PEANUT BUTTER COOKIES

1 cup smooth peanut butter
3/4 cup sugar
1 egg
1 teaspoon vanilla
Confectioners' sugar

Mix peanut butter, sugar, egg, and vanilla. Form into balls, and roll in confectioners' sugar. Bake at 350° F. for approximately 8 to 10 minutes. Store in an airtight container. Makes about 3 dozen cookies.

Jessica Tice, Currituck County

These melt-in-your-mouth cookies are a favorite with my children. When they want cookies, they ask for these bite-sized treats. They like to help me form the balls and roll them in the confectioners' sugar. (You should see us when we've finished!) The cookies are so easy to make and have so few ingredients that they are a favorite with me when I have to make cookies for different events—and especially at Christmas.

RICE KRISPY COOKIES

1 cup sugar
1 cup brown sugar
1 cup margarine
1 egg
3/4 cup cooking oil
1 teaspoon vanilla flavoring
3 1/2 cups all-purpose flour

1 teaspoon baking soda
3/4 teaspoon salt
1 teaspoon cream of tartar
1 cup coconut
1 cup chopped nuts (I use
    pecans)
1 cup Rice Krispies

Cream together sugars and margarine. Add egg, cooking oil, and vanilla. In separate bowl, mix together flour, baking soda, salt, and cream of tartar. Gradually add dry ingredients to cookie mixture. Lastly, stir in coconut, nuts, and Rice Krispies. Roll into 1 to 1 1/2-inch balls, and flatten with a fork. Place on ungreased, nonstick cookie sheet, and bake at 350° F. for 10 to 12 minutes, or until cookies are lightly brown. Remove and cool on wire racks. Makes approximately 100 cookies.

Nancy Miller, Catawba County

This recipe makes a lot of good cookies. I make them each year to sell at our church bazaar. They also have been a real hit at covered-dish dinners at church and work.

AUNT ADDIE'S TEA CAKES

1/2 cup butter or margarine
1 cup sugar, granulated
1 egg, well beaten
1 teaspoon vanilla

1 3/4 cups all-purpose flour
2 teaspoons baking powder
1/4 teaspoon nutmeg

Cream butter and sugar thoroughly. Add the egg and vanilla, and mix well. Sift together the flour, baking powder, and nutmeg, and add to the mixture. Mix until dough is formed. Cover, and chill in the refrigerator for 1 hour. Roll out on a well-floured surface to 1/8-inch thickness. Shape with a biscuit or cookie cutter, and place on nongreased cookie sheet. If desired, brush the cakes with milk, and sprinkle with colored sugar. Bake in a preheated 325° F. oven for 8 to 12 minutes. Bottom of cakes will brown slightly. Remove from sheet immediately, and let cool on wire racks. Makes 3 dozen tea cakes.

Sylvia I. Pate, Robeson County

Aunt Addie was my great-great-aunt. She was born in 1864 and lived until 1951. All the nieces and nephews who visited her for generations would head immediately for the old stoneware churn on the kitchen table to get some of her tea cakes.

—

MAMA'S TEA CAKES

2 cups self-rising flour
3 eggs
1 cup sugar
1 stick butter

1 teaspoon vanilla flavoring
1/2 cup milk (or more if
   needed)

Place flour in a large bowl. Make a hole in the center of the flour. Add eggs, sugar, butter, and vanilla. Stir, and gradually add milk until batter is cookie dough consistency. Pinch off and roll golf-ball size cookies, and flatten with hand. Place on cookie sheet about 2 inches apart. Bake at 350° F. for 10 to 12 minutes, or until golden brown.

Alice Green Connor, Columbus County

This recipe was passed down from my grandmother, Alice Duncan.

OLD-FASHIONED TEA CAKES

2 1/2 cups flour
2/3 cup butter, softened
1 egg

1 cup sugar
1/4 cup milk
1 teaspoon vanilla

Sift flour. Add other ingredients to form a medium dough. Roll thin about 1/3 of dough at a time. Cut with a round biscuit or cookie cutter. Bake on a cookie sheet at 400° F. for 10 minutes.

Margaret H. Jackson, Sampson County

This recipe brings back childhood memories. My mother would have the tea cakes waiting for me when I came home from school.

Butter the Size of an Egg?

Old recipes often call for butter the size of an egg. After all, butter was churned; it didn't come packaged in sticks. The people at Land 'O Lakes say that 1/4 cup is the approximate equivalent.

SOUTHERN TEA CAKES

1 cup shortening	3 cups flour
1 1/4 cups sugar	2 teaspoons baking powder
2 eggs	1/2 teaspoon salt
Grated rind of 1 lemon	1/2 cup milk

Cream the shortening and sugar; add the eggs gradually and the lemon rind. In a separate bowl, sift together flour, baking powder, and salt. Add alternately with the milk to shortening-sugar mixture. Turn onto a floured board, roll out 1/4- inch thick, cut into rounds, place on greased baking sheet, and bake at 350° F. for 12 to 15 minutes. Note: Dough will work better if chilled for several hours before rolling out.

Rachel A. Sigman, Catawba County

This is the basic recipe Grandmother and Mother used for sugar cookies. Grandma laid out cookies on a flour sack towel in the drawer of the china cabinet. The horse-shaped cookie was my favorite.

OLD-FASHIONED TEA COOKIES

1/2 cup butter	1 egg, beaten
2/3 cup sugar	2 1/2 cups sifted flour
1/2 cup shortening	1 teaspoon vanilla extract

Cream butter, sugar, and shortening thoroughly. Add egg, and blend well. Sift flour; add with vanilla extract to first mixture. Blend thoroughly. Drop by level teaspoonfuls on ungreased cookie sheet. Press to 1/8-inch thickness. Bake at 400° F. for 6 to 8 minutes. Makes about 60 cookies.

Betty Mathews, Perquimans County

These cookies are great anytime.

SIMPLY OUTRAGEOUS COOKIES

1 stick margarine	1 14-ounce can condensed
1 1/2 cups graham cracker	milk
crumbs	12 ounces chocolate chips
	1 cup pecans or walnuts

Melt stick of margarine in a 9 x 13-inch pan. Mix remaining ingredients in a mixing bowl, then add the melted margarine. Press into the 9 x 13-inch pan. Bake in preheated 350° F. oven for 25 to 30 minutes. Cut into squares when cool.

Karen Scalf, Duplin County

APPLE-NUT SQUARES

2 eggs	1/2 teaspoon salt
1 1/2 cups sugar	2 teaspoons baking powder
1 teaspoon vanilla	2 cups chopped apples
1 heaping cup flour	1 cup chopped nuts

Beat eggs; add sugar and vanilla. Sift flour with salt and baking powder. Mix with egg-sugar mixture. Stir in apples and nuts. Spread in 9 x 13-inch pan. Bake at 350° F. for 30 minutes.

Ann Kilian, Warren County

A delicious snack with no added fat.

BABY RUTH BARS

1 cup sugar	6 1/2 cups Rice Krispies
1 cup light Karo syrup	12 ounces chocolate chips
1 3/4 cups crunchy peanut butter	1 block wax

Mix sugar and syrup. Heat until sugar is dissolved. Remove from heat. Stir in peanut butter and Rice Krispies. With hands, make small balls or long finger rolls. Melt chocolate chips and wax in small pan. Use fork to dip balls. Place on waxed paper on tray. Freeze about 5 minutes until chocolate firms. Serves 15.

Debbie Smith, Wayne County

My two sons love these for an after-school snack.

Home Grown

Based on farm cash receipts in 1999, the North Carolina Department of Agriculture lists the top 10 North Carolina counties as Sampson, Duplin, Union, Wayne, Wilkes, Johnston, Randolph, Robeson, Henderson, and Bladen.

BANG THE DRUM BROWNIES

1/2 cup butter
4 squares semisweet baking
  chocolate
2 eggs
1 cup brown sugar
3/4 cup flour

1/4 teaspoon baking powder
2/3 cup coarsely chopped
  pecans
1/3 cup coarsely chopped
  walnuts

Melt butter and chocolate together; set aside to cool. In a large mixing bowl, beat the eggs and sugar together until light. Stir in cooled chocolate mixture. Stir in flour and baking powder. Fold in pecans and walnuts. Pour into a 9-inch greased baking pan. Bake for 40 to 45 minutes at 350° F. Serves 12.

Frances Milks, Wayne County

I remember the reaction people had after eating my grandmom's Bang the Drum Brownies.

BLONDIES

1 cup white sugar
1 cup light brown sugar
4 eggs
1 cup oil

1 1/2 cups self-rising flour
1 teaspoon vanilla
1 cup pecans
1/4 cup walnuts

Mix all ingredients, and bake in a greased 9-by-13-inch pan at 350° F. for 35 minutes.

Jeannette Draughon, Sampson County

Blondies are easy to make and very good.

BUTTERSCOTCH BARS

1 stick butter, melted
2 cups brown sugar
2 eggs
1 teaspoon baking powder

1 1/3 cups all-purpose flour
1/2 teaspoon salt
1 cup nuts, chopped

Melt butter; add sugar and eggs, and beat well. Add dry ingredients, then nuts. Spread batter in a greased and floured 8 x 8-inch baking pan. Bake 35 minutes at 350° F. Cut into squares to serve.

Brenda Hutchins, Buncombe County

CARIBBEAN ISLAND BARS

1/2 cup margarine, softened	8 tablespoons margarine
3 large eggs	8 ounces light cream cheese
1 box yellow cake mix	1 16-ounce box powdered
1 cup coconut	confectioners' sugar
1 cup pecans, chopped	1 teaspoon pure vanilla

Mix first 3 ingredients together, and spread batter in a 9 x 13 x 2-inch pan. Top with coconut and pecans. (If desired, you can vary the cookies by adding raisins or chocolate chips.) Mix 8 tablespoons margarine, cream cheese, powdered sugar, and vanilla, and spread on top of first layer. Bake at 300° F. for 1 hour. Let cool and cut into bars.

Shirley B. Wright, Cleveland County

This is such an easy recipe. It is not very pretty when cooked, but it is delicious.

GOLDEN SQUARES

1 box graham cracker crumbs	1 cup black walnuts
1 small package semi-sweet chocolate chips	1/2 cup margarine
	1 can Eagle Brand condensed milk

Combine 3/4 box of the graham cracker crumbs with the chocolate chips and nuts. Melt margarine in a 9 x 13-inch pan. Add margarine to graham cracker mixture, and mix well. Blend in milk, making sure all crumbs are moist. Put in the greased 9 x 13-inch pan. The mixture will be very thick. Bake at 350° F. for 20 minutes.

Sandra Vann, Northampton County

MAPLE NUT BARS

1 box yellow cake mix
(reserve 2/3 cup for filling)
1/4 cup brown sugar,
pressed into the
measuring cup
2 tablespoons margarine
1 egg
1/4 cup chopped nuts
Topping:
2 eggs

2/3 cup reserved cake mix
1/4 cup brown sugar,
pressed into the
measuring cup
3 tablespoons margarine
1/2 cup white corn syrup
1/2 teaspoon maple
flavoring
1/2 cup chopped nuts (I
prefer pecans)

Combine the first four ingredients. Mix until crumbly. Stir in 1/4 cup nuts. Press into 13 x 9-inch greased pan. Cook at 350° F. for 8 to 10 minutes. *Prepare topping:* Beat 2 eggs until foamy, add next five ingredients. Beat for 1 minute at low speed. Pour over crust, and sprinkle 1/2 cup of nuts on top. Bake at 350° F. for 15 to 25 minutes. Let cool, and cut into small bars. Can be stored in covered container for 2 or 3 days. Makes 25.

Marie Joyner, Nash County

These are good with Coke or coffee for family or any time friends get together. It is also a good dish to share with neighbors.

SWEET POTATO CHEWY BARS

4 eggs, beaten
3/4 cup cooking oil
1 cup coconut
1 teaspoon vanilla
1 16-ounce box light brown
sugar

2 cups Bisquick
1 cup pecans, chopped
1 cup sweet potatoes, raw,
finely shredded

Combine all ingredients, and pour into lightly greased 9 x 13-inch baking pan. Bake at 350° F. for 45 minutes.

Betty Jo Thigpen, Jones County

Everyone in the family enjoys this recipe. It is a big disappointment to see nothing left but crumbs!

MAMA'S APPLE PIE PUDDING

2 eggs beaten
1/4 cup melted butter or
  margarine, melted
1 cup sugar
1 cup flour
1 teaspoon baking soda

1/4 teaspoon salt
3/4 teaspoon cinnamon
1/2 teaspoon nutmeg
2 cups apples, peeled and
  chopped

In medium bowl, combine eggs with butter and sugar. Beat until smooth. Stir in flour, soda, salt, cinnamon, and nutmeg. Stir in apples. Turn into a buttered 9-inch pie plate. Bake at 350° F. for about 40 minutes. Serve warm or cold. Delicious with vanilla ice cream. Serves 6 to 8.

Ruth Morgan, Buncombe County

NO-COOK BANANA PUDDING

1 box vanilla instant
  pudding
2 cups cold milk
1 12-ounce carton Cool
  Whip

1 8-ounce carton sour
  cream
1 box vanilla wafers
Bananas, sliced

Mix pudding and milk as directed on box. Add Cool Whip and sour cream. Place layer of vanilla wafers in a dish, then a layer of bananas, and then a layer of the pudding mixture. Repeat until all mixture is gone. Chill about 1 hour before serving.

Donna Bailey, Rutherford County

GRANDMA'S BANANA PUDDING

1/2 cup granulated sugar
1/3 cup all-purpose flour
Dash of salt
4 egg yolks, at room
  temperature
2 cups milk
1/2 teaspoon vanilla extract

35 to 45 Nilla Wafers
5 to 6 medium bananas,
  sliced
Meringue:
4 egg whites
1/4 cup sugar

Combine sugar, flour, and salt in double boiler. Stir in egg yolks and milk; blend well. Cook, stirring constantly, until thick. Add vanilla. Spread a small amount of the custard in the bottom of a

1 1/2-quart casserole dish. Cover custard with wafers and then sliced bananas. Continue to layer custard, wafers, and bananas, ending with custard. *Prepare meringue:* Beat egg whites until stiff but not dry. Gradually add 1/4 cup of sugar, and beat until stiff peaks form from the spoon. Spoon on top of the pudding; cover the entire surface. Bake at 425° F. for 5 minutes or until brown. After the pudding has cooled, garnish with wafers and bananas. Serves 6 to 8.

Carrie Martin, Wake County

I found this wonderful recipe on the Nilla Wafers box. Our family enjoys this fun dessert on weekends as a pick-me-up or as a quick and easy dish when company comes.

—

MAMA'S COCONUT PUDDING

1 1/2 cups sugar	1 teaspoon vanilla
1/4 cup flour	Ritz crackers
4 egg yolks	1 6-ounce package coconut
1 large can evaporated milk	*Icing:*
1 can water	4 egg whites
1/2 stick margarine, melted	1/4 cup sugar

Mix all ingredients except coconut and icing ingredients. Cook until mixture thickens. Add coconut. Pour mixture into a buttered 13 x 9 x 2-inch baking dish or pan lined with Ritz crackers. *Prepare icing:* Beat egg whites and sugar until stiff peaks form. Spoon over top of pudding. Bake at 350° F. until brown.

Joan J. Grimes, Harnett County

My mother-in-law, who passed away in 1997, made this pudding quite often. It was passed on to her by her mother. It always serves as reminder of what a great cook she was and how much she loved to cook for her family.

Brown Sugar

Brown sugar gets its color from molasses. Dark brown sugar has the most molasses. Store brown sugar in an airtight container in a cool spot. It will harden if the moisture in the sugar evaporates. Recipes that call for brown sugar may also call for white sugar. In this case, the white sugar is granulated, not confectioners'.

FRENCH CUSTARD

1 tablespoon butter	1/4 teaspoon salt
1 tablespoon flour	5 egg yolks, beaten
3 cups milk	1 teaspoon vanilla extract
1/3 cup sugar	

Melt butter in top of double boiler. Blend in flour, and add milk slowly. Cook over direct heat stirring constantly until boiling point is just reached. Stir in the sugar and salt. Stir slowly into the well-beaten egg yolks. Then pour back into the double boiler, and cook over simmering water, stirring constantly until custard just coats a metal spoon. Remove from heat. Stir in the vanilla, and chill before serving. Serves 5.

Betty Jean King, Warren County

Mary "Pollie" Newman Hilliard made this recipe in the late 1800s because it was a favorite of her husband, John Hilliard. They lived in Warren County near the Drewey community.

Persimmon Pudding is an old-fashioned North Carolina favorite. Explore the half dozen recipes given here and find your family's favorite.

GLAZED PERSIMMON PUDDING

3/4 cup butter or margarine	1 teaspoon baking soda
3/4 cup sugar	1 teaspoon baking powder
2 tablespoons brown sugar	1 teaspoon vanilla
3 eggs	3/4 cup buttermilk
2 cups persimmon pulp	*Glaze:*
2 cups sifted all-purpose	1/3 cup sugar
flour	1/3 cup water

Cream butter and sugars together until fluffy. Add eggs, and beat. Add persimmon pulp, dry ingredients, vanilla, and milk. Mix together well, and bake in a 9 x 13-inch pan for 45 minutes at 350° F. *Prepare glaze:* Boil sugar and water together. Pour over pudding as soon as it is removed from the oven. Serves 12 or more.

Emily Clapp, Guilford County

This old favorite farm dish is good any day of the year.

OLD-TIMEY PERSIMMON PUDDING

1 cup flour
1 1/2 cups sugar
1 quart persimmons
3 cups milk
2 eggs

Butter size of an egg, melted
Pinch of salt
Spices if you like (such as
  cinnamon, cloves, nutmeg)

Mix flour and sugar. Put raw persimmons through a sieve. Mix persimmons with milk. Add flour-sugar mixture and eggs. Add spices, if desired. Bake at 350° F. until pudding is firm, approximately 30 minutes.

Lizzie Mock, Forsyth County

PERSIMMON PUDDING

1/2 cup butter
1 1/2 cups persimmons
1 1/2 cups sugar
1 1/2 cups flour
1/2 teaspoon baking soda
1 teaspoon baking powder

1/2 teaspoon cinnamon
1/2 teaspoon mixed spices
3/4 cup milk
3/4 cup buttermilk
2 eggs

Mix well, and bake in greased and floured baking dish at 300° F. until pudding turns loose of pan at edges.

Mary Coletrane Gray, Guilford County

REESE FAMILY PERSIMMON PUDDING

2 cups sugar
2 cups all-purpose flour
1 teaspoon salt
1 teaspoon cinnamon
  (optional)
1/2 cup margarine, melted
1 small can evaporated milk

1 egg, slightly beaten
1 cup buttermilk
2 cups persimmon pulp
1 teaspoon vanilla
2 cups sweet potatoes,
  grated

Mix dry ingredients together. Add remaining ingredients, and mix well. I usually grate my sweet potatoes in the milk in the blender. Bake in a greased, floured 12 x 8-inch pan, or two smaller pans at 300° F. for 1 1/2 hours. Serves 16.

Benelia Reese, Catawba County

The recipe is my mother-in-law's. My family and many other people have enjoyed this persimmon pudding for years.

MOCKSVILLE PERSIMMON PUDDING

1/2 cup (1 stick) butter or
  margarine
2 eggs
1 cup sugar
1 cup persimmon pulp

1 cup self-rising flour
2/3 cup evaporated milk
1 teaspoon vanilla
1/2 teaspoon cinnamon
  (optional)

Melt half a stick of butter in each of two 9-inch pie pans. Beat eggs. To the eggs, add sugar and persimmon pulp. Mix well. Add cooled, melted butter. Mix in flour. Add milk, vanilla, and cinnamon, if desired. Pour into pie pans. Bake at 350° F. for 35 to 40 minutes, or until firm.

Martha B. Edwards, Nash County

My mother and her sisters would gather at one of the sisters' homes in Mocksville when the persimmons were ripe. They would prepare the pulp, freeze it, and divide it among themselves. My mother always shared some with me so my family could enjoy persimmon pudding. Once all the one-cup containers were gone from the freezer, we eagerly awaited the next persimmon season. I have never seen any persimmons or pulp on sale in a store.

SOUTHERN PERSIMMON PUDDING

1 pint persimmon pulp
1 tablespoon cinnamon
1 teaspoon vanilla
Dash of nutmeg
1 cup buttermilk

2 1/2 cups sugar
1 stick butter or margarine,
  melted
4 eggs
3/4 cup self-rising flour

Beat all together until smooth. Pour into a greased 9 x 13 x 2-inch Pyrex pan. Cook for 1 hour at 300° F. Let cool, and cut into squares. Serves 12. (Note: 1 pint is 2 cups.)

Betty Brown, Randolph County

I make this persimmon pudding all the time and wouldn't change to any other recipe. My family loves it, and everyone else who eats it does, too.

BAKED WHOLE PUMPKIN

1 pumpkin, 5 to 7 pounds
6 whole eggs
2 cups whipping cream
1/2 cup brown sugar
1 tablespoon molasses

1/2 teaspoon nutmeg
1 teaspoon cinnamon
1/4 teaspoon ginger
2 tablespoons butter

Cut top off pumpkin. Remove seeds. Mix the remaining ingredients except butter. Fill the pumpkin, and top with the butter. Cover pumpkin, and bake at 350° F. for 1 1/2 hours until set like custard. Serve from the pumpkin, scraping some of the pumpkin off with each serving.

Watauga County Extension and Community Association

QUINCE PUDDING

2 level cups flour
3 level teaspoons baking
 powder
1/2 level teaspoon salt

1 egg, beaten
1 cup milk
2 tablespoons butter, melted
1 cup quince preserves

Sift flour, baking powder, and salt together. Beat the egg, and add milk and melted butter. Mix with dry ingredients. Batter will be stiff. Add preserves, and beat well. Turn into a greased 8-inch baking pan. Bake at 325° F. for 30 minutes. Pudding may be served with sweet cream.

Helen Mae Hilliard King, Warren County

Mary White Hilliard had her husband, Armstead Barlette Hilliard, plant several quince bushes near the path between the house and the stable in the early 1900s. The bushes are still living, but they do not produce much fruit now.

STRAWBERRY PUDDING

2 eggs
1/4 pound butter, softened
1 1/2 cups confectioners'
 sugar

1 pound vanilla wafers
2 quarts fresh or frozen
 strawberries
1 can dessert topping

In a small saucepan, stir eggs, butter, and sugar together. Cook over low heat, stirring constantly until mixture bubbles in one or two places. Remove from heat. Let cool. Crush three-fourths of the vanilla wafers, and place in the bottom of serving dish. Add cooked mixture. Add a layer of strawberries. Cover the strawberries with dessert topping. Top with remaining vanilla wafers. Let stand in refrigerator overnight. Serves 8 to 10.

Johnsie C. Cunningham, Granville County

This dessert is not just a pretty dish...it's a family favorite.

GRATED SWEET POTATO PUDDING

3 cups grated sweet
  potatoes
2 1/2 cups milk
1/2 cup butter or
  margarine, softened

1 1/2 cups sugar
2 eggs
1 teaspoon salt
2 teaspoons vanilla extract
1 cup coconut

Grate sweet potatoes into milk, which will keep them from turning dark. Blend butter, sugar, eggs, salt, and vanilla extract together. Add grated sweet potatoes, milk, and coconut. Mix well. Pour into a greased oblong pan, and bake at 350° F. for approximately 1 hour, or until potatoes are tender when tested. Serves 6 to 8.

Emily Clapp, Guilford County

This recipe has been a favorite in our farm family for over 60 years.

SWEET POTATO PUDDING

3 large sweet potatoes,
  sliced
2 1/2 cups water
2 tablespoons vanilla
  flavoring

1 cup sugar
1 teaspoon cinnamon
1 1/2 sticks margarine,
  divided
1 box yellow cake mix

Slice potatoes, and place in 9 x 13-inch pan that has been greased or sprayed. Put vanilla flavoring into water, and pour over potatoes. Mix sugar and cinnamon, and pour over potatoes. Melt 1/2 stick margarine, and pour over sugar mixture. Spread dry cake mix over top, and dot with 1 stick margarine. Bake 1 hour at 350° F.

Nelda Draughn, Surry County

BUTTER PECAN ICE CREAM

1/4 cup butter or margarine
2 cups chopped pecans
7 cups milk, divided
1 14-ounce can sweetened
  condensed milk
2 cups sugar

6 large eggs, lightly beaten
1 5.1-ounce package of
  vanilla instant pudding
  mix
1 teaspoon vanilla extract

Melt butter in large, heavy saucepan over medium-high heat. Add pecans. Cook, stirring constantly for 3 minutes, or until lightly browned. Drain and set aside. Combine 1 cup milk, sweetened condensed milk, sugar, and eggs in saucepan. Cook over medium heat, stirring constantly for 5 minutes, or until mixture coats back of a spoon. Cool. Stir in remaining 6 cups milk, pudding mix, and vanilla. Add pecans; stir well. Pour mixture into freezer container of a 5-quart ice-cream freezer. Freeze according to manufacturer's instructions. Pack freezer with additional ice and rock salt. Let stand 1 hour before serving. Makes 1 gallon.

Sue Knowles, Duplin County

FRESH PEACH ICE CREAM

1 quart milk
1 10-ounce package of
  marshmallows
2 cups sugar
1 14-ounce can sweetened
  condensed milk

2 cups Half & Half dairy
  creamer
3 cups mashed fresh
  peaches

Combine milk and marshmallows in Dutch oven. Cook over medium heat, stirring constantly until marshmallows melt; remove from heat. Add sugar and remaining ingredients; mix well. Chill. Pour mixture into freezer container of gallon hand-turned or electric ice cream freezer. Freeze according to manufacturer's instructions. Pack freezer with additional ice and salt, and let stand for 1 to 2 hours to ripen before serving.

Rita Clark, Vance County

Safe Ice Cream

While many old-fashioned ice cream recipes use uncooked eggs, today's food safety experts recommend only recipes that cook the eggs.

FRESH STRAWBERRY FROST

3 pints fresh strawberries,
  hulled
2 cups sugar
1 1/2 cups orange juice
1/2 cup lemon juice
1/4 cup Grand Marnier or
  Cointreau

In electric blender, put half of the berries, sugar, orange juice, and lemon juice. Cover, and blend at high speed for 30 seconds. Turn mixture into 8 x 12-inch dish. Repeat, using remaining berries, sugar, orange juice, and lemon juice. Pour into baking dish and stir in Grand Marnier. Freeze until partially frozen. Turn mixture into large mixing bowl, and beat smooth with electric mixer at medium speed. Put into freezer containers, and store in freezer. Yields 9 cups.

Alice Graham Underhill, Craven County

CHOCOLATE SOP

(serve with hot biscuits, or use to flavor milk or as a cake icing)

1/2 cup cocoa
1 cup sugar
1 cup water
1/2 teaspoon salt
1 tablespoon flour
1/2 cup or less water
4 teaspoons butter
1/2 teaspoon vanilla

Mix cocoa, sugar, and 1 cup water. Boil. Add salt. Mix flour and 1/2 cup water; stir into boiling mixture. Add butter and vanilla.

Josephine Worsley, Edgecombe County

I was first served this at a friend's house in the 1950s.

M'M'M DESSERT

2 6-ounce boxes instant
  pudding
5 cups milk
Graham crackers
8-ounce container frozen
  whipped topping

Beat puddings in milk until smooth and beginning to thicken. Layer pudding and graham crackers alternately in an 8 x 8-inch casserole dish, starting with crackers. Spread pudding thinly. Top with frozen topping. Chill several hours or overnight before serving.

Pat Jones, Pitt County

My grandchildren enjoy this dessert and many times choose it instead of cake for their birthday celebrations.

—

CHERRY YUM-YUM

1 1/2 sticks butter or
  margarine, melted
3 cups graham cracker
  crumbs
3/4 cup sugar

8 ounces cream cheese,
  softened
2 packages Dream Whip
2 cups milk
2 cans cherry pie filling

Mix melted butter and graham cracker crumbs. Spread half of this mixture in a 9 x 13-inch pan. Mix sugar with cream cheese. Beat Dream Whip into milk. Add cream cheese mixture to milk mixture. Spread half of the mixture over the graham cracker crust. Spread cherry pie filling on top of filling. Top with remaining graham cracker mixture. Chill in refrigerator for 24 hours before serving. Serves 12.

Josephine Costello, Pitt County

This recipe is one of my sister's standards for bridge, covered-dish dinners, and family reunions.

STRAWBERRY-BANANA WHIP

2 cups fresh strawberries
3 large bananas
1 cup sugar

1/4 cup fresh lemon juice
1/2 pint heavy cream

Wash and hull strawberries. Peel bananas. Force fruit through a sieve. Place in saucepan. Add sugar and lemon juice. Bring mixture to a boil, but do not boil. Mixture will thicken. Chill completely. Refrigerate overnight. Next day, whip cream, and fold into fruit mixture. Serve in dessert glasses. If desired, top each serving with a whole strawberry. Serves 8 to 10.

Juanita Fisher Lagg, Rowan County

I've enjoyed this dessert for at least 40 years. I now use Cool Whip instead of whipping cream. This dessert took first place at the Patterson Farm Strawberry Festival in 1999. I freeze strawberries in May for use in December. This is a perfect light Christmas dessert after a heavy meal.

BLUEBERRY DESSERT

1 cup flour	1 cup sugar
1 stick margarine, softened	1 teaspoon vanilla
1 cup chopped nuts	1 can blueberry pie filling
8 ounces cream cheese	(or 1 pint fresh berries, 3/4
1 large container Cool	cup sugar, and 1
Whip	tablespoon cornstarch)

Mix flour, margarine, and nuts. Press into a 9 x 13-inch glass baking dish. Bake at 350° F. for 10 minutes. Cool. Beat cream cheese, Cool Whip, sugar, and vanilla until smooth. Spread on cooled crust. Top with 1 can blueberry pie filing. (If using fresh or frozen berries: Fresh or frozen blueberries may be used, but do not add sugar to frozen berries. Wash the blueberries and drain. Mix 1 cup sugar and 1 tablespoon cornstarch with enough water to moisten. Pour in blueberries. Cook on medium heat, stirring constantly until thick. Cool completely. Pour on cream cheese mixture.) Refrigerate. Serves 10.

Wanda H. Powell, Nash County

Mrs. Estelle Strickland brought this dessert to Kenneth Powell's homeplace when his grandmother died.

BLUEBERRY CREAM CHEESE DELIGHT

Crust:	1 teaspoon vanilla
1 stick margarine, melted	8 ounces Cool Whip
1 cup all-purpose flour	*Topping:*
1 cup nuts, chopped	2 cups blueberries
Filling:	1 cup sugar
8 ounces cream cheese,	4 tablespoons flour
softened	1 tablespoon lemon juice
2/3 cup sugar	

Melt margarine; add flour and nuts. Press crust into a 9 x 13-inch pan or glass baking dish. Bake at 350° F. until lightly browned. Let crust cool *completely* before spreading filling. To prepare filling, mix cream cheese, sugar, and vanilla until smooth. Fold in Cool Whip. Spread filling over cooled crust. To prepare topping: mix topping ingredients in saucepan, and cook until thickened. Let completely cool; then spread over filling.

Martha W. Warner, Bladen County

FROZEN SALAD/DESSERT

1/2 cup chopped pecans
3/4 cup sugar
2 bananas, diced
10 ounces frozen
  strawberries, thawed

1 cup of chunk or tidbit
  pineapple, drained
1 8-ounce package cream
  cheese
1 large container Cool
  Whip

Mix all ingredients except cream cheese and Cool Whip. Add the
softened cream cheese, and fold in Cool Whip. Pour into 9 x 13-
inch baking dish. Cover with aluminum foil and freeze.

Joyce Ann McFail, Granville County

*I've always made this for most of my club special dinners and have
shared the recipe with many friends.*

PEANUT BUTTER AND HONEY FUNDOUGH

1 cup peanut butter
1 cup honey

2 cups powdered milk

Mix all ingredients together in a bowl. Add more powdered milk if
necessary to make a workable dough. Form the dough into a ball
and then into other shapes, then eat. Makes 2 1/2 cups.

Sandra Vann, Northampton County

*Kids make, shape, and eat this edible dough. It's a fun project on a
rainy day.*

RECIPE FOR HAPPINESS

Take 2 heaping cups of patience
1 heart full of love
2 hands full of generosity
Dash of laughter
1 head full of understanding
Sprinkle generously with kindness
Add plenty of faith and mix well
Spread over a period of a lifetime
And serve to everybody you meet

Susan Harper Britt, Nash County

Index

APPETIZERS

Appetizers, Finger Foods, Snacks
Boiled Green Peanuts, Babs Wilkinson, Wake, 3
Boiled Peanuts, Babs Wilkinson, Wake, 4
Cheese Straws, Vicki Walton, Wake, 4
Cheese Straws, Lottie Lou Dickens, Nash, 5
Holiday Meatballs, Susan Harper Britt, Nash, 5
Miss Evelyn's Crab Cakes, Rosie Patton, Dare, 6
Shrimp Appetizer, Georgine Armstrong, Pasquotank, 6
Spinach Tarts, Ann Clarke, Lee, 7
Stuffed Mushrooms, Kay Greene, Hertford, 7
World's Best Deviled Eggs, Nancy Johnston, Buncombe, 8

Cheese Balls
Cheese Ball, Sue Arnette, Duplin, 8
Dried Beef Ball, Elizabeth Harper, Edgecombe, 8
Ham and Cheese Ball, Ruth Morgan, Buncombe, 9
Nutty Cheese Ball, Juanita T. Cannon, Gaston, 9
Nutty Fruit Ball, Mary Alice Brooks, Union, 9
Olive Cheese Ball, Hannah Cox, Craven, 10
Olive-Stuffed Cheese Balls, Patricia Herring, Wayne, 10
Orange-Date Cheese Ball, Hilda Ray, Columbus, 10
Party Cheese Ball, Wilma B. McCollum, Union, 11
Pepper Jelly Cheese Ball, Betty Wood, Craven, 11

Dips
Cheese Dip. Vickie Guin, Wake, 13
Chip Dip, Wanda Simmons, Wake, 13
Hot Onion Dip, Tina Brown, Cabarrus, 14
Mexican Dip, Kristy Easter, Surry, 14
Sausage Dip, Barbara Braswell, Union, 14

Spreads
Crab Spread, Jennifer Britt Crumley, Nash, 11
Pimiento and Cheese, Juanita Fisher Lagg, Rowan, 12

BISCUITS, BREADS, & STUFFINGS *(continued)*

CAKES

CAKES *(continued)*

Pound Cakes

CAKES *(continued)*

Pound Cakes *(continued)*
Caramel Nut Pound Cake, Laura B. Wooten, Wake, 256
Colonial Pound Cake, Margaret Helton, Rutherford, 257
Crisco Pound Cake, Paula Williams, Duplin, 256
Kay's Black Walnut Pound Cake, Kay Carswell, Rutherford, 256
Million Dollar Pound Cake, Jerrie Hasty, Union, 258
My Mother's Pound Cake, Bettie H. Hodges, Davidson, 258
Myrtle Ashley's Pound Cake, Susan E. Pope, Wake, 259
One-Half Pound Cake, Harriett Coleman Edwards, Wake, 260
Pound Cake With Fruit And Icing, Paul Taylor, Alamance, 260
Red Velvet Pound Cake, Anna Lee Poe, Ashe, 261
Velvet Pound Cake, Gladys Patton, Clay, 261
Whipped Cream Pound Cake, Mrs. Vollie Dalton, Rutherford, 259

Fruit Cake
Grandma Slate's Fruit Cake, Nancy C. Sapp, Forsyth, 262
Old-Fashioned Dark Fruit Cake, Isabelle M. Fletcher-Perry, Lenoir, 263
Plantation Fruit Cake, Jennifer Mitchell, Harnett, 264
White Christmas Fruit Cake, Jane Stuart, Wake, 265

CAKE FROSTINGS, ICINGS, & FILLINGS

7-Minute Icing, Hattie Sessions, Columbus, 254
7-Minute Icing, Evelyn Stevens, Wake, 254
Buttermilk Icing, Mrs. Roland Beck, Burke, 247
Carrot Cake Frosting, Elizabeth Parrish, Chowan, 224
Carrot Cake Icing, Marie Joyner, Nash, 223
Chocolate Frosting, Iris S. Conner, Rockingham, 235
Coconut Cake Filling, Laura B. Wooten, Wake, 211
Coconut Frosting, Carnell Autry, Sampson, 229
Coffee Icing, Helen Mae Hilliard King, Vance/Warren counties, 232
Cream Cheese Frosting, Hilda McGee, Davidson, 214
Cream Cheese Frosting For Carrot Cake, Dot Ballance, Wayne, 222
Fresh Apple Cake Glaze, Dale Evans, Union, 216
Frosting For Coconut Cake, Maxine Jordan, Bladen, 228

CAKE FROSTINGS, ICINGS, & FILLINGS
(continued)

COOKIES & DESSERTS

Drop Cookies

Shaped or Sliced Cookies

COOKIES & DESSERTS *(continued)*

COOKIES & DESSERTS *(continued)*

Miscellaneous Desserts (continued)

FRUIT

PIES & COBBLERS

PIES & COBBLERS *(continued)*

PIES & COBBLERS *(continued)*

POULTRY, MEATS, & MAIN DISHES

POULTRY, MEATS, & MAIN DISHES

POULTRY, MEATS, & MAIN DISHES *(continued)*

Brunswick Stew (continued)
Jim Graham's Tar Heel Brunswick Stew, Jim Graham, Wake, 105
Mom's Brunswick Stew, Evelyn Stevens, Wake, 109
St. Lewis Brunswick Stew, Elbert Ray Pitt, Edgecombe, 109

Cheese
Cheese Pudding, Mrs. Leroy Whitfield, Greene, 143
Macaroni And Cheese Casserole, Mary Warren, Cleveland, 143
Macaroni and Cheese, Debby McGilvery, Guilford, 144
Vegetable Lasagna, Carol Skroch, Ashe, 144

Chicken
Aunt Nell's Chicken 'n' Dumplin's, Linda Reasor, Durham, 92
Chicken And Dressing Casserole, Nancy Plummer, Brunswick, 95
Chicken And Dressing For One, Jennifer Mitchell, Harnett, 97
Chicken And Dressing Casserole, Eva S. Pridgen, Wilson, 96
Chicken And Egg Casserole, Pearl Freedman, Columbus, 97
Chicken Casserole, Juanita Cannon, Gaston, 96
Chicken Casserole With Corn Bread Dressing, Patricia Herring,
    Wayne, 96
Chicken Gumbo, Vernon Tyndall, Duplin, 90
Chicken 'N' Dumplings, Della Stephens, Forsyth, 93
Chicken Pie, Linda Dalton, Stokes, 91
Chicken Puffs, Sandra Vann, Northampton, 99
Chicken-Rice Casserole, Eva S. Pridgen, Wilson, 98
Chicken Squares, Dennis Furr, Cabarrus, 91
Chicken Supreme, Pearl Ange, Craven, 98
Chicken With Swiss Cheese And Stuffing, Linda H. Harris, Vance,
    97
Curry Chicken Salad, Nancy Johnston, Buncombe, 100
Dixie Grilled Chicken, Dayle Oakley, Wake, 89
Elegant Chicken Salad, Laura B. Wooten, Wake, 100
Fiesta Chicken Lasagna, Jean Richardson, Wake, 98
Fried Chicken, Barbara Braswell, Union, 89
Golden Chicken Nuggets, Kristen Elizabeth Britt, Nash, 92
Hot Chicken Salad, Mrs. Kathryn Ort, Wake, 101
Individual Chicken Pies, Elizabeth Harper, Edgecombe, 90

POULTRY, MEATS, & MAIN DISHES *(continued)*

Sausage
Chili-Sausage Squares, Jerrie Hasty, Union, 131
Mexi-Muffins, Wanda H. Powell, Nash, 130
Sausage And Corn, Thelma Shore, Yadkin, 129
Sausage And Grits Breakfast Casserole, Laura B. Wooten, Wake,
  131
Sausage And Rice-A-Roni Casserole, Tina Brown, Cabarrus, 129
Sausage-Cheese Lasagna, Rita Clark, Vance, 130

Seafood
Crab Quiche, Hilda Ray, Columbus, 135
Farmer's Wife Salmon Loaf, Wilma B. McCollum, Union, 140
Fish Stew, Nancy Lilley, Onslow, 136
Holiday Oysters, Alice Graham Underhill, Craven, 137
Millie Tice's Crab Casserole, Jessica Tice, Currituck, 135
Millie's Shrimp Creole, Jessica Tice, Currituck, 139
Oyster Casserole, Faye S. Bunn, Nash, 138
Pete's Oyster Delight, Pete and Gael Jaeger, Chatham, 139
Scalloped Oysters, Sarah Odom, Harnett, 139
Scalloped Oysters, Mrs. J. S. Payne, Hyde, 138
Scalloped Oysters, Ethel Pitt, Edgecombe, 139
Shrimp-Rice Casserole, Hilda Ray, Columbus, 140

Turkey
Turkey And Oyster Dressing, Emily Clapp, Guilford, 103
Turkey And Wild Rice Casserole, Mildred Moxley, Alleghany, 104
White Turkey Chili, Zoe C. McKay-Tucker, Wake, 104

Variety, Organ Meats
German Hash, George Daniel, Halifax, 128
Liver Mush, Mrs. Roland Beck, Burke, 126
Liver Pudding, Hazel Koonce, Wake, 126
Liver Pudding Or Liver Mush, Norene Hill Moll, Henderson, 127
Scrapple, Ellen Teague Miller, Guilford, 128
Scrapple Or Panhaus, Pam Staton, Clay, 129

SALADS

SALADS *(continued)*

SAUCES

SOUPS

VEGETABLES

Asparagus

Beans

Beets

Broccoli

VEGETABLES *(continued)*

VEGETABLES *(continued)*

Mixed Vegetables
Veg-All Casserole, Patricia Herring, Wayne, 84
Vegetable Casserole, Lula Mae Tyndall, Sampson, 84
Veggie Bars, Anne W. Harper, Edgecombe, 85

Onion
Dilly Onions and Cucumbers, Laura B. Wooten, Wake, 66
Onion Casserole, Bee Simpson, Union, 65
Stewart's Onions, Juanita Fisher Lagg, Rowan, 66

Peas
English Pea Casserole, Bee Simpson, Union, 66

Peppers
Pepper Relish Chow Chow, Nancy Beck, Burke, 67

Poke Greens
Poke Greens, Othola Thompson, Rockingham, 67

Potatoes, Irish
Hash Brown Casserole, Nancy Johnston, Buncombe, 68
Hash Brown Potato Casserole, Mildred M. Harper, Edgecombe, 68
Irish Potato Casserole, Donna Edsel, Wilkes, 69
Irish Potato Casserole, Witt Fogleman, Alamance, 68
Oven-Fried Potatoes, Margaret Clark, Wake, 69
Overnight Potato Casserole, Barbara Ross, Haywood, 69
Parslied Potatoes, Velma McClure Poe, Ashe, 70
Potato Pie, Debby McGilvery, Guilford, 70
Potato Supreme, Carol Cox, Wake, 71
Potato-Tomato Scallop, Lizzie Mock, Forsyth, 71

Pumpkin
Pumpkin, Dorothy C. Fisher, Nash, 71

Rice
Baked Rice, Juanita McKnight, Wayne, 72
Christmas Rice, Jane H. Ross, Bladen, 72
Pineapple Rice, Dorothy Fender, Alleghany, 73
Rice Casserole, Laura B. Wooten, Wake, 72

VEGETABLES *(continued)*

VEGETABLES *(continued)*

Wild Rice
Wild Rice Supreme, Ruth Nesbitt, Buncombe, 85

Zucchini
Fried Zucchini, Debby McGilvery, Guilford, 86

HAPPINESS
Recipe for Happiness, Susan Harper Britt, Nash, 148

*Many thanks to all the wonderful cooks
who shared their recipes!*

To Order Another Cookbook

Each copy of *Jim Graham's Farm Family Cookbook* costs $19.95.
You may choose between regular mail delivery (allow 2 to 3 weeks
for delivery) for $4 and Priority Mail (one week or less) for $6. Add
$2 for each additional book in the same order.

Quantity	Regular mail	Priority mail
1 book	$23.95	$25.95
2 books	$45.90	$47.90
3 books	$67.85	$69.85
4 books	$89.80	$91.80

Sales tax for North Carolina residents is extra.
Add 6.5% sales tax ($1.30 per book; Mecklenburg
County residents must add 7%, or $1.40 per book).

To order by credit card, call 1-800-472-0438 toll free. We accept
MasterCard and Visa. Or place your order at:
www.abooks.com/cookbook

To order by check or money order (payable to aBOOKS), fill out
the following form, and send it along with the full amount due to:
Jim Graham Farm Family Cookbook
c/o aBOOKS
65 Macedonia Road
Alexander, NC 28701

Please send me _____ copies of *Jim Graham's Farm Family
Cookbook*. I am enclosing $_____, which includes $19.95 for
each book ordered, postage, and sales tax (if in North Carolina).

Mail my books to:

Name _____

Address _____

City _____ State _____ Zip _____

Orders will be shipped by the U.S. Postal Service.